TRANSFORMATION OF THE MORMON CULTURE REGION

Transformation of the Mormon Culture Region

ETHAN R. YORGASON

UNIVERSITY OF ILLINOIS PRESS

Urbana and Chicago

Library of Congress Cataloging-in-Publication Data
Yorgason, Ethan R., 1965–
Transformation of the Mormon culture region /
Ethan R. Yorgason.
    p.   cm.
Includes bibliographical references and index.
ISBN 0-252-02853-8 (cloth : alk. paper)
    1. Mormons—Utah—Social life and customs.
    2. Mormons—Utah—Social conditions.
    3. Mormons—Utah—Politics and government.
    4. Utah—Social life and customs. 5. Utah—Social
conditions. 6. Utah—Politics and government.
    7. Regionalism—Utah—History. 8. Group identity—
Utah—History. 9. Conservatism—Utah—History.
    I. Title.
F835.M8Y67   2003
979.2′34′88283—dc21   2003000547

CONTENTS

PREFACE

As with most historical work, contemporary concerns inform this book. Researchers rarely if ever undertake historical research simply to find out "what happened." We also look to history to provide greater insight into the present state of affairs. This book is no exception. It analyzes the transformation of the Mormon culture region around the turn of the twentieth century, but it does so to illuminate today's Mormon culture region. The key contemporary question prompting this study is why such a strongly conservative set of sociocultural norms marks the present-day Mormon culture region. Each election year shows that Utah is among the most politically conservative states. Visitors and newcomers are often struck by the depth of political conservatism. Social movements, such as those for gender rights, workers' rights, and antiwar sentiment, struggle mightily in the region. Run-of-the-mill Democratic Party liberalism easily gets branded as wild-eyed socialism, feminism, or anti-Americanism that attempts to take away individual rights.

It seems reasonable to suppose that Mormon conservatism naturally produced a politically conservative region. Mormonism has conservative tendencies, many of which relate to regionally conservative political norms. But Mormonism also possesses radical stances toward mainstream American culture in, for example, its communitarian doctrines and its distinctively gendered theology of the origin of human beings.[1] In the nineteenth century, these nonmainstream elements produced strong antipathy among most non-Mormons. Fundamental Mormon conservatism therefore cannot by itself explain current regional conservatism, nor can the fact that inhabitants of the Mormon culture region also inhabited the larger American West. Although a kind of conservative economic individualism in the Mormon region appears very much like that phenomenon in the larger West, Mormon history demonstrates that such a convergence was not inevitable.

To explain contemporary regional conservatism, one must examine regionally specific history, particularly the period of so-called Americanization (1880–1920). This process of Americanization gave Mormon defenses
of mainstream American institutions and norms an upper hand over Mormon critiques and placed the Mormon culture region as a subregion in the
American West. It produced a regionally distinctive tendency toward conformity that only later became elaborated as a strong regional political conservatism. This is to say that the Mormon culture region acquired a regionally specific cultural trajectory pointing toward conservatism during
the process of Americanization. While much has happened since 1920, cultural norms in the Mormon region have elaborated this logic and have not
established a different trajectory. In particular, regional inhabitants have
not forgotten the lessons learned about how to establish and maintain peace
between Mormons and non-Mormons. Foremost among these lessons is
the sense that public life needs to build on commonalities between the two
groups and that critical social visions of American life are to be shunned
and ignored.

This book also derives from my own position in society. My family heritage extends on all sides to the nineteenth-century Mormon culture region.
In one sense, this book constitutes a partial attempt to understand my own
family. Even more significant, this study derives from the interaction of my
own Mormonness and other identities with my political commitments. I
consider myself a white, heterosexual, western, Utah, male Mormon. But
unlike many people with a similar identity, I hold radical leanings. In particular, I believe society has basic problems of inequality and oppression,
and I think these problems can be solved only by a fundamental redistribution of power. I do not claim to know exactly how such a redistribution
could occur or be maintained (though I tend more toward the political left
than the right in seeking answers). I simply think that society ought to search
for egalitarian means to effect such a redistribution and that a conversation
with those holding similar goals (even if there is disagreement on the means)
would be beneficial.

This book is partially an attempt to bring my Mormon identity and heritage into conversation with people who are not likely to equate Mormonism with egalitarian critique. Often—too often it seems—I meet people with
similar political leanings who express amazement that I hold onto my religious identity and faith when so much and so many in Mormon culture are
politically conservative. This is not the place to address that question fully,
but I hope this book shows that Mormonism can encompass critical social
thought. Reasons exist, just as they do for American black churches, for not

wanting to erase Mormonism from radical thought. I hope this study hints at why engagement with Mormonism by those seeking greater social egalitarianism might be politically productive. For Mormon readers, I hope this book encourages greater social and theoretical critique and a deeper understanding of regional cultural history. I myself am searching for a committed political stance that can derive partially from and sit comfortably beside an ethical Mormon engagement with the world. I hope—following Cornel West's (1994) argument on African American identity—that Mormon identity will come to imply a way of ethically relating to others as much as it constitutes a way of differentiating oneself from non-Mormons.

Nevertheless, the primary objective of this book is not to retrieve a politically progressive Mormon history or ethic but to contribute to regional history and regional geography. It points to the challenges anyone would face in trying to reconstitute regional and Mormon cultures. In particular, it shows how their conservative-tending trajectories emerged in response to a very real need for regional peace. Mormon culture cannot simply be re-radicalized vis-à-vis the American mainstream (assuming that such a project is both possible and desirable) without addressing the need to find ways for Mormons to live peaceably with non-Mormons. Mormon critique of American society was largely a separatist project. The regional question is how different groups can live peaceably and nonoppressively in the same space without basing such peace on least-common-denominator solutions (individualist liberty, nationally dominant social relations, and nationalist xenophobia). This book does not answer that question, but by explaining why the Mormon culture region's attempt at regional peace moved in a nationally conformist direction, it provides insight into what must be considered before trying to answer it.

ACKNOWLEDGMENTS

I owe many people more thanks than I can possibly provide here. Laurence Yorgason helped instill in me a curiosity for Mormon studies. He and Kay Lynne Yorgason have provided intellectual, emotional, and economic support throughout this project. I could not dream of having more supportive parents. Many members of my family have also encouraged my work.

I have been blessed to work with many wonderful teachers, friends, and colleagues at the University of California at Los Angeles and the University of Iowa who helped shape my ideas on Mormon regional culture. David Reynolds, in particular, deserves special thanks for showing faith in my abilities during a crucial moment in my academic training, for taking on (advising) a project related to a western religion/religious group with a reputation for authoritarianism and conservatism, and for being a true friend. Others also deserve special intellectual and personal thanks: Claire Pavlik, Randy Wilson, Joe Nevins, Gerry Hale, Jane Moeckli, Kat O'Reilly, Laura Donaldson, Rebecca Roberts, Rex Honey, Gail Hollander, Steve Herbert, Mark Lawrence, Chris Merrett, Jeremy Brigham, Toby Moore, Larry Diamond, Larry Knopp, LaChee Payne, and Don Oberdorfer. John Durham Peters was such a good friend that I decided to leave him off my dissertation committee; nevertheless, this project owes more than he can ever know to his charity, grace, faith, and intellectual acumen. Lynn Rowell and Verna Johnson gave me space to write most of the early version of this book and were good friends.

Many archivists and librarians provided professional service at the University of Utah's Marriott Library, Brigham Young University's Harold B. Lee Library, the Utah State Historical Society, and the Church of Jesus Christ of Latter-day Saints Historical Department. Many other people provided support at various points in this project. Thomas Alexander, Donald

Meinig, and John Agnew read some version of the whole manuscript and have helped me become a better historian and geographer. Don Mitchell, Jeanne Kay Guelke, John Seagroves, and John Sillito read parts of the manuscript and provided invaluable feedback and encouragement. Sharon Snow Carver and Rick Phillips provided helpful information and ideas. Many of my colleagues at Brigham Young University at Hawai'i also gave intellectual and moral support: Chad Compton, Michael Allen, Jeff Belnap, Phillip McArthur, David Beus, Yifen Beus, Kathy Ward, Jim Tueller, and Jim Allen. Thanks also go to Liz Dulany at the University of Illinois Press for her patience and faith in the ideas of this book. Jane Mohraz improved the manuscript's readability greatly and saved me from many small mistakes.

Portions of the arguments in this book appear in articles recently published in the journals *Antipode* and *Cultural Geographies;* I thank reviewers and editors. I also thank the Historical Department of the Church of Jesus Christ of Latter-day Saints for allowing me to quote from its archives.

Most of all, I thank my wife and children. Chiung Hwang has borne with patience and grace my absences, strange ideas, and preoccupations. In a household with two academics and two children, one parent's project always cuts into the other's time for his or her own interests. Chiung Hwang's sacrifices have made this book possible. Thanks also to Chenoa and Annika for reminding their daddy of what is truly important.

TRANSFORMATION OF THE MORMON
CULTURE REGION

INTRODUCTION:

A Narrowed Regional Conversation

Preparations for the Salt Lake City 2002 Winter Olympics demonstrated that people considered the area a unique place. There were charges (and hopes) that those Olympics would become known as the "Mormon Olympics." The bribery scandal accompanying the Olympic location-bidding process deeply shamed the area. Many people equated Utah and Salt Lake City with Mormons, and Mormons expected to demonstrate superior morality. This was hardly the first incident that brought Mormonism and its region to the fore. News from the recent past provides example after example of social issues being read through Mormonism and debates between Mormons and non-Mormons: a gay club in a Salt Lake City high school, charges of anti-Mormonism at the University of Utah, claims that the Mormon church effectively controls much of the state legislature, antigambling campaigns, right-to-work laws, the Equal Rights Amendment, and the MX missile. Most regional inhabitants could probably provide many more examples. A personal favorite is how Dennis Rodman and his distaste for Utah/ Mormons almost upstaged Michael Jordan when the Chicago Bulls and the Utah Jazz battled for the National Basketball Association championship a few years ago.

A "Mormon culture region" exists.[1] There, Mormons dominate. Others need to learn their language and ways. Regional distinctiveness resides in more than just religious life itself, however, at least if religion is confined to matters of individual spiritual conscience. It also exists in deeply rooted conservative social ideologies. Such conservatism did not always mark the Mormon culture region. Not much more than a century ago, the Mormon culture region seemed to pose such a threat to the nation that the federal government brought the Church of Jesus Christ of Latter-day Saints to its figurative knees. In the eyes of non-Mormons, rampant sexual immorality, anti-Americanism, and coercive communalism characterized this region. Here men and women held unnatural relations with one another, white non-Mormon Americans felt like strangers, and frontier capitalism could not fully flourish. To most Americans, the central problem of the region then, as now, was Mormon dominance. But a little over a century ago, Mormon dominance produced an excess of radical challenge to the nation; now it accompanies an excess of conservatism. How did this change occur? This book attempts to answer that question.

The Mormon Culture Region and Americanization

Years ago, Donald Meinig (1965) wrote of the creation and expansion of what he called the Mormon culture region. To geographers studying Utah and the Mormons, Meinig's work remains a classic.[2] He charted the spread of Mormon settlement and church influence in the western United States during the latter half of the nineteenth century. He focused on the migratory streams through which Mormons came into the area and their expanding patterns of settlement. Most of the significant inflow and expansion came while Brigham Young was president of the church. Meinig's post-1877 (post–Brigham Young) analysis focused on smaller geographical shifts in Mormon population and church influence. Meinig's paper described an unparalleled process in American history. The creation of a Mormon culture region is remarkable in many ways. American society oppressed many minority religious groups, but only the Mormons were driven out of American territory and went on to establish America's most numerically successful homegrown religion. Not even the Baptists so directly influenced the growth of an American regional culture. Only struggles in the American post–Civil War South and those in immigrant-rich eastern cities and California were more important than those around the turn of the twentieth century in the Mormon region in determining what Americanism has come to mean.

Meinig's study focused on one part of this story of regional creation. His paper was less a work of cultural analysis than of geopolitical mapping. He focused less on the content and derivations of cultural values than on identifying where Mormon power was most prevalent. His paper centered on the power of the Mormon church as an institution. It paid less attention to cultural values inculcated and contested in the region. While he treats the establishment of Mormon culture as a historical process, once that culture is in place, it does not appear to evolve or undergo much historical change. The sense that Mormon culture and regional culture constituted shifting and contested terrains does not come through clearly. One learns, for example, that relations between Mormons and non-Mormons improved around the turn of the century, but one learns little about how this change affected the cultural socialization of regional inhabitants.

The present work argues that understanding the Mormon culture region, its current conservative characteristics, and its place within (while still somewhat apart from) the American West, depends on understanding the struggles over and transformation of the cultural values of the region's inhabitants since the nineteenth century. The meaning of regional habitation changed since then. The social moral orders (conceptions about right and wrong) that undergirded regional culture changed in subtle but very important ways during that period. By 1920, people possessed a set of cultural orientations that led them to perform and tolerate very different actions than they would have in 1880 (for an early analysis of LDS culture itself along some similar lines, see Ericksen [1922] 1975).

Many scholars describe this as a period of "Americanization."[3] Utahns and Mormons adopted many cultural conventions by choice or force, and other Americans no longer saw the Mormon culture region as un-American. LDS polygamy ended officially in 1890. Within a few years, Mormon leaders disbanded the LDS political party, and non-Mormons dissolved their anti-Mormon political party. These moves paved the way for Utah's statehood in 1896. Prior to the 1890s, largely because of the crippling power of antipolygamy legislation, the Latter-day Saints deemphasized their communitarian and separatist economic ideals. The Americanization of the region meant that Mormons and non-Mormons joined forces in political parties, social clubs, and economic pursuits. It meant that Mormon church leaders no longer monopolized political and economic activities regionally. Thus Utah and Mormons clearly were Americanized. But, as in the rest of the country, Americanization did not preclude the development of regional difference.[4] Inhabitants sought to retain a sense of regional distinctiveness. They emerged from the period more strongly Americanized but also strongly regionally socialized. The region did not disappear in the process of Americanization, but it surely was transformed.[5]

Dynamics of Regional Transformation

Meinig centered his definition of the Mormon region on the influence of the Mormon church. He concentrated on geographically defining the expanding or shifting of Mormon influence and the strength of that influence. My analysis changes the focus a bit. I do not want to confront Meinig's arguments and conclusions directly; for example, I do not take issue with his regional boundaries. Instead, I pay more attention to the cultural and social conditions driving the creation of regional difference in this era of Americanization (approximately 1880–1920). It is not enough to say that the area where Mormons dominate defines the Mormon culture region; the social and cultural implications of that dominance must be examined as well.

I argue that the Mormon–non-Mormon dynamic, set into motion by Mormon dominance, was the key element of regional creation and transformation.[6] It is hard to overestimate the drive to categorize people as either Mormons or non-Mormons and to base social difference on this distinction as a producer of regionality. Tensions existed between Mormons and non-Mormons in the area since the 1850s, just as there were patterns of cooperation and understanding between the two groups. But the areas of tension and bases of cooperation changed significantly over time. Non-Mormons residing both inside and outside the region struggled against Mormons over social practices and cultural meanings. This Mormon–non-Mormon dynamic was not static, and, as a result, regionally distinctive norms and cultural meanings shifted from when Mormons first dominated a geographical area in the Intermountain West.

In 1880, tensions between Mormons and non-Mormons were far more apparent than were areas of cooperation and commonality. These tensions structured regional society. Regional inhabitants' Mormon or non-Mormon identity came close to determining their stances on various sociocultural debates. Non-Mormons in the region generally shared with those outside the region a critique of the Mormon religion and Mormon social power. Mormon and non-Mormon sociocultural structures were considered incompatible, and most members of each group expended considerable energy trying to establish the regional dominance of their structures. The stakes were so high that they seemingly had little choice. Non-Mormons worried that Mormons would establish an anti-American society in the heart of the western United States, while Mormons, who felt they were implementing American ideals, feared for the existence of their church and their faith. Regional inhabitants thus viewed virtually all social questions through this prism. They structured issues seemingly far removed from the debate—woman suffrage, for example—around regional efforts to either establish or break down Mormon power.

By 1920, this dynamic had changed substantially. The distinction between Mormon and non-Mormon was still significant, but it no longer structured people's lives so completely. Being a Mormon or a non-Mormon no longer determined stances on the day's social debates. Moreover, non-Mormons residing outside the region had much less to say about how non-Mormons and Mormons related to each other within the region. By 1920, these "outsiders" no longer participated so directly in the dynamic. The Mormon–non-Mormon dynamic itself possessed a much different logic. In 1920, the collective memory of past tensions between Mormons and non-Mormons and the fear of returning to these battles structured the region culturally. Both sides made strong efforts (even if they were more understood than stated) to ensure that the area did not again become a site of these unmanageable battles. This regional understanding allowed Mormons and non-Mormons to work together peacefully on the basis of a broad range of social commonalities. By 1920, they shared much more than a notion of white racial superiority. They also agreed on most other fundamental social categorizations. And they both felt the need to develop and support their increasingly unified regional economy. But the price regional inhabitants—both Mormons and non-Mormons—paid for such a compromise was the capacity to question seriously the fundamental categories upon which they agreed. Questioning was too risky. It might open old wounds; previous polarizations might return. In essence, the culture region had been transformed, and it set off on a twentieth-century trajectory toward cultural conservatism. Regional inhabitants effectively banished the potential for fundamental critique of American society that the nineteenth-century region had seemed to represent. The accomplishments of regional transformation were immense—and I would not wish to return to the nineteenth-century Mormon culture region, with its polygamy and difficult struggles between Mormons and non-Mormons, any more than anyone else. Yet I think the region lost something valuable.

Many of the social roots of the Mormon culture region's transformation can be easily identified. Historians and social scientists who write about the Americanization of Utah or the Mormons point to most of the same elements. The death of Brigham Young in 1877 marked the end of an era in Mormonism. No Mormon leader thereafter possessed so much power and influence over the lives of church members. No other individual could capture the respect church members had for his feats of saving the church in its hour of apparent collapse, of leading its exodus across the "Great American Desert," and of establishing a growing and prospering Zion in the "desert" valleys of the mountains. By the time he died, the membership of the Mormon church had grown so large that leaders could no longer effectively use the personal style he preferred. After Young's death, Mormon leaders could not shape relations with non-Mormons as completely as he had. Nor could they command as much obedience as he had through the strength of his persona. Consequently, ideas about the Mormons' place in the nation and the economy were increasingly up for grabs. In addition, a younger generation had grown up within Mormonism, which meant they did not share with their parents the experience of gathering and separating from the rest of the world.

Regional and national forces outside Mormonism also played an important role in regional transformation. The expansion of American capitalism (already under way in the area before Young's death) can hardly be overemphasized. While Mormons had never completely rejected capitalism, they attempted at various times between 1830 and 1880 to repudiate its cultural logic. They attempted to shunt fundamental economic relationships and moral orders in communal/communitarian, as well as mercantilistic, directions. Maintaining these challenges to the individualistic capitalistic economy became increasingly difficult after 1880, when capitalist relations were expanded in the region and the region's economy was more fully linked to the national economy. During this time, two other institutions joined forces to transform Mormonism. The federal government and much of organized Protestantism finally determined that the Mormon church was too foreign to exist in the United States without significant change. In this quest, they found willing allies in most non-Mormons of Utah and the surrounding area. By the 1890s, these allied forces were able to make the Mormon church fear for its institutional existence and concede that it would abandon polygamy and give up control over Utah politics. Demographically, the area was also changing. The American West underwent rapid population growth during this period, and many newcomers were non-Mormons.

These social forces combined with unstable nineteenth-century Mormon and non-Mormon cultures to produce regional change. By unstable, I mean only that both Mormon and area non-Mormon cultures possessed attributes that facilitated their own modification. They were not less coherent or meaningful than other cultures. Cultural instability, I believe, is endemic. But different cultures possess their own specific contradictions, and the combined working out of Mormon and non-Mormon cultural contradictions produced regionally specific effects. Cultural contradictions can exist over long periods without creating cultural tension if the opposing elements are segmented from one another. Attacks on Mormonism and the maturing of Mormon culture made these contradictions widely apparent by the 1890s, however. They became problems in need of resolution.

The most important contradictions of nineteenth-century Mormon culture were these (see also O'Dea 1957):

1. a concept of patriarchal authority (this authority was less systematized and more personal than the regularized priesthood system

that later developed) versus a view of the church as an instrument of progress, independence, and freedom;

2. communitarian economic tendencies, led by strong central authority, versus the need to "demonstrate the truth" of Mormon doctrine through the regional economic superiority of the Mormon Zion; and

3. loyalty to the American nation versus an almost utter indifference to national political and social concerns.

These contradictions developed over the second half of the nineteenth century but became widely viewed as problems only once the strong attacks on Mormon culture and power commenced in the 1880s and 1890s.

Many non-Mormons who lived in the region tended to be more individualistic, more conservative on gender, and more nationalistic than most other Americans. They were an "advance guard" for the national movement toward the political right beginning in the 1890s.[7] Their culture also possessed contradictions that appeared problematic only as the struggle to change Mormonism developed. These included:

1. support for "American" political institutions in theory, which by definition included local majority control, versus a desire to install minority control in Utah because of distaste for Mormon norms and LDS political power;

2. a sense that attacking Mormon polygamy was working toward the progress of women versus an inability to see Mormon women as more than dupes of Mormon men and the church hierarchy; and

3. charges that Mormons lacked independence versus insistence that Mormons conform to American cultural norms and ways of thinking.

Regional inhabitants resolved most of these contradictions between 1880 and 1920. By 1920, these contradictions were no longer (or no longer seen as) problems. Inhabitants reached a new regional compromise. This compromise entailed a new set of tensions, but few people noticed these new contradictions at the time because no major pressures forced confrontation between contradictory elements. The contradictions "bore fruit" only in subsequent decades. These new regional tensions included:

1. a generally unquestioning acceptance of American capitalism versus an increasing peripheralization and colonization of the regional economy (May 1974; Alexander 1995b);

2. an inability to question some fundamental social structures versus a regional conception that this was a leading progressive region;
3. a social structure increasingly dominated by capitalist class differentiation versus the somewhat different norms of privilege and social commonality of a still-powerful LDS religion; and
4. a regional belief that tolerance for cultural differences had been achieved versus a regional "politics of home" that worked against acceptance of many kinds of difference.

Regional Movement away from Critical Perspectives toward Dominant Relationships

Regional inhabitants worked these social pressures and cultural contradictions into a new set of dispositions in which citizens grew increasingly incapable of radically approaching (especially through discourse) social practices or institutions dominant in the region and nation. In particular, these dispositions placed some fundamental power structures relating to identity beyond question. The power differentials men held over women, whites held over nonwhites, capitalists held over workers, church leaders held over church members, and Americans held over non-Americans were naturalized. Few people any longer questioned the national government's agenda, the Mormon social hierarchies, and capitalism's economic structures. One might work to reform some social practices through recourse to basic nationally dominant norms, but one would not ask about the desirability of the dominant norms or structures of power. Partly because these norms became so strongly inscribed in Mormon culture itself (and thus given a quasi-canonical status), the Mormon culture region set off on its own cultural trajectory, leading at first to middle-of-the-road conformity with national ideals. As this culture of conformity was further removed in time from the social conditions that had called the culture into existence, conformity tended toward conservatism. By the mid-twentieth century, a regional culture of superpatriotism and political conservatism had emerged.

Things could have turned out differently (contrary to Leone 1979). The dislocations produced between 1880 and 1920 opened many possibilities; a conformist-conservative trajectory was not the only one. Because of the differences between Mormons and non-Mormons and the challenge nineteenth-century LDS ideals posed to American norms, one of the possibilities might have encompassed more fundamental critiques of dominant power relations. A regional politics that tolerated difference and sought more egalitarian social and cultural structures could have resulted. To be sure, not all of nineteenth-century Mormonism could have fed into such a politics. Mormons and non-Mormons alike embraced American racist and colonialist attitudes and practices toward Native Americans, for one important example. Nevertheless, a respect for difference in other fundamental social categories might have emerged. Such a politics did not develop; instead, possibilities for such a politics were closed off. Regional inhabitants learned between 1880 and 1920 to shun such a politics.

Let me be clear. This argument does not apply only to Mormon culture. While Mormon values contributed to a conformist culture by sometimes advocating unquestioning obedience, regional non-Mormons also promoted this emergent regional culture. Ironically, non-Mormon attacks on Mormonism helped instill this regional culture of conformity. This culture arose from interaction between Mormons and non-Mormons. In 1880, habits of probing received wisdom and structures of privilege existed regionally (even if in an overly partisan manner) in the debates between Mormons and non-Mormons. By 1920, for the most part, such questions were no longer effectively posed regionally.

Three areas in which nineteenth-century Mormons and non-Mormons had substantial disagreement were the most important elements of regional transformation. Nineteenth-century contests raged over issues of gender authority, economic responsibility, and loyalty to the American nation. These debates related most directly to nineteenth-century Mormon polygamy, Mormons' communitarian experiments, and the political power of the church and Mormon distrust of the national government. The debates affected more than just Mormon institutional policy. The struggles over polygamy raised broad questions of men's and women's social authority (Gordon 2002). Debates over Mormon communitarian economic activity brought fundamental assumptions about social responsibilities inherent in economic life into question. Questions regarding Mormon political power addressed basic questions of what a nation was and what it meant to be loyal. Taken together, these debates allowed regional inhabitants to raise fundamental social questions.

In each case, regional inhabitants resolved the debates in ways that inculcated a narrow set of dominant norms: they rendered strongly differentiated gender authority unquestionable, they figured capitalist individualism as the properly dominant economic ethic, and they no longer debated national loyalty. Even the power of the Church of Jesus Christ of Latter-day Saints itself grew increasingly unquestionable in some ways. Concurrently, regional inhabitants grew unwilling or unable to conceive of Mormonism as a social (and not just a religious/moral) alternative to dominant structures of power. Meanwhile, older oppressive ideologies—such as those involving racial hierarchies—remained beyond question. The regional transformation strengthened faith in the inevitability of social progress. The three regional debates affected one another. Together they mitigated against regional inhabitants' making space for social difference beyond pluralistic, somewhat privatized religious belief.

In claiming that regional inhabitants rendered fundamental social structures increasingly unquestionable by 1920, I do not mean that regional inhabitants lacked the capacity for social criticism. Both Mormons and non-Mormons spoke out ably on many important issues. My point is, rather, that the scope of some particularly basic debates narrowed considerably between 1880 and 1920. Distinctions hardened between masculine and feminine, individual and cooperative, and loyal and disloyal. Only issues that did not much threaten these fundamental categorizations remained. By 1920, regional debate focused on such issues as prohibition; prostitution; Mormon truth claims; the power structures of political parties; workers' wages, hours, and safety; morality; and the League of Nations. These issues were important, but debates did not possess as much fundamentally transformative potential vis-à-vis American society as those of 1880 had.

* * *

Subsequent chapters detail these arguments. Chapter 1 explains the work's conceptual and methodological underpinnings. It suggests why "region" is at the center of the story. Chapter 2 explores the fortunes of regional feminism and struggles for greater female authority after polygamy officially ended. The first part describes the newly opened potential space for coalition between Mormon and non-Mormon women in the struggle for greater female cultural authority. This potential foundered as Mormon feminists found difficulty in retaining what I call their "radical edge." The second part of chapter 2 describes more precisely what Mormon critiques of gender authority lost during the region's transformation. Chapter 3 turns to regionalized norms of economic responsibility. Nineteenth-century communitarian experiments provided Mormons with an alternative economic tradition/ethic. But Americanization-era interaction between Mormons and non-Mormons created regional norms of conservatism and conventionality. The first part of the chapter details the convergence of Mormon and non-Mormon norms of wealth and wage labor; the second part centers on discourses of self-sufficiency and egalitarianism. Chapter 4's theme is regional norms of national loyalty. The region's political "liberalization" did not produce free individuals as much as Mormons and non-Mormons who better knew how to conform to national norms. The first part explores shifts from a rights-oriented discourse to a responsibility-oriented discourse; the second part argues that regional inhabitants came to understand national loyalty as political uniformity and cultural conformity to national trends. Chapter 5 relates the emergent regional norms of gender authority, economic responsibility, and national loyalty to one another by reading the transformation of the Mormon culture region through the discourse of the home and as a "politics of home." The major shifts in LDS culture—from challenge to embrace of Victorian gender relations, from communal to individual economics, and from political protest to identification with national power and might—facilitated and justified one another. In the afterword, I relate the contemporary Mormon–non-Mormon dynamic to the one that emerged a century ago and look for possibilities of contemporary progressive regional change.

CHAPTER ONE

THE REGION AS THE UNIT OF ANALYSIS

To describe and explain the historical transformation of the Mormon culture region, I utilize regional geographic analysis. The so-called new regional geography contributes to theorizations of the spatiality of social life. In so doing, it continues the project of many of the best "traditional" regional geographers who prioritized concept formation and explanation (Jonas 1988; Entrikin 1991). New regional geography breaks with traditional (see J. Hart 1982) particularly by addressing debates in social theory and (in recent years) cultural studies.

Regional Theory

One important concern of new regional geography is how regions come into existence or are transformed as a social category.[1] Regions are sets of social and cultural relations with spatially specific effects or patterns; regions can be thought of as "agents of social change" (Reynolds 1994, 234). In other words, new regional geography concerns itself with the processes whereby regions acquire sociological fixity and distinctiveness (as races or ethnicities might[2]), how they come to be considered important, and the effects produced by such spatially rooted processes and beliefs. It focuses on the creation and transformation of such regional processes through struggles and conflict. Regional historians addressing issues of regional existence make fewer philosophical claims than do geographers, but they have come to similar issues of cultural struggle and contest through multiculturalist concerns.[3] Ten assertions related to region point to many of this book's subthemes. A view of regions as dynamic, persistent, normative, porous, and process-dependent emerges (see also Cartier 2001, especially 18–30, 260–69).

Social Relations Occur in Place

Geographers insist that understanding where things occur is vital to understanding what occurs. Since the 1980s, scholars from other disciplines have slowly begun to acknowledge the point as well (see, for example, Gregory and Urry 1985; and Agnew and Duncan 1989). Mormon history makes this point obvious. Joseph Smith began proclaiming the LDS gospel in New England and the Upper Midwest. The consequences of this beginning differ from those that could have obtained if he had started somewhere else—the American South or Formosa, for example. Many argue that the LDS movement could not have even started anywhere else. Similarly, a place where the church grew—pre–Civil War Missouri—may well have influenced the development of the Mormon ban on blacks holding the priesthood (Bush and Mauss 1984). Likewise, as any LDS missionary will attest, the church's home in the United States influences the present-day reception of it throughout the world.

Place matters in many ways. The effects of *location* are perhaps most obvious. Location influences what is possible through proximity or lack of proximity. Brigham Young's perception that the Great Salt Lake Valley was far away from the rest of American society influenced his decision to end the Saints' exodus there. Just as surely, the increasing proximity of the Great Basin to other parts of the United States (because of migration and the railroad, for example) affected the subsequent drive to Americanize Mormons. But place is more than just location. It is also the *physical environment,* especially in relation to social processes (FitzSimmons 1990). The American West's arid and vast physical environment, for example, may have helped westerners justify white colonizers' monopolistic systems of water distribution (Worster 1985; not all agree: Pisani 1992). Perhaps most important to the present work, place matters as a *context* of social and cultural relations. As Michael Curry argues, places exist when people can claim "that's how we do things *here*" (1999, 99–100). Places represent the social practices and cultural understandings people have in different parts of the world. The social and cultural relations marking the American "frontier" strongly affected the shape Mormon culture assumed in the twentieth century, for example. Places do not determine action or meaning, but they are more than the background noise against which social and cultural processes operate. Places always partially constitute such processes.

In this book, I center on the Mormon–non-Mormon dynamic. This dynamic was not abstract or without context. Instead, it very literally assumed its structure in place. Its key features by the decades surrounding the turn of the century were that Mormons continued (but by an ever-shrinking margin) to hold a numerical majority in a certain area, that they remembered their persecutions and separatist goals, that non-Mormons considered themselves an oppressed minority in this area, and that most of these non-Mormons (Native Americans excepted, of course) had the federal government on their side. It mattered very much that most people in a specific part of the world lived this dynamic and could not escape from it. People sensed that they were in a unique part of the world and acted in ways that reproduced this uniqueness.

Region Is an Important Type of Place

Places, as contexts with a geographical structure, occur in many forms and in a variety of scales. Places can cover small spaces—such as a bedroom, a guard tower, or an LDS Relief Society room. They can be large—such as nation-states—or megaregions—such as "Asia." For some, the world constitutes a place. Regions—in the sense of the Mormon culture region—constitute a particular kind of place. Regions in this sense possess attributes distinguishing them from most small-scale places or places like the nation-state. The key distinctions do not directly relate to spatial size, however.

Anssi Paasi (1991) argues that region and (what I have called small-scale) place are both historically and geographically constituted, but they are distinct categories that differ temporally. Place refers to individually experienced "situated episodes of life history" (248). Region, to Paasi, precedes place. It has a longer historical duration and is "a representation of 'higher-scale history' into which inhabitants are socialised as part of the reproduction of the society. . . . [It is] a *social and cultural category* with an explicit collective dimension representing institutional practices sedimented in the *history of the region . . .*" (249). Regions are not simply mental constructs; they become institutionalized and produce communication and symbols common to most in the region, though the meanings associated with these differ according to individual situations. Regions, Paasi also suggests, exist through generations.

Regions—like nations (Benedict Anderson 1983)—exist only through the widespread act of imagining a community; regional inhabitants cannot possibly know most other inhabitants personally, but they can feel affinity for those unknown fellow citizens. I want to distinguish regions from nation-states, however, and even from nations with unfulfilled political aspirations. Such places share many attributes with regions, but the goal of state sovereignty so pervades the constitution of nations and nation-states that one needs to be reminded (through the concept of region) that such communitarian/territorial imaginations often result from other means. This distinction also emphasizes that regions do not necessarily arise from formal political boundaries.[4]

The unit of analysis in this book is the region (the space where the Mormon–non-Mormon dynamic had continued social significance), not the state of Utah. The Mormon culture region shaped human action, identity, and consciousness over the span of more than a generation. The practices, ideologies, and symbols represented by the region were socially powerful on a broad scale, not just individually experienced or dictated within state boundaries. Awareness of this region's distinctiveness existed both locally and extralocally and shot through relations between Mormons and non-Mormons.

Regions Are Socially, Culturally, and Historically (in Addition to Geographically) Constituted

A strength and a weakness of traditional regional geography (as well as traditional regional history) lay in its integrative objectives. It sought to synthesize a bulk of information about an area into a coherent whole (Minshull 1967). At its best, it created elegant regional pictures; at its worst, it accomplished little beyond cataloguing. The new regional geography still synthesizes. But, as Anne Gilbert (1988) argues, synthesis now serves analysis instead of existing as a goal in itself. In particular, many look for conflict, struggle, dominance, and oppression before identifying regional homogeneity (although see Holmén 1995).[5] Thus, in Gilbert's words, "the region under analysis will be relevant on the basis of the social processes it brings into perspective" (222)—in the present case the struggles between Mormons and non-Mormons.

New regional geography requires synthesis because region (as a type of place) distills multiple social, cultural, and natural processes (Sack 1997). This book synthesizes in two ways. On the one hand, it integrates arguments about gender, the economy, and the nation. On the other hand, it insists that each of these topics comprises simultaneously interacting social, cultural, and historical processes. Gender relations, for example, consist in social opportunities available to women, cultural imaginations of men's and women's relations with each other, and efforts to remember or forget the past (polygamy and woman suffrage, for example). Similarly, the regional economy encompasses increasingly pervasive capitalist social relations, cultural ideologies of proper wealth creation, and the memory of LDS communitarianism.

A divide exists within geography between scholars who see places/regions primarily as social structures and those who regard them fundamentally as imaginative abstractions. Many political and economic geographers regard relations between social groups as both the key ingredient and the product of regional processes. J. Nicholas Entrikin (1996) suggests that this vein of writing leaves us with little more than a sense of regional conflict, important as such conflict is. We do not see how people create meaningful ties and moralities through cultural processes. Humanist cultural geographers emphasize such meanings and identities, while many nonhumanist post-structuralists prioritize imaginations of regions, with little concern for the social relations that exceed discourse (I believe these exist). Many of these latter scholars rightly question strong distinctions between materiality and representation (see, for example, Matless 1995; and K. Anderson and Gale 1992), but too many collapse materiality into representation.

I do not wish to declare either social relations or cultural imaginations as most fundamental; rather, I hold them in productive tension (see also Peet 2000). While the social and the cultural help constitute each other, they are not the same thing.[6] Regions interest me precisely because territorial imaginations and territorially organized social processes (as well as territorially organized uses of history) hold mutually constitutive relationships (Agnew 1999). Within regions, cultural imaginations and social processes are always historically constituted. The past is always present in some form.

The literature on Mormons/Utah/the region has not often effectively brought cultural imaginations into analytical relation with social processes. We currently understand Americanization's social processes much better than cultural ones. We know the political changes forced on the region. We know about the church's dissociation from polygamy. We know how the church abandoned communitarian economics. We know when and why periods of distrust arose between Mormons and non-Mormons. We know about the successful battle for woman suffrage. We know many Mormon leaders were successful capitalists. We understand the rough outline of the regional economy's shift from relative self-sufficiency toward reliance on raw material extraction and dependence within the American economy. We know whites continually marginalized Native Americans through displacement and exploitation. We know of non-Mormon immigrants' increasing role in the area's socioeconomic patterns. But we know very little about changing cultural imaginations and meanings. If this book concentrates on the cultural more than the social, it is because a larger void exists there.

Regions Require Identity

The common words *place* and *space* become slippery when used conceptually. Is there a difference between space and place? If so, what? Are areas of the earth simultaneously spaces and places? When does a space start being a place? Many scholars do not clearly delineate these terms. Yet distinguishing between place and space aids regional analysis. Years ago, Yi-Fu Tuan (1977) proposed a distinction. A place can only exist when people identify themselves as belonging to it. If no strong identity or sense of belonging exists, it is a space, not a place (see also P. Taylor 1999).

Region means that people regard an area as a home. Feminists justifiably criticize the home—or at least certain types of homes—as a site of oppression, especially for women and children. Yet *home* still conjures up images of safety and refuge (hooks 1990; Reagon 1998). Even most people who want to escape dysfunctional homes or oppressive traditional homes desire not homelessness but a home more nearly matching the images of safety and refuge (Sack 1997, 263). Regions, like homes, incorporate feelings of belonging, even if these feelings are unequally distributed. Regional identity connotes a sense of belonging in a particular area (Cuba and Hummon 1993) or shared historical experience, memory, or struggle (Milner 1992; Worster 1992). Identity utilizes intersubjective meanings associated with symbols. Although symbols have multiple and shifting meanings, people share meanings and use them to determine who is or is not one of "us" (Kelley 1994). Regional identity links the "we" to the "here" in Curry's "that's how we do things here" place-identifying phrase.

Of course, identifying a "we" involves more than asserting solidarity and fellowship. Regional identity is always relational (Berdoulay 1989; Massey 1994). By asserting it, people "negotiate a meaningful life space" and simultaneously "position themselves within a situation of power," according to Allen Chun (1996, 69). It positions people in relation to others both outside and inside the region. It identifies a "them," who are not "us," through other identities outside the region. It also creates an internal "them"—those who do not properly conform to dominant practices in the region. The creation of the latter "us" and "them" has gradations, with hierarchies implying that certain people epitomize regional citizenship while others hold more marginal or imperfect identities. American society typically creates hierarchies along lines of social difference—gender, race, class, ethnicity, religion, sexuality, and the like. Thus affective rewards and oppressive marginalizations simultaneously pervade the creation of regional identity.[7]

An important aspect of the Mormon region's transformation is the development of a stronger regional identity incorporating both Mormons and (at least white, native-born) non-Mormons. Regional identity is never fully finished but instead is subject to continual renegotiation (Anglin 1992; Oakes 1993). Regional relations in the Mormon culture region of the late 1800s can be compared with relations in a dysfunctional home. Most Mormons were extremely wary of non-Mormons, while non-Mormons shunned most things Mormon and insisted that the church needed to dissolve or change substantially. By 1920, though some uneasiness remained, Mormons and non-Mormons sensed that they shared a common regional destiny and that they could jointly call the region home. To their credit, regional inhabitants acquired this sense without destroying the LDS Church or LDS cultural identity and with decreasing non-Mormon alienation. But here, as elsewhere, exclusions and oppressions also resulted. Marginalizations of Native Americans did not improve, for example. Immigrant groups experienced much alienation. The resultant regional identity privileged whiteness and more clearly differentiated the roles of male and female regional citizens.

Regions Are Real

The assertion that regions are real is theoretically contentious. A brief theoretical foray may help explain the claim. Two related theoretical commitments open up space to view regions as real. First, social theory has long insisted that structures affect human behavior. Second, transcendental realism claims that nonempirically verifiable structures exist and invest objects and agents with causal powers (Sayer 1992; Sack 1997, 53–56; Entrikin 1991, 20–23). Structures that can be grasped only through an intellectual abstraction of multiple processes and manifestations, such as capitalism, are nevertheless real. To claim that regions exist is to claim, most fundamentally, that they produce effects. Regions are not inconsequential imaginations or the surface spatial manifestations of a more fundamental social reality. Regions exist in much the same sense that nations exist, and they produce similar types of effects.

Regions produce effects because regional identities matter in the United States (Onuf 1996). They produce effects because the spatial structuring of social processes opens some avenues of social intercourse and closes others. Perhaps most important, they produce what Paasi calls "structures of expectation" (1991). Structures of expectation refer to the ways people organize their knowledge of the world and use that knowledge to interpret new information. Paasi derives the concept from Raymond Williams's (1961) "structure of feeling" and Pierre Bourdieu's (1977) "habitus." Structures of expectation relate to the practices and ideological dispositions regional inhabitants take for granted, those they often utilize less than completely consciously. Through the process of regional socialization, regional inhabitants incorporate specific ways of being in the world and pass these dispositions on (if imperfectly) through generations.

The Mormon culture region's transformation meant a fundamental re-casting of structures of expectation. People knew much had changed re-gionally because of Americanization, but few grasped how substantial the change was. Yet the strong regionally contentious attitudes and ideologies of the 1880s had been transformed into unquestioned agreement by 1920. Regional inhabitants took the capitalist ethic for granted, for instance, as the only possible one upon which the economy could effectively operate. Sim-ilarly, dispositions that were in the mainstream of regional debate in 1880 moved to the fringes by 1920. For example, conceptions of national loy-alty now precluded assertions that the United States did not extend enough rights. Much changed in structures of expectation, and the lack of regional commentary on the breadth of the changes is remarkable. To be sure, both Mormons and non-Mormons claimed the regional climate between the two groups had vastly improved, but neither group saw itself as having changed much. Nevertheless, change was profound; the new expectations reverber-ated throughout the twentieth century in approaches to social difference.

Regions Are Like Conversations or Debates

The argument for the reality of regions does not imply that regions are pre-ordained, eternal, or immutable. Scholarship in the 1980s debunked essen-tialized claims for nations (Hobsbawm 1990; Benedict Anderson 1983; Gell-ner 1983). Nations change; some hold similar form over time only when people continually reproduce them through practice and ideology. Regions likewise change their content, contours, and geographical and social bound-aries over time. Allan Pred (1986) argues that places are processes, not static geographical entities. Michael Curry takes issue with following the process metaphor too far but agrees that places exist only as long as processes keep them "alive" (1999, 102). He similarly argues that we err if we think of place most fundamentally as location. Doing so prioritizes boundary identification and map drawing. Such exercises obscure the fact that people must contin-ually maintain regions for them to exist. Instead, Curry believes, comparing regions to conversations is more useful.

Conversations change, Curry reminds us. Participants do not always re-main the same. The central topic may shift over time. Those involved might have pleasant relations, or there may be bitter acrimony; these relations often shift. In such ways, regions resemble conversations. Basically, people must continually maintain and reproduce the key processes and dynamics if the region is to exist over time (see also Woods 1998, 25). If processes or dynamics change substantially, the region transforms. Others make similar arguments, though some shift the metaphor toward "debate," since the sides are often clearly drawn and antagonistically arrayed against each other (see, for example, Massey 1994; and Oakes 1993).

The Mormon–non-Mormon dynamic was a fundamental producer of regionality and a key indicator of regional change. Distinctions between Mormons and non-Mormons held great importance during the period under study (as they have ever since then). This dynamic was not at that time primarily a theological disagreement disconnected from social reality.[8] Regional "conversations" have social, material, practical, and ideological implications. This dynamic changed between 1880 and 1920. The topics debated, the key participants, the relationships between participants, and the tone with which participants conducted the conversation all shifted substantially. The dynamic itself, however, never ceased to exist and to produce effects. I thus refer to regional "persistence" as well as to "transformation" and "trajectory."

There is another similarity between regions and conversations. Very rarely do close-to-equal power distributions exist (Massey 1994). The real world has not achieved Jürgen Habermas's ideal conversation situation. Power differentials shoot through regional life. This book points to key inequalities: whites holding more power than nonwhites; native-born more than nonnative-born; men more than women; capitalists more than workers; and Mormons sometimes more than non-Mormons locally but generally less nationally. The contours of these power relations shaped the changing regional conversation.

Regions and Moralities Help Constitute Each Other

This book emphasizes one type of regional cultural structuring: morality. In recent years, mostly theoretical analyses of the mutually constitutive relationship between place and morality have proliferated.[9] Regions incorporate the positioning of people in society, (sometimes less-than-conscious) practices people engage in, and senses of regional identity. Each of these attributes implies that people make moral judgments when creating and maintaining regions. They point to the creation and establishment of regional moral orders. Moral order is a set of definitions, usually not explicated, regarding what is proper to do and what can reasonably be expected from others or the sense of what people feel they owe one another as members of a community (Hughey 1983; Wuthnow 1987). In a simple sense, morality involves distinguishing right from wrong. The moral order of a group represents a popular consensus on which practices are and are not legitimate. Moral order may or may not correspond to actual practices, but its norms are those around which leaders can most easily motivate widespread action (Thompson 1971).

In spite of many academics' modern and postmodern distrust of ordering narratives of social life, people continue to seek moral order. Through social contestation, people clarify norms guiding their everyday actions. These norms define what is and is not permissible for "good" members of society. They organize disparate cultural categories into a "system" of shared meanings and symbols (Dudley 1994). Historical analysis of moral orders examines the norms and values people in particular contexts link with strong connotations of propriety. How do particular norms and values gain dominance? How are others marginalized? Too often—especially in the United States, with its supposed separation of religion from politics—discussions of morality assume an ethereal, disconnected quality. But moral orders are ideological in the most materially relevant sense of that term; they constitute a kind of politically interested discourse (Eagleton 1991). Analysis of changes in such orders reveals much about society's conflicts and contests.

The debates structuring this book involve three types of moral order: gender authority, economic responsibility, and national identity. Regional transformation fundamentally depended on shifts in each. Gender systems constitute moral orders because such systems comprise expectations about what is proper and the kind of relations people owe one another as gendered individuals. The concept of moral order helps us understand the strength and durability of particular gender systems. People view gender ideologies as more than simple cultural conventions that they can easily alter or replace. Instead, they see violations to these moral orders as, in Nancy Eberhardt's words, "disturbing transgressions, an invitation to chaos and evil" (1988, 6). Or, to use a metaphor currently popular on the political right, people believe gender systems are a central "thread" in the "social fabric." Weakening this thread places the whole fabric in jeopardy. Gender as a moral order acquires strength and durability through embodiment (Moi 1991). Economic systems also encompass moral orders. Such systems incorporate a set of expectations about morally proper and improper economic action. Much scholarship explicates the "moral economy" of groups faced with the onslaught of capitalist or colonialist systems (Scott 1976; Thompson 1971; Gosner 1992). In addition, Robert Wuthnow argues that the capitalist market system provides people with a sense of self-worth and structures much of their participation in public life. "It is," he contends, "an integral aspect of our basic values and our assumptions about reality" (1987, 79; see also Zukin 1991). Threats to the system challenge not only those who benefit most from the system but also widely distributed and deeply held social expectations accompanying the system. Ideals of national loyalty/identity also make strong claims about proper behavior and attitudes; they, too, incorporate moral orders. Nations not only demarcate a community to which one does or does not belong but also imply proper dispositions toward this imagined entity (Benedict Anderson 1983). As with gender and economy, specific moral orders of national loyalty are more often than not naturalized and considered to be the only possible set of proper dispositions.

Regions Are Porous but Not Diffuse

The processes affecting a region exceed any spatial limits it might possess. While this statement sounds banal, it has received significant theoretical acknowledgment and justification only in recent years. Doreen Massey, for example, claims that "what is specific about a place, its identity, is always formed by the juxtaposition and co-presence there of particular sets of social interrelations and by the effects which that juxtaposition and co-presence produce. Moreover . . . a proportion of the social interrelations will be wider than and go beyond the area in any particular context as a place" (1994, 168–69).[10] Regional stories cannot be told only from the inside. While distinguishing between a region's "inside" and "outside" by the co-presence of specific processes and the identity accompanying this co-presence (regions are not completely diffuse), analysis must include the outside.[11] Notions that a culture region represents the relatively unimpeded elaboration of a single group's culture within space are inadequate. The Mormon culture region cannot be fully understood if it is seen most fundamentally as the product of an evolving or maturing LDS culture.

Geographers often analyze how large-scale capitalism creates local places or regions. The expansion of capitalist relations played a key role in the Mormon culture region's transformation, but I also point to other extraregional processes. The federal government had a keen interest in reforming the region politically and socially and exerted power in multiple ways. Contests between mainstream Protestantism and Mormonism were important, as were American/Protestant understandings about the boundaries of religion. Movements with centers outside the region produced effects—I discuss woman suffrage and socialism in some detail—and region-exceeding ideologies—such as those of Victorian romanticism, progress, civilization, liberalism, and the American frontier—influenced the regional transformation. Because of all these processes, operating simultaneously with different logics and with varying intensities (Appadurai 1990), the Mormon culture region must be regarded as porous.

Robert Sack (1997) suggests that the degree of porosity varies; it, too, deserves analysis. The Mormon culture region's porosity diminished between 1880 and 1920 in at least one key way. To be sure, porosity increased in some

ways as regional inhabitants became more involved in national economic processes, political debates, and social issues. Nevertheless, the fundamental
Mormon–non-Mormon dynamic operated much more solely within the region by 1920, primarily because it became difficult to see Mormons as a significant threat to the nation and because regional non-Mormons simultaneously desired less extraregional assistance. Extraregional actors seemed to
lack the deftness for rapid changes that regional habitation provided.

Regions Overlap with and Are Structured Hierarchically in Relation to Other Places

Regions are not mutually exclusive territorial entities. Sometimes geographers and others identify mutually exclusive territories within regional
schemes, but such efforts emphasize one or a few set of relations over others. The region always depends on the social relations the researcher emphasizes. Someone who focuses on the capitalist economy's structure would
likely specify a region spatially incongruent with the one I base on the
Mormon–non-Mormon dynamic.[12] Or someone else might emphasize relations between whites and Native Americans to produce an altogether different regional space. But the reality of these regions (or the fact that they
produce significant effects) does not diminish because differing, though spatially overlapping, regions can and should be identified. I thus do not claim
that this book constitutes the definitive treatment of the turn-of-the-century
Mormon culture region.[13] The notion that regions overlap has another implication. Emphasizing some social processes means deemphasizing others.
While I do not totally ignore Native Americans, for one example, neither
do I position them as fundamentally in my account as other narratives prioritizing other social relations should. I regrettably (but probably unavoid-
ably given the focus) treat them as historical objects more than as historical subjects. In this sense, historical regional geographies are not simply
historical summaries of events (or even geographical events) within specified
spatial boundaries.

Similarly, although unlike the case for nation-states, there is no single regional scale. Regions both overlap and nest within one another. This book
points to the Mormon culture region's increasingly comfortable residence
within the American West. Western norms and agendas—so antithetical to
many Mormons during Brigham Young's day—appeared to both Mormons
and non-Mormons as a logical common base for the two groups' interactions by 1920. The Americanization of the Mormon culture region thus promoted its regionalization (regional persistence). As with today's globalization and proliferation of local identities (Massey 1994; Kong 1996; Wang

1997), the larger process does not always obliterate (though it surely affects) the smaller. In many respects, Americanization and regionalization required each other (Onuf 1996). Today, regional differences and identities remain, even if American commonalities and globalization have obliterated the original reasons for their existence. Spatially uneven development, migration, and ecological destruction, for example, promote distinctiveness in the Northeast, "New" South, California, Pacific Northwest, and South Florida. Likewise, regional political habits do not die easily (Elazer 1994; Johnston 1991).

Institutions and Collective Memory
Help Regions Persist over Time

I have already suggested that socialization processes facilitate the persistence of regional "conversations" in a generally similar form. Institutionalization (Paasi 1991) and collective memory (Milner 1992) provide channels for maintaining a structured flow of regional conversations. Institutions retard the speed at which social change occurs in much the same way that the built environment creates inertia and decreases the ability of local places to react to rapid flows of global capital (Harvey 1985); in both instances, local distinctiveness persists. Collective memory of jealousies, mistrust, and competitiveness can likewise slow social change. Of course, change may occur quickly when institutions or collective memories undergo substantial shifts.

Even as the Church of Jesus Christ of Latter-day Saints embraced much of the region's rapid social and political change, it was the primary institution promoting regional identity. The church and Mormon culture more generally retained a sense of inhabiting a regional home. The most central regional collective memory was that of nineteenth-century struggles and fights between Mormons and non-Mormons. This collective memory pushed other potential (and potentially controversial) memories—such as "radical" Mormonism—to the margins. Regional inhabitants found the memory of past animosities too bitter to countenance other memories that might call the achieved regional peace into question.

Finding the Region

This is a study about regional cultural transformation. As such, its central concern is the manner in which meanings and norms shifted over a period of time and structured a new sense of regionality through persistent struggles between Mormons and (primarily white) non-Mormons. It deals with issues of Mormons, non-Mormons, radicalism, conservatism, liberalism, gender, nation, economy, Utah, and the like, yet my central conceptual and topical concerns are not these but rather region and moral order. Thus, for example, an obvious gender topic during this period—Mormon polygamy—receives little analysis (instead, see Van Wagoner 1986; Carmon Hardy 1991; and Daynes 2001). Polygamy simply was not very important to the regional norms created by 1920, except as a continuing worrisome memory.

Yet how does one find an abstraction like region through historical analysis? It must be inferred from the study of more concrete objects and events. I examine regionality through seven major events, institutions, and issues as well as a few smaller ones. These topics bring into focus moral norms dearly valued by nineteenth-century Mormons and deeply resented by most non-Mormons. Each sheds light on the regional accommodations and consensus reached between Mormons and non-Mormons. I do not tell the whole story of any of these institutions, events, or issues; rather, I combine them to tell a comprehensible regional story. Specific sources used on these topics illuminate broad social thinking—what Nigel Thrift (1994) calls the regional public sphere—more than institutional debates or the views of individuals.

The Mutual Improvement Associations

These LDS-sponsored youth organizations, divided by gender, were an important part of a powerful system of religious and social training for church members. The organizations were conceived toward the end of Brigham Young's life and contributed to his strategy of resisting increasing non-Mormon regional influence. Despite their beginnings, they held much autonomy within Mormonism. While today's successors to these organizations look inward, the early twentieth-century mutual improvement associations involved Mormon youth in leading social and moral causes of the period (Alexander 1986). The Young Ladies' Mutual Improvement Association socialized young women into expectations of LDS motherhood and introduced them to arguments from the women's movement, among other things. The Young Men's Mutual Improvement Association trained young men particularly for Mormon missionary service early in the period and later on in economics, especially vocational training. Both associations had strong educational foci—literature, science, and history, for example, were taught alongside LDS doctrine; Mormons did not yet regard public schools as a desirable option. Key sources I utilized are the manuals used for weekly instruction as well as the journals published for association members (initially the *Contributor* and later *Improvement Era* for the Young Men's Mutual Improvement Association; *Young Woman's Journal* for the Young Ladies' Mutual Improvement Association).

The Aftermath of the Woman Suffrage Movement

Utah women gained the right to vote twice—in 1870 and with statehood in 1896 (Van Wagenen 1994). Between those years, the federal government took their vote away (in 1887) as part of its crackdown on Mormon polygamy and theocratic power. In 1870, the church initiated or at least approved the idea of suffrage. Many non-Mormons also supported suffrage then, assuming that female LDS voters would revolt against polygamy. This hope never materialized; Mormon women joined Mormon men in voting for church-nominated political candidates and continued to support polygamy publicly. Congress therefore revoked woman suffrage in 1887 as one strategy of breaking LDS power. If all women in Utah could not vote, it reasoned, the LDS women's vote would not dilute the non-LDS vote. In spite of fervent protests, Utah women had to wait until after statehood to regain the franchise.

During these years, most of the suffrage movement's Mormon spokeswomen were involved in polygamy. Their messages extended beyond the right to vote. They expressed views that resonate somewhat with recent cultural feminist critiques of Victorian ideals of romantic love, female friendship, and gender roles. They grounded these views in a polygamous social system and therefore provoked much criticism from polygamy's opponents. Nevertheless, they established political connections with some national suffrage and women's rights leaders. By the late 1880s, however, the battle against polygamy reached such a pitch that national women's rights leaders could no longer politically afford to seek even limited common cause with polygamous Mormon suffragists. Thereafter, a new generation of mostly monogamous Mormon women led suffrage battles. In the 1890s, Mormon and non-Mormon women fought together for suffrage at statehood; they also lent support to the national movement after 1896. My research looks at the claims about gender made, particularly by Mormon women, after suffrage in Utah was achieved. The *Woman's Exponent,* a monthly journal published by Mormon women, contains the most important statements.

Speeches by Mormon Leaders

I prioritize speeches by LDS leaders in the church's semiannual general conferences because they were widely heard and recognized as representing the church's position (see also Shepherd and Shepherd 1984).[14] Members came to Salt Lake's Tabernacle to hear "counsel" from church leaders in these three-day conferences. Although this particular source does not reveal all the behind-the-scenes maneuvering by church leaders, it effectively relates "official" church stances. These official stances mattered to both Mormons and non-Mormons and reveal much about regional culture. Mormon leaders often responded, at least indirectly, to charges made by the non-Mormon community. Even in the twentieth century, church leaders remained among the region's most influential people. They still commanded respect and obedience from many church members, several leaders played strong roles in business, and a few held significant political influence.

Opening of the Uintah Indian Reservation

The Uintah Indian Reservation, located in the northeast corner of Utah, near the Colorado-Wyoming border, opened to white settlement in 1905 (see Fuller 1990). The federal government expended much effort on the reservation on teaching farming and individual self-sufficiency to the Ute (for a history of the Ute, see Conetah 1982). The allotment of the reservation also gave whites opportunities to grab land and to provide an "example" to the Ute (MacKay 1995; Lang 1954). Unlike the adjacent Ouray Indian Reservation, the Uintah Indian Reservation was reputed to have large amounts of arable land. Although these reports proved unduly optimistic, the opening provoked great excitement. It also gave Mormons and non-Mormons one of their first opportunities to settle an area together. Federal records show the government's role in the opening and the kind of pressures it faced from private individuals and groups.[15] Newspaper accounts of the opening, particularly from those located in northeastern Utah, provide other viewpoints.

The Relationship between Utah Socialism and Mormon Communitarianism

In the 1850s-70s, Brigham Young led attempts to establish communal, cooperative, or communitarian economies; all eventually succumbed to more capitalistic systems. Some recent observers see values strongly resembling socialist ideals underlying such efforts. While most contemporary Mormons have resisted comparisons of nineteenth-century Mormonism with socialism—indeed have shunned socialism—the question was much more open one hundred years ago. For example, John McCormick found that about 40 percent of Utah Socialist Party activists were Mormons during this era (1982, 232). Socialism was a topic of great interest in Utah during the early years of the twentieth century, as it was elsewhere in the United States, although the Socialist Party itself was never powerful there. Several newspapers published a regular socialist column for a time. Many such columns lasted only a short while, but the *Ogden Morning Examiner*'s weekly columns spanned nearly four years (1905–9); they are my most important source on this topic. LDS Church leaders also mentioned socialism, and Christian socialism was very influential in Utah's socialist movement.

Patriotic Celebrations

In the nineteenth-century Mormon culture region, rancor between Mormons and non-Mormons over the celebration of patriotic holidays was endemic. Non-Mormons typically accused the Saints of a lack of American patriotism during Fourth of July celebrations. Mormons, for their part, held their own Independence Day ceremonies, during which they simultaneously proclaimed loyalty to America and protested their treatment at the hand of the American government. Pioneer Day is the second major patriotic holiday for Mormons. The first company of Latter-day Saints completed its journey to the Salt Lake Valley on 24 July 1847, and the day has been commemorated in Utah ever since. I used newspaper accounts to examine this topic. I looked at celebrations in sampled years as reported in the *Salt Lake Tribune* (the early name was the *Daily Tribune*) and the *Salt Lake City Deseret News* (the early name was the *Deseret Evening News*). The latter paper was an organ of the church, while the former, though not ostensibly organized as anti-Mormon, consistently positioned itself as an opponent of the church.

Smoot Hearings

In 1903, Utah's legislature elected the Mormon apostle Reed Smoot as U.S. senator. A number of Salt Lake City citizens protested that Smoot could not honestly defend the U.S. Constitution because he was one of the top fifteen men in the Mormon hierarchy. The Senate therefore, in Thomas Alexander's words, "conducted what many observers consider the most wide-ranging investigation of a religious organization in American history" (1995b, 254; see also Flake 2000). The ostensible issues were whether Mormon church leadership continued to countenance plural marriages and whether leaders used ecclesiastical authority to control members' politics, but many more issues surfaced. The hearings coincided with the revival of an anti-Mormon political party in Utah. Until the early 1890s, Utah politics split along religious lines: the Mormon People's Party versus the non-Mormon Liberal Party. The Liberal Party dissolved only after the People's Party had disbanded and Mormons had joined the two major national political parties. By the early years of the twentieth century, some people, primarily former Liberals, regarded the church's Americanization efforts as disingenuous and formed the American Party in 1904; one of their major goals was to oust Smoot. The Senate committee that heard the complaint against Smoot recommended denying him a seat in the Senate. The full Senate, however, voted in 1907 to seat him, probably more out of partisan politics than any single issue that arose from the hearings.

*   *   *

I rely on these topics because of an ethnographic desire to represent norms and values in many different situations and an historiographic desire to tell a story that makes contextual sense. The topics I researched influence the story I tell in this book. If I had focused on different topics, my regional story would surely be different.[16] I therefore do not claim to have produced the final word on the Mormon culture region's turn-of-the-century transformation. Instead, I believe historical research is fundamentally about finding plausible meaning. History has the dual purpose of suggesting how people may once have created meaning and hinting at how contemporary readers can make sense of their own situations. The point, then, of this work is to offer a plausible interpretation of how the Mormon culture region was transformed through shifting moral orders and to provide further insight into such issues as the regional constitution of social life, Mormon history, Utah history, Mormon culture, and American culture.

CHAPTER TWO

MODERATING FEMINIST IMAGINATIONS

Much LDS female youth literature from 1880 to 1920 addressed the qualities young men and women ought to possess as potential marriage partners and what to expect from each other. Leaders of Mormon youth felt that the ways young people associated with members of the opposite sex should not be left to chance. The attributes the leaders tried to instill are apparent in this literature. A prominent figure in this literature is the pure and innocent Latter-day Saint young woman.

Despite variations in different stories, several common qualities characterize this figure. This innocent Mormon young woman typically works hard and is unselfish. She keeps busy during her teenage years by working in the home to benefit her family. She is mostly unfamiliar with the vices that tempt young women who have more time on their hands. In spite of her innocence, she has a solid education and appreciates civilization's niceties. She typically has lived on the edge of poverty and knows that her own hard work makes the difference between her family's comfort (if minimal) and desperation. She likely grew up in a rural setting and is strongly bound to her family and community. Many authors strengthen and regionalize these ties by setting her hometown in mountainous areas. She is eminently capable as a housewife and possesses a sweet, undemanding personality, making her attractive to young men seeking a wife.

In some stories, she exhibits no character weakness. In others, she can be tempted by suitors with the sophistication and material advantages the young men in her community lack. When she displays weakness, it invariably lies in her attraction to non-Mormon city boys, who have smooth public manners and promise her a life of greater sophistication and comfort than she has hitherto enjoyed. The point of stories with such a figure is to show how she overcomes or occasionally is destroyed by her attraction to such characters. She realizes that staying in her community is the best course before marriage, or (if she marries her temptation) she regains, and often wins her husband over to, the values and lifestyle of her upbringing. Authors of literature for young Mormon women repeated this general story over and over.

This figure's continuity makes it easy to overlook an important shift over these years. The pure and innocent young LDS woman loses a good deal of her autonomy from men (and desire for autonomy) by 1920. "The Western Boom," printed serially in the first volume of the *Young Woman's Journal,* provides a good example of the figure early in the period. The story's heroine marries a non-Mormon and moves with him to a California boomtown. She soon realizes that the promise of greater wealth elsewhere was misleading; she lived much more comfortably in her Utah home. But she eagerly goes to work, and soon she and her husband prosper. Her regional identity comes under attack when a neighbor advises her that for the sake of her social status she should not let others know she is from Utah. She responds by defending polygamy (her own family was polygamous) and her upbringing: "I shall never stoop to sail under false colors, nor permit my parents to be vilified in my presence. I should feel like a traitor if I cast undeserved opprobrium upon the soil that nurtured me" (Jakeman 1890–91, 1:243). The author also marks her regional identity by her later realization that Californians differ from Utahns in their generosity. She becomes a community oddity for giving tramps food willingly and consistently. When her husband disapproves of her actions, she stands up to his criticism. She convinces him that she has a mind and a will of her own and is not some servant to be ordered around (see similar independence exhibited in May Stapley's diary [Bate 1992]).

Contrast this young woman with one in a story published thirty years later (Stone 1920). Maizie is an innocent country girl, living and working in the city for the first time. Here a young man attracts her attention. He "knows how to treat a lady, and that's more than I can say for most of the swains back home. The home boys are good enough, but they wouldn't know what to do with a dress suit if they had one, and they don't know what a salad fork is made for" (607–8). He tempts her to go away for the weekend with him, and only the clever thinking of her wise female work supervisor saves her from doing so. She extricates herself from the situation only with a weak excuse to her suitor that she has to leave temporarily. After showing interest in the young man, she apparently possesses little power to stand by her convictions and back them up with her own authority. Maizie is "an outdoor blossom withering in the greenhouse of city existence." She is simultaneously "capable of making some good man happy" and susceptible "to becom[ing] a toy" in the city boy's hands (608).

The contrast between these two characters exemplifies shifting LDS conceptions of gender authority that affected regional conversations on gender. Moral orders of gender changed in Mormonism between 1880 and 1920. Women's cultural authority declined. The balance of gendered authority shifted toward men. The range of permissible models of gender authority narrowed, and these models became increasingly hardened and irrefutable. By the end of the period, little cultural space existed regionally from which to question or even discern alternative conceptions of gender hierarchy.

This claim may seem unusual or even absurd, given the usual narrative of women's rights. After all, wasn't this an era of progress? Didn't the end of polygamy free Mormon women from their bondage? Didn't U.S. women win suffrage after long struggles and finally enter into previously unattainable forms of public participation? Indeed, women accomplished great things during this period, and women's involvement in the "public" sphere took many new forms. The constitution of Utah guaranteed woman suffrage. That same year, Utah voters elected the country's first female state senator. While Martha Hughes Cannon did not win the most votes in her Democratic Party, she defeated a large pool of Republican candidates, including her husband. Women gained education and membership in professions as never before. Women and men joined forces in conserving the natural environment (Alexander 1995a). Women's clubs proliferated, with some women becoming increasingly involved in public debates (Carver 2000). Many women enjoyed the fruits of local and national struggles for opportunities outside the home. But while many women benefited from the period's social opportunities, LDS young women were simultaneously offered increasingly restricted cultural/ideological choices. They found ever-narrowing expectations of women's cultural authority. Women's and men's social roles hardened. Notions about the proper family and gender roles outside and inside the home converged around a few dominant themes. The range of culturally acceptable male roles narrowed, just as it did for women, but in these shifts men gained more cultural authority.

Nineteenth-century Mormon "feminism" forms the starting point of this chapter's examination of the causes, extent, and implications of these changes. Despite the problematic nature of LDS women's feminism if judged by today's standards, LDS women opened the possibility of questioning basic societal structures of gender authority. The first part of the chapter argues that the persistence of such questioning was vital if any fundamentally critical regional feminist movement was to persist within American-ization. It explores how forces, both within and outside Mormonism and inside and outside the region, made such persistence difficult. The second part charts the gradual weakening of LDS feminism. It shows in five major ways that cultural expectations about gender authority underwent subtle changes. This period was a heyday of female opportunities regionally. But while many women were enjoying unprecedented opportunities, the LDS moral order of gender was simultaneously narrowing in scope and creating conditions not conducive for producing a regional movement willing to question fundamental gender hierarchies.

Mormon Feminism's Importance to Regional Feminism

Mormon Feminism

Many religious movements originated in nineteenth-century America, but none matched Mormonism's combination of distinctive practices, sense of historical destiny, involvement in members' lives, community building, and numerical success. Mormonism, more than any other indigenous American religion, produced a "people," even a near-nation (O'Dea 1954). Mormonism did not simply occupy a place in its members' lives; it encompassed their lives. Consequently, attacks on Mormonism were often framed and perceived as attacks on Mormons. For polygamous women, this was certainly the case. Mormon women propounding women's rights and independence had no doubt that their religion produced female improvement. But their religion (and, for many, their individual identity) was also polygamous. Celestial marriage necessarily implied women's advancement, they believed.[1] Attacks on polygamy offended their very identity and led to counterarguments that polygamy advanced women's causes.

From Mormonism's inception, LDS women shouldered a heavy load in community creation and maintenance. Before his death, Joseph Smith established the Women's Relief Society, which strengthened women's organizational and administrative skills. Throughout much of the nineteenth century, the Relief Society enabled women to participate in certain forms of priesthood power (Newell 1992a and 1992b; Beecher 1976 and 1992; Burgess-Olsen n.d., 9). Many leading women in the society had gained quality educations before converting to Mormonism. The exodus to the Great Basin and the need to construct a new society there helped them develop practical capabilities. Nineteenth-century Mormonism contained many capable and talented women who regularly made broad-ranging community contributions (Beecher 1992; and 1993, 129–30). Many of these women entered into polygamy. It pained them to realize that most Americans viewed them primarily as dim-witted drudges and sexual playthings (Bunker and Bunker 1991; Iversen 1984, 511; Bunker and Bitton 1983, 33–56). After all, they believed, their religion opened up greater opportunities for personal development and community involvement than did the larger American society (Dushku 1976, 194).

Mormon women easily politicized themselves, starting with an 1870 mass demonstration protesting the antipolygamy Cullom bill. Lola Van Wagenen argues that at least a few women were politicized before 1870 and struggled for women's advancement (1994, 8–24). Emmeline Wells emerged as Mormon feminism's intellectual and political leader in the 1870s. Her centrality to the movement continued through at least the mid-1890s. She edited these women's major mouthpiece, the *Woman's Exponent*, until the *Relief Society Magazine* replaced it in 1914. Judith Dushku and Patricia Gadsby describe her as "a Christian and a Mormon, a humanist and a feminist. . . . She supported a fairly radical school of thought within the church at that time. This philosophy held that woman's role was one of strength and purpose and that this role was an eternal truth that had been restored through Mormonism" (1977, 15). According to Sarah Kimball (1891), an early Mormon suffragist, women's emerging rights lay within God's unfolding plan. These women devoted most of their intellectual and political energies to two causes—promoting woman suffrage and defending polygamy. In both cases, they asserted that women deserved more social authority than American society allowed.

Polygamy's opponents in 1870 hoped LDS women would use their newly won franchise to "break free" from polygamy and Mormonism's "bands." Mormon women did no such thing. Some commentators thus discredit LDS women's commitment to female causes. Beverly Beeton claims that LDS suffrage activists were little more than "pawns" in church leaders' cynical attempts to gain statehood with polygamy intact (1976, 57–58). Peggy Pascoe argues that Mormon women's quarrels with Protestant mission women—their would-be saviors from polygamy—constituted a denial of female societal authority and reasserted male authority (1990, 21–22). Although these critiques offer some insight, they depend too much on liberal, individualistic notions of freedom and authority and do not allow for more communalistic conceptions. More accurate is Joan Iversen's conclusion. She notes that these Mormon women's position was profoundly complex, contradictory, and probably not a "true feminism" (such a notion could still be called upon in the 1980s) by today's standards (1984; see also 1997). But she also argues that it produced many positive outcomes, particularly by promoting an enlarged female sphere.[2]

Mormon women of the 1870s stood in a position akin to that of American women after World War II. In the 1940s, large numbers of men returned from the war to assume old employment patterns and displace "temporary" female workers. In the Utah of the 1870s, community relations changed rapidly, especially in the larger population centers. Women's place in communities eroded when non-Mormons relocated to Utah and community relations assumed a more secular tone. In this context, activist Mormon women viewed enfranchisement not "as a mechanism for securing change in their religious practices, but rather as the means for participating in the civil life of the community," according to Van Wagenen (1994, 48). Beeton is partially correct in arguing that "the franchise as viewed by the Mormons was not an innate human right as expressed in the liberal credo; rather it was a privilege bestowed upon some citizens by the governing body" (1976, 85). She rightfully recognizes that Mormons did not adhere to the tenets of classical liberalism, but she fails to consider how women asserted rights and authority within a communalistic philosophy. As Van Wagenen argues, "[Mormon suffragists'] loyalty to the church did not outweigh their individual interests or take precedence over their women's rights concerns; rather, they saw no dichotomy between their interests and those of the church. . . . Mormon women were not asserting individualism through the vote, they were reinforcing community" (1994, 49). These activists felt that women played important community roles. Women could maintain or even create such participation, they argued, only through the vote.

Mormon women, along with all women in the Utah Territory, voted from 1870 until 1887. The Edmunds-Tucker bill removed the franchise, ostensibly to destroy polygamy and church power. In response, Mormon activist women argued that they had responsibly exercised this right. Emmeline Wells argued in 1885, for example, that Utah women used the franchise well when they had it. She addressed women's importance to community by pointing to the disproportionate number who owned homes and paid taxes (J. White 1975, 86). In an 1886 mass protest by Mormon women,[3] Marilla M. Daniels claimed the right to the vote in community-oriented terms: "If the suffrage was universally given to woman it could not but result in good. Who has the interest of mankind more at heart than woman? She would vote for good moral men, who would use their influence to protect virtue and denounce vice" ("Mormon" Women's Protest [1886], 61).

If Mormon women used communalistic reasoning to construct suffrage rights, they saved their most distinctive and creative arguments about women's authority to defend polygamy. They claimed that polygamy did not subjugate women to men's whims; on the contrary, it gave plural wives freedom and opportunities monogamous women could never experience. Polygamy, they argued, helped relieve loneliness, provided opportunities for intimate female friendship, made sharing household and child-care responsibilities possible, and emancipated wives from many marital duties. Some even maintained that polygamy meant that women need not live for men, nor men for women (though this latter belief was not dominant) (Dushku 1976, 194–95).[4] "When the women of the *Woman's Exponent* defended plural marriage, they challenged the contemporary view of dependent womanhood, urging a vision of more competent womanhood," Iversen observes (1984, 512). She asserts that women's defense of polygamy called the ideology of romantic love into question and strengthened female bonding, female independence, and mother-child bonds.

These justifications of polygamy stood in uneasy tension with Mormon women's suffrage rhetoric, however. Their suffrage rhetoric relied primarily on universalistic arguments. They argued that women deserved to vote because they equaled men in all essential respects. Plural marriage's defense depended on the contemporary notion that women surpassed men morally. Men and women possessed different natures, they argued. Depravity and lust characterized men. In monogamous society, husbands turned to wife abuse, desertion, divorce, prostitutes, and other evils. Polygamy better accommodated men's and women's different sexual natures; it also gave women a better chance of marrying men of similar moral caliber (Dunfey 1984, 527–31).

Nevertheless, defending polygamy never took most LDS women far from traditional female roles. Although they consistently sought to enlarge women's sphere, they did not shift its central parameters. Home and motherhood remained pivotal. Polygamy did not free women from these duties; rather, it afforded opportunities to spend less energy on these marital demands and more on societal interests.[5] Their feminism was not "complete" enough to allow serious questions about either the family's or their church's patriarchal nature. Their Mormon faith led to the belief that even if God had not specified much else concerning gender relations, he had at least made women more morally upright than men and home and children women's primary responsibility. Men would hold the priesthood and preside over, though not dictate to, their families. These distinctions implied neither natural nor social male superiority, Mormon feminists reasoned; rather, they imposed a necessary order in governing these important activities. Mormon feminists often called on the same Victorian notions of womanhood, family, and purity that those attacking polygamy used (*Home Writer*, 9 October 1882; Iversen 1984, 509–10). Moreover, they questioned the romantic love ideology much more in theory than practice. In fact, most LDS women, including the staunchest activists, wanted romantic connubial relationships with their husbands and were profoundly disappointed when their marriages fell short of the ideal, as often happened (Dunfey 1984, 532–35; Fox n.d.).

In spite of the contradictions, LDS feminists found genuine pride in examples of female independence and social authority. Mormon women disproportionately owned homes, they claimed. They participated strongly in economic and intellectual activities outside the home, suffrage work, and groups promoting women. To them, this independence and authority derived not only from their support for women's rights but also from their church membership. Utah women enjoyed greater social, religious, and political freedom than women elsewhere, they argued ("Editorial" 1877; Z. Young 1894; E. S. 1894). The physician Romania B. Pratt could thus reasonably argue that "[h]and in hand with celestial [polygamous] marriage is the elevation of women. In the church she votes equally with men, and politically she has the suffrage raising her from the old common law, monogamic serfdom, to political equality with men. Rights of property are given her so that she, as a married woman, can hold property in her own individual right. . . . If any woman at an advanced period of her life wishes in a measure to retire from her husband's society with his consent, this is her own individual privilege with which no one has the right to interfere" (*"Mormon" Women's Protest* [1886], 31). According to Emmeline Wells, "That greater liberty has been given to women in our church than elsewhere is indeed true; that now equality of sex prevails is undeniable. . . . The aim and influence of our institutions has been to lift women up to a higher standard of thought and intelligence, to protect and guard virtue, to promote self-reliance and individual development; and it is a principle of our religion to teach our girls, as well as our boys, self-protection, and to instruct our boys, as well as our girls, that virtue and chastity are just as essential in man as in woman" (*"Mormon" Women's Protest* [1886], 76–77). Mormon feminism, like many movements with transformative potential, was neither completely conservative nor wholly radical. Its conservatism emerged most strongly in relation to the church, but it represented radical potential vis-à-vis the broader American society.

Opportunities for Regional Feminism

While these "feminist" ideas never became official LDS doctrine, they existed well within mainstream Mormon culture. Most women advocating the advancement of women had authority in the church and faced no strong opposition from Mormonism. Their leadership positions in the church's Relief Society, Young Ladies' Mutual Improvement Association, and Primary Association helped them spread their ideas. They mobilized LDS women for suffrage and other causes. Late-nineteenth-century Mormonism contained a significant impulse to question and struggle against nationally dominant norms of gender authority.

This feminism's regional appeal (encompassing both active and nonactive Mormons, as well as non-Mormons) was limited in the nineteenth century by polygamy. No matter how much non-Mormon women agreed with LDS feminists' goal of increasing female social authority, polygamy proved an insuperable barrier to most alliances between Mormon and non-Mormon women. Struggles against polygamy and Mormon power occupied most non-Mormons' energies far more than attempts to forge even provisional alliances with their Mormon sisters. This antipolygamy movement prodded those involved to disregard concerns in America about monogamous gender relations in favor of insistence on narrow, monogamous, and Victorian norms of purity (Gordon 2002, 29–54; see also Iversen 1997). Protestant reformers, such as Angie Newman, who founded the Salt Lake City Industrial Christian Home for "escaped" polygamous wives, waged an all-out war against polygamy and the Mormon church's power. Non-LDS suffragists, such as Jennie Froiseth, most often found cooperation with Mormon women too difficult. Mormon and anti-Mormon suffragists competed to represent Utah's women in national suffrage organizations (Van Wagenen 1994, 300–351, 387–91, 410–18; Pascoe 1990, 23–26). Charlotte Ives Cobb Godbe Kirby was among the few women prior to the mid-1890s who supported the LDS feminists' agenda, forged ties (although sometimes strained) with them, and carried their concerns to non-Mormons inside and outside Utah.[6] In general, however, Mormon feminists found few non-Mormons willing to sympathize with their efforts. Their main allies before polygamy ended came from the National Suffrage Association; such leaders as Elizabeth Cady Stanton and Susan B. Anthony argued that the association could support Mormon women's struggles for women's rights without advocating polygamy.

The church's renouncement of polygamy in 1890 shifted the terrain for regional cooperation.[7] Mormon feminists, in particular, faced a complex situation. On the one hand, the end of polygamy greatly enhanced opportunities to make alliances with others struggling to increase women's rights and authority. Likewise, for all but the most hardened church opponents, the end of polygamy and the simultaneous diminishment of church power over members' temporal affairs removed major impediments to cooperating with Mormons. Mormon feminists eagerly renewed old alliances and created new ones with local and national suffrage advocates and with other women's groups (Madsen 1995). On the other hand, polygamy's demise significantly undercut LDS women's philosophical reasoning for increasing female authority. They still could claim (and did so at every opportunity) that LDS theology accorded women increased honor, responsibility, and opportunity for individual development. But the practical basis on which LDS women felt they developed their individual talents, exercised greater cultural authority, and forged special female bonds was collapsing. Mormon women claimed that polygamy provided social space apart from men to develop greater authority. Though few Mormon women mourned polygamy's passing, for plural marriage caused many women great pain, some fondly remembered sisterhood ties that developed between wives or even nonrelated polygamous women (Gates 1911).

Mormon women thus faced options that were not entirely compatible. On the one hand, if they developed stronger alliances with non-Mormon women, they could do so only by abandoning their defense of polygamy and by leaving behind practices through which they had developed social authority. A model of monogamy, burdened with numerous ways of limiting female authority, stood ready as a replacement. On the other hand, if they valorized polygamy's socially empowering implications, they risked marginalization by non-Mormon women and even among the Saints. Of course, Mormon women had experience juggling contradictory social positions. Their simultaneous support for women's rights and polygamy is just one example. My point is that competing positions can produce progressive social action, depending on how people negotiate them.

Paul Smith argues on the level of (what he believes is wrongly labeled) the "individual" that "the necessary existence of various and different subject-positions in the interpellated 'subject' produces resistance to the logic of domination while still being in a sense part of, or a by-product of, that logic" (1988, 152). Negotiating these contradictory influences on one's identity (both consciously and unconsciously) produces the human agent and opens a space for active resistance to these influences. Derek Gregory extends this argument sociologically by noting that colonial and postcolonial societies usually produce pronounced levels of the dissonance that promotes resistance (1994, 188–205). Late nineteenth- and early-twentieth-century Utah and the surrounding area constituted precisely that—a colonial society becoming postcolonial (Morin and Guelke 1998). In its developing regionality, this area could have resisted and challenged status-quo social formations and practices, but such a regionalized habitus depended on negotiating between the contradictory influences emergent in regional society.

Mormon feminists of the 1870s and 1880s kept the available, contradictory influences in enough creative tension to challenge some patriarchal practices. In Smith's terms, they were human agents, in whom ideological resistance was expressed (1988, xxxv). To be sure, they produced this resistance without switching ideological contexts. Mormon women did not reject but instead inhabited the discourses of polygamy, marriage, and LDS patriarchal priesthood authority. But this is precisely Gregory's point. Resistance cannot completely escape the conditions to which it responds; one should not expect it to do so, despite the difficulty of inhabiting such marginal positions (hooks 1984; Spivak 1988, 102–17; Bordo 1993, 224–25). Neither does resistance often directly confront power. Rather, it utilizes tactics, in the de Certeauian sense, to "toy" with or "mock established grids" of power. LDS women never mocked established power to the extent of losing social respectability; indeed, they wished to maintain their influential positions in Mormon society. But in simultaneously defending women's rights and LDS polygamy and theology, they challenged both monogamous women's lack of independence and authority and LDS society's tendency to privilege patriarchal and hierarchical modes of action.

The end of polygamy disrupted their previous juggling pattern. The potential for resistance did not vanish, however. Rather, its locus shifted from Mormonism to the emerging regional social formation. Regional society, after polygamy ended, could have challenged dominant gender authority patterns. Competing influences still existed. Polygamy's death opened a space for a regional feminist alliance between Mormons and non-Mormons where it had not previously existed. The combination of Mormon feminists' wariness about American monogamous women's opportunities, non-Mormon feminists' faith in monogamy, and the strategic necessity on each side to ally around suffrage and other objectives could have produced creative resistance. Both sides of the ideological tension—the non-Mormon advocacy of monogamy and the Mormon distrust of it—would have had to remain potent. Smith argues that present-day feminism's creativity and resistant power derives precisely from feminists' ability to negotiate the contradictory positions available to them (for example, poststructuralism's decentered subject and the empowered, politically active female agent). They skillfully forge solidarity among the various positions without insisting on any single position's absolute priority. If Smith is correct, it would follow that powerful regional feminist alliances could have arisen if each side maintained its position's political potency while simultaneously respecting the other side and allowing it to innovate and mobilize political action.

Such a creative alliance did not result. Instead, the specific regional negotiation of these contradictory influences and ideological positions suppressed opportunities to resist dominant gender orders. Instead of showing how the contemporary gender system limited women's social authority, the new regional alliances obscured its oppressive operation and made challenges to it much less likely. The LDS women's community, in particular, experienced substantial pressures that made retaining a critique of American norms difficult.

Pressures for Change

Communities with a significant LDS population underwent great change around the turn of the century. The battle against "unfortunate" Mormon regional features (polygamy, bloc voting, and communitarian/separatist economic practices) consumed non-Mormon attention both inside and outside Utah. Eradicating these features meant that Utah could occupy an unstigmatized place in the nation and could optimistically point to future regional progress. Most Mormons also greeted the changes hopefully, for now their beliefs would cause them little day-to-day disadvantage. They no longer needed to defend their church membership at every turn; they could now fully experience solidarity with other Americans. Nevertheless, both Mormons and non-Mormons had concerns during this period. Non-Mormons feared that the LDS Church's accession to change merely constituted a strategy to consolidate power and reduce opposition; they surmised the church would later reinstate offensive practices. Mormons worried about "their" communities' deterioration as LDS control withered. They suspected that Mormonism's opponents intended to eliminate not only offensive Mormon features but also Mormonism itself. They thus feared for their religious and cultural identity.

These fears profoundly affected the potential to challenge dominant gender norms and worked with other changes undermining Mormon women's ability to critique monogamy's norms. The end of polygamy played a major role. While opening space for alliances between Mormons and non-Mormons, it undermined the practical basis of the Mormon critique of monogamy. Still, the end of polygamy, by itself, could not sufficiently produce LDS women's acquiescence to dominant American gender practices. After all, monogamous LDS women were already activists for women's rights. When polygamous LDS women's position waned in the National Suffrage Association (antipolygamy sentiment grew in that organization during the mid- to late 1880s, as it did in the country as a whole), monogamous Mormon women assumed leadership of local chapters. Led by such women as Emily Richards, they reasserted that suffrage was a God-given right and women's advancement brought about God's plan (Van Wagenen 1994, 398–411; Madsen 1987, 214–15). A challenge to dominant norms might have remained, even from within LDS monogamy, but other changes also transformed Mormon women's radical edge into support for the gender status quo. These changes included a generational shift in LDS women's leadership, mainstream Christianity's continuing challenge to Mormon women, the LDS Church's altered public relations priorities, the women's movement's overreliance on suffrage, a growing disparity between elites and nonelites in Mormon society, and hardening economic roles in proletarianizing Mormon families.

A CHANGING GENERATION OF LDS WOMEN LEADERS   Polygamy ended as the early generation of Mormon feminists aged. In 1893, Sarah Kimball, who had been most critical of national gender norms, resigned from leadership in Utah suffrage organizations due to age. The most widely known Mormon feminist, Emmeline Wells, was aging and losing influence. Though younger than Kimball, Wells identified more closely with older LDS women activists than with the younger generation. Personal acrimony developed between her and Emily Richards and Ellen Ferguson over the Utah Woman Suffrage Association's strategies (Van Wagenen 1994, 458–60; Madsen 1987, 217–18). In 1895, Wells wrote the president of the Beaver County Woman Suffrage Association, warning against women of this younger generation. In her opinion, they were recklessly trying to push woman suffrage without courting the broad support she and others had carefully cultivated (E. Wells 1895a). Her journal, the *Woman's Exponent,* increasingly noted the deaths of women's rights supporters (see, for example, Dye, Lyons, and Freeman 1907; and Stimson, Thornton, and Taylor 1908). An anonymous author, presumably Wells, worried that the younger generation might not adequately carry on its pioneer mothers' legacy ("Women Past and Present" 1913). Mormon activists' aging thus shifted the framework of Mormon feminism. While younger women carried on suffrage and women's rights traditions, they had different views about the movement's strategy and purpose. They also lacked experience with the female authority and interdependence that the older women had gained through polygamy and community building (Beecher 1993, 123, 132–33). This generational difference did not splinter Mormon women or weaken their commitment to women's issues, but it became more difficult for younger Mormon female leaders to carry forward the older critique of monogamous women's authority.

THE CHRISTIAN FIGHT AGAINST POLYGAMY   Mainstream Christianity's persistent critique of the LDS Church and LDS women also made maintaining the Mormon critique of monogamous gender norms difficult. Even after polygamy ostensibly ended, reports (some true) reached Christian churches that Mormons were perpetuating old plural relations and undertaking new polygamous vows. Some religious organizations therefore castigated the church and its members at every opportunity. These groups included the Woman's Christian Temperance Union, Salt Lake City's Ministerial Association, the National Reform Association, and the International Council for Patriotic Services (originally named the Interdenominational Council of Women for Christian and Patriotic Service), among others (Alexander 1986, 64; U.S. Congress 1906; Vermilye 1912). Other church and polygamy opponents not connected with Christian organizing (including some unsympathetic to organized Christianity) tended to repeat the religious groups' accusations.

The problem for Mormon women was that these groups not only attacked polygamy but also consistently questioned LDS women's intelligence, capacities, and honor. Statements of solidarity and support notwithstanding, these critics invariably implied that Mormon women were not fully competent social actors and that the Mormon hierarchy had duped them. Mormon women were said to be incapable of extricating themselves from the oppressive chains binding them to Mormonism (Givens 1997). (Critics of polygamy tended not to concern themselves with nuptial bonds per se.) A 1904 political speech quoted in the Smoot hearings by William Hyde Stalker of Boise, Idaho, was typical: "[A] woman under this system has no voice in matters that concern her own happiness and welfare. A woman is a nonentity under this system. We in north Idaho regard women as the embodiment of virtue. We look to her for the ennobling and refining element in our social condition. We regard her as equal in every sense of the word. Her consent is required before we attempt to do anything of any importance; not so under the Mormon system" (U.S. Congress 1906, 2:636–37). Even many who considered polygamy a dying political issue believed plural wives to be deluded (U.S. Congress 1906, 2:673, 679–80). Few opposed polygamy without denigrating those involved. Most Mormons could not agree that Henry W. Lawrence accurately represented dominant non-Mormon sentiment (though he may have accurately spoken for himself[8]): "Those who have opposed this system are not opposing the people. They have nothing but kind feelings toward the masses of the Mormon people. Barring polygamy, the Mormon community will compare very favorably in morals, in sobriety, and in industry with any other class of people of the same intelligence" (U.S. Congress 1906, 4:120).

Mormon women had difficulty counteracting the notion that polygamy's female proponents were ignorant. Charges leveled against Mormons exhibited great continuity over time (Smoot 1997; Gordon 2002). Florence Merriam, a visitor to Utah in the early 1890s, clearly articulated what many non-Mormons were thinking. She noted that intelligent and cultured women existed in Salt Lake City, but she still felt that polygamy's only cure was greater education. Mormonism, she claimed, "was built up to appeal to the emigrant class, not to the intelligent American citizen" (1894, 109). Modernization could occur only by combating the Mormon woman's ignorance and delusion:

> [T]he education that we owe to her is to the highest and broadest that we have attained. It must develop her reasoning powers by the most careful scientific training, teaching her that the universe is governed by immutable laws, not set aside by revelations . . . ; enabling her . . . to recognize the futility of modeling the civilization of the future upon the outgrown institutions of the past; the danger of turning to the past for the ethical ideals of the future. For above all, it must teach her that the hope of the world lies in the evolution of moral and spiritual life. (138–39)

LDS women found charges from Christian groups the most revolting. These attacks typically contended that polygamy relied on duped girls or (implicitly ignorant) foreign women (Mason 1909 and 1911). LDS women continually felt obliged to defend themselves against such statements. While they did not often dignify the continuing attacks with direct rebuttal, they responded in three major ways: they closed ranks with LDS men and lapsed into old defensive patterns (Spalding 1911);[9] they tried to ensure that nobody could criticize their monogamous relations; and to counter charges of ignorance, they continued emphasizing their social achievements.

DIMINISHING INSTITUTIONAL CHURCH SUPPORT   While Mormon women felt compelled to defend their intellect and character, the LDS Church itself created obstacles to their continued alliance with the national women's movement. The church faced serious debt early in the twentieth century because of the effects of polygamy-era legislation and questionable subsequent financial decisions (Arrington, Fox, and May 1992, 337). These problems, along with the church's changing social circumstances, led to altered financial priorities. The church had long attempted to create positive publicity about itself, particularly since it attached so much importance to gaining converts. One nineteenth-century way it sought positive press was supporting its female leaders' participation in national and international women's organizations. By the second decade of the twentieth century, polygamy and its associated disabling legislation had ended, and suffrage was an old issue in the West. Women's social aspirations no longer benefited the institutional church as much (Van Wagenen 1994, 474). The church for many years had provided funds for Relief Society, Primary Association, and Young Ladies' Mutual Improvement Association leaders to attend national and international conventions, but these moneys began evaporating toward the end of the opening decade of the twentieth century.

Nevertheless, the Relief Society itself, which was not yet wholly reliant on the church for its funding, continued to desire national alliances. Organization representatives and some individual women continued to travel when expenses allowed (E. Wells 1908; B. Smith and Wells 1909). Whatever their private concerns, Mormon women leaders did not publicly protest against the changed priorities. They surely knew that the average Mormon woman's support for national organizations had diminished after the 1896 suffrage victory in Utah and that women's energies diffused in many directions thereafter (Gates [1920a]; Van Wagenen 1994, 481; Carver 2000). They must have realized that withdrawal of financial support was likely, if not inevitable.

Church leaders' support for women's rights began to waver publicly during the debate over reinstating suffrage.[10] Female activists had relied on the church leadership's solid bloc of support for their efforts in the past (in spite of private individual differences of opinion), but the suffrage debates revealed public division among the leadership. During these debates, for example, Emmeline Wells (1895a) assumed that the often-used behind-the-scenes lobbying of church leaders would produce a message (direct or implied) of church support for woman suffrage. Such a statement never came. Instead, B. H. Roberts, the politically popular member of the church's Quorum of the Seventy, made an impassioned plea against woman suffrage (*Salt Lake Tribune*, 29 March 1895 and 30 March 1895), which was an early indication that LDS women did not have all church leaders publicly on their side. Church president Wilford Woodruff reprimanded Roberts, and many other leaders (including Joseph F. Smith, church president from 1901 to 1918) publicly supported suffrage as individuals, but Wells felt that the church no longer supported the cause as directly as it had (Alexander 1991, 311; Van Wagenen 1994, 461–64).

Although leading LDS women were disappointed by church leaders' withdrawal of financial assistance and diminished formal political support, they continued their individual national and international participation with suffrage groups. Nevertheless the institutional changes weakened this engagement, both by reducing the numbers and frequency of LDS representation and by lessening the sense that those women who participated did so from a specifically LDS viewpoint. LDS women consequently moved away from the cutting edge of women's activism.

ELITE ALLIANCES AND OVERRELIANCE ON SUFFRAGE   Like many others, LDS women placed great faith—too much faith—in the vote's power to expand female opportunities. The vote, S. A. Boyer wrote, holds the key to gender equality: "I am not superstitious to the extent, that it will right all the wrongs of women any more than it has righted all the wrongs of men, but it is the golden gate to every opportunity, and precisely the same advantage it gives to one sex it will give to another" (1893, 66). Most LDS feminists held similar views. Suffrage might not automatically position women equal with men, but it gave women opportunity to gain such station.

This faith in suffrage's power affected LDS women's ability to critique mainstream monogamous marriages in two important ways. First, it reduced support among average LDS women for fighting other gender inequalities. While a certain cultural elite dominated most LDS theorizing and active alliance-building, their Relief Society sisters consistently backed them up. The great women's mass meetings in the 1870s, 1880s, and 1890s (especially those in 1878 and 1886) show large numbers of Mormon women involving themselves in women's activism. They mobilized primarily to work for suffrage and to protest perceived persecution. Woman suffrage associations in the Utah Territory during the early 1890s, for example, usually met at LDS meeting houses in conjunction with Relief Society meetings ("Minutes" n.d.; Beeton 1976, 131–32). Interest in these associations decreased after state suffrage in 1896, and no cause emerged to take its place among ordinary LDS women. While female LDS elites struck alliances with non-Mormon elites and moved on to other paths of female development (Carver 2000; Thatcher and Sillito 1985; Van Wagenen 1994, 481), ordinary LDS women refocused on the day-to-day demands of family life (Beecher 1993). During this period, LDS economic elites felt freer to follow capitalist economic patterns and less compelled to temper capitalist practices in their religious community. Mormon and non-Mormon elites increased alliances in business and social interests. Although local wards and stakes still bound together Mormons of different classes, Mormonism's "latent diversity" began to manifest itself (Shipps 1987, 347). LDS female elites' activities diverged from the experiences of the majority of their LDS sisters.

Second, overreliance on suffrage circumscribed possible alliances (or even conversations) between LDS and non-LDS women. Because ending polygamy did not dissolve all old prejudice and wariness, alliances and friendships formed only slowly; even social clubs had some religious divides (Carver 2000, 33). Suffrage had been a major impetus to interreligious alliances. But because so few years (just over five years) elapsed between the end of polygamy and the gaining of suffrage in Utah and because suffrage dominated women activists' agenda, opportunities to construct a broad-ranging gender debate did not emerge. This led to a seeming paradoxical situation: many (especially elite) twentieth-century women took advantage of the widely increased social opportunities for which nineteenth-century women had struggled, but few women continued to fundamentally question gender hierarchies.

HARDENING OF ECONOMIC ROLES IN THE HOUSEHOLD   Utah, like the rest of the western United States, developed a more "mature" economy as its population grew and its transportation and communication links increased. This meant that a wider range of capitalistic roles became available to individuals. Fewer survived on household production. More hired themselves out in manufacturing, retail, and service. Employees increasingly conformed to employers' demands—such as punctuality, regular attendance, and separation of employment time-spaces from other time-spaces. Flexibility to resolve life's demands diminished in the process. The increasingly rigid environment of employees, most of whom were men, necessarily affected women, as well. Male employees with reduced flexibility increasingly expected their wives to handle household duties. While notions of men's work and women's work had long influenced Mormon families, society's growing proletarianization fortified gender distinctions. No longer could families easily alter the sexual division of labor. The economic flexibility of the 1870s no longer existed. As Maureen Beecher argues, the Americanization of Utah brought "overwhelming shifts in lifestyle for individual Latter-day Saint women" (1993, 132). Their assumed duties increasingly centered on the household. With an economic system that presumed a strong separation between men's and women's work, Mormon women found criticizing gender norms more difficult. Many women had fewer opportunities to experience other norms or even experiment with gender roles at monogamy's margins.

Loss of Mormon Feminism's Radicalism

In this chapter, I claim that a Mormon feminism existed in the latter part of the nineteenth century. Though conservative in some ways and strongly centered on defending Mormonism, it offered an expanded view of female social authority in both theory and practice. Polygamy's demise and other social changes opened up a twentieth-century possibility to construct a regional feminism capable of continuing to press for fundamental change. Such a regional feminism would have needed creative tension between non-Mormon women's rights activists (who tended to accept dominant American marriage norms) and Mormon feminists (who traditionally questioned those norms). Such a regional feminism did not develop, however, because of Mormon women's failure to extend earlier critiques of nationally dominant gender norms (especially those associated with monogamy) and regional society's failure to provide an environment in which they could do so. These were social, not individual, "failings."

This section more closely examines changes within Mormonism's gender culture that made it difficult for Mormon women to carry on earlier critiques. It explores how Mormons (and non-Mormons, where appropriate) addressed gendered authority, gender difference, and gender norms of action. The possibility of a vibrant regional feminism depended on LDS women's perpetuating a serious critique of mainstream gender norms in the midst of a rapidly changing regional society. Their failure to maintain this critique can be seen as a result of five key changes: (1) diminished radicalism in Mormon suffrage work, (2) strong differentiation of male and female spheres by socially privileged women, (3) reassertion of male privilege, (4) "retreat" to Victorian ideals of love, and (5) codification of family gender roles.

Diminished Radicalism in Mormon Suffrage Work

When B. H. Roberts made his series of speeches critical of women's enfranchisement during Utah's 1895 constitutional convention (*Salt Lake Tribune*, 29 March 1895 and 30 March 1895), suffrage advocates were surprised, not because they did not know of Roberts's opposition but because they did not expect a member of the LDS hierarchy to speak so strongly and publicly against suffrage (Van Wagenen 1994, 461–62). The church had officially supported the suffrage movement between 1870 and the early 1890s, and unsupportive leaders had generally kept their opposition low-key. Emboldened by the church's withdrawal from politics, however, Roberts felt free to oppose suffrage publicly. It turned out that his ecclesiastical influence did not damage the suffrage cause much—many LDS leaders supported suffrage and willingly said so (see, for example, Whitney 1895; *Salt Lake Tribune*, 30 March 1895; and F. Richards 1895). But many people also regarded Roberts as one of the state's best political minds. He had political friends and was known as a skillful orator. His arguments energized suffrage opponents (mostly non-Mormons), many of whom had regarded suffrage as a foregone conclusion. His arguments alarmed suffrage proponents, who had also foreseen a certain suffrage victory; to that point their strategy consisted largely of avoiding offending voters and key politicians (J. White 1975, 90–97; Van Wagenen 1994, 463).

One response to Roberts came from Ruby Lamont (1895) in the *Woman's Exponent*. Lamont began by claiming the supposedly masculine ground of superior logic for herself:

> Truly "oratory is not argument nor rhetoric reason!" . . . When I learned that there would be serious opposition [to suffrage] I expected that opposing champions would arm themselves with a comprehension of the subject and that their arguments would be well-nigh unanswerable, never dreaming that we should only have a re-hash of the old ignorant prejudices and bug-bears connected with the proper attention of women to the creature comforts of their families, and the wreck of homes. . . . And as the "gentleman from Davis" [Roberts] was so lionized we must examine his arguments and ascertain what they are worth. Argument! Oratory there may have been to such as sat under the spell of his voice. But logic! Argument! Are they not mainly conspicuous by absence? (6)

Lamont then mockingly cut down Roberts's arguments about women's aspirations being confined to the home, his interpretation of Eve's curse, and his implication that chivalry drove his interest in the suffrage issue. Continuing sarcastically, she reached her central point—female authority:

> Ah, no, woman must have her *rights;* her rights to bear children in sorrow and to rear them in a like manner; to yield gently, willingly to the rule of her husband, to keep dutifully within the sphere which he may limit and, in addition, bear a heavy share of his burden beside. *His* sphere who shall limit; *his* actions who shall criticise, *his* unerring judgment who shall question.
>
> Poor woman! There is danger to society, to the home, to the children, if she should be trained to think; if her mind should wander beyond her care of socks and buttons and puddings, beyond fashion and the tiresome dullness of conventional society. Danger to society if she should be given a personal incentive to study anything but fashion and housekeeping. She *may* study government for the sake of her influence over male relatives, but it must be purely from such feminine standpoint—not with any hope of casting a personal vote for what she may feel in her soul to be right. Influence! If her *influence* is of any use, or if it *can* be admitted what is the danger of her personal ballot with it. But that would be unwomanly, and some one else might have to rock the cradle or hold the baby while she cast it. There is danger to society if she gain a little ascendancy over her ages and ages of subordination and oppression; if, by giving her the ballot, whereby she could help protect herself and the interests of her fireside, she should gain a little respect of her brother who knows too well, and does not always forget to remind her, that she may have ever so earnest and anxious convictions, when *he* goes to the polls any valueless son of Adam so long as he can stagger there, if it

be in a drunken stupor, is worth more than the whole union of intelligent womanhood. (7)

Women need authority to protect their own interests and promote the good of all. Although female authority most obviously affects the home, she conceded, such authority needs to be spread throughout the whole society.

This desire to strengthen female social influence and weaken gender hierarchies (along with the defense of polygamy and concomitant critique of monogamy) was nineteenth-century LDS feminism's radical edge. Mormon women's activism reinforced the status quo in many respects, though. It maintained a conspicuous silence on LDS male priesthood authority, for example.[11] And, to be sure, many LDS women never exhibited this radical edge. But the strong demand for societal influence disturbed many non-LDS and LDS men, especially as the locus of political action shifted from the Mormon community to individuals and nuclear families (see chapters 3 and 4). Mormon feminists felt they were creating a new society, and, in a very real sense, they were. The fight for suffrage helped many women gain opportunities for educational, professional, and political influence that few previously enjoyed. But Mormon feminists' insistence on greater societal influence gradually withered after 1896. Their radical power, their capacity seriously to question society's fundamental gender norms, had eroded by 1920.[12]

Many early articles published by the *Woman's Exponent* presented similar demands for increased female social authority. An 1894 editorial (presumably written by Emmeline Wells) is typical; though not strident, it insists that society's advance depends on increased female influence:

> [W]oman will be called to *act* as well as to use a *silent* influence, and the better prepared politically, morally, mentally and spiritually she may be, the greater helpfulness she can render in the coming struggles where mankind will assuredly stand in need of her wise counsel and aid, her economy, her tenderness, fortitude and endurance, and where she will have abundant opportunity to prove her ability as a help meet to man not only in the home, but in the public arena of life itself, taken in its largest and most comprehensive sense. ("Woman's Opportunity" 1894, 148)

This editorial and the many other articles like it suggested that women have a right to exercise authority in all aspects of life.

This insistence on authority derived from certain assumptions and beliefs. First, like many of their contemporary suffrage allies, Mormon women believed that biological differences between men and women implied gendered distinctions in personality and character. Women were purer and more virtuous, men more hard-nosed. From this belief, Ruby Lamont

(1895) deduced an argument for a more equal distribution of social authority. The male-female domestic relationships God envisioned ought to also exist in society, she argued: "The nature of men and women cannot be changed by the ballot. True to that nature, they unite in the home as in politics, one complementing the other: subduing, assisting, fulfilling, completing what neither can do alone—what neither was ever intended to do alone. Helpmeet, companion, queen in the home, as he is king, with superiority to neither, God designed that companionship, that bearing of one another's burdens, sharers of each other's fortunes, for no narrow sphere" (7). This gender distinction meant that men and women could make useful social contributions in ways the other could not (M. Cannon 1894, 114). It meant that men could not control society alone without serious deficiencies arising. Second, Mormon feminists believed in men's and women's equality. "God created us equal," Isabella Horne told a national audience: "[W]e stood side by side when mankind was created and man has no right to say 'I am master'" (1895, 77). To LDS women, equality did not preclude difference but implied that women's voices should be heard in all matters. Third, Mormon women strongly believed that social progress would inevitably perfect this different but equal relationship. The LDS gospel was the foremost agent of this progress. Women recognized that Mormon society had not yet achieved gender equality, but they believed that the joint influence of the women's movement and the LDS gospel would produce this equality (Editorial 1894a). Hopes that perfect equality would soon reign depended on faith in the millennium's imminence (C. Pratt 1889, 54; Cactus 1894, 210).

Although LDS women continued to support suffrage after 1896, many ordinary women abridged their involvement. The movement became more hierarchically organized, and the leaders of the church's female organizations played a greater role. These leaders continued fostering institutional ties to national suffrage and other women's organizations (Anthony 1900; Sewall 1901; A. Allen 1909; A. W. Cannon 1911). Through the alliances, they felt they could correct national prejudices against Mormons. A few LDS women, such as Susa Young Gates, gained significant organizational influence. Nevertheless, their insistence that women must gain more social authority and break down hierarchies began to weaken during this period.

In 1902, the Utah Woman Suffrage Association noted that while some ambitious women sought publicly visible achievements, the benefits of suffrage to most women were much more personal (E. Richards and Smith 1902). Most women, it argued, modestly contented themselves with influencing legislation connected with their own or their family's living environment: "Such women constitute the majority of the sex who rejoice in the privilege to cast a free and equal ballot and ask no more. What more should they ask? Is not this the vital spirit of equal rights, the very soul of suffrage?" (quoted in E. Richards and Smith 1902, 22). The association found it perfectly acceptable for the vast majority of women to seek greater influence over domestic, even personal, concerns (for an early example of this sentiment, see L. Smith 1890, 176). I do not want to imply here that "personal" concerns are socially unimportant or that the public-private dualism is stable and coherent. The twentieth-century feminist slogan that "the personal is political" reminds us that increased control over one's personal environment is a fundamental social and political concern, but the slogan also suggests that authority in "personal" matters ought to lead to greater consciousness of the concerns of others in society. The association's statement contains no suggestion that personal authority leads women to enlarged concerns about society or other women's place in it. Instead, it justifies the notion that women properly exercise authority within a small circle and argues that female votes do not greatly increase female social involvement for most women.

An editorial in the *Relief Society Magazine* in 1920 contemplated female gains through national suffrage. It celebrated women's political voice and noted that women needed additional education to consider broad social issues responsibly. But it contentedly implied that the right to vote gave women sufficient authority. They need not participate in civic activities much beyond voting and motherly influence: "Woman will rise to the heights of her womanhood in the simple and honest use of the ballot. She will vote in local matters as well as in national matters for the very best men and the very best measures that she can discover with her more or less limited opportunities. She will learn, she will progress, she will achieve, and her *sons* and *sons' sons* will be the better for her striving, her mistakes, and her final intelligent use of power" ("What Women Will Do with the Suffrage" 1920, 294, emphasis added). In a 1908 speech to the International Woman Suffrage Alliance, Romania B. Penrose explained suffrage's effects in Utah. She noted that Utah women gained influence to increase social morality and initiate reforms without losing "womanliness" or neglecting "home duties," contrary to the suffrage opponents' expectations. But she also implied that female authority was naturally circumscribed; male authority better resides in some political offices: "There are offices in the gift of the people for which women are especially adapted. There are others which can be better filled by men" (R. Penrose 1908, 15). These messages (see also "Women Recognized" 1912) do not carry the same strength as

earlier demands that women ought to claim authority everywhere in public life.

Mormon women throughout the period consistently maintained that
women's greatest influence resided in the home. But outside the home, they
gradually restricted the sites where female authority was properly exercised.
They limited themselves to the same ideal of civic housekeeping that marked
mainstream American women's groups—such as the League of Women Voters—throughout most of the century (Carver 2000). A 1912 article claimed
that in suffrage states, women's unselfish work "is making itself felt in all
matters pertaining to the uplift and betterment of humanity" ("Four More
States for Suffrage" 1912, 12, emphasis added).[13] The article continued: "It
is seen that the women give intelligent thought and study to economics and
are endeavoring to obtain through public sentiment those reforms that will
bring the greatest benefit to the *home*, the *school*, and the *commonwealth*"
(12, emphasis added to mark the order). The article suggested that women
need greater educational and other opportunities but primarily to exercise
effective authority in an increasingly narrow set of sites.

In one sense, the message to LDS women remained constant from the
early 1890s to 1920: motherhood and wifehood are important and necessary foci of female social influence, and suffrage strengthens needed female
authority elsewhere in society. Although the message's dual substance persisted, its tone changed after 1890 in understandable, yet important ways.
Restatements of this message invariably prioritized one of the two parts
over the other. They relied on the common rhetorical device of contrasting
what one takes for granted with what needs action. Essentially, the messages contain a "but." The following sentences emphasize both social authority and motherhood:

1. Women have more influence through motherhood than in any
   other capacity, *but* they can only reach their highest potential
   with the additional social authority that comes with the vote.
2. Women rightly have increased social authority through the vote,
   but they can reach their highest potential only by realizing that
   their greatest influence comes with motherhood.

What comes before and after the "but" changes the import of the argument.
The first example's emphasis dominated late-nineteenth-century suffrage ar-
guments (C. Pratt 1889; Lamont 1895, for example). Thereafter, however,
LDS suffrage discourse tended toward the second example ("Progress of
Women in the Last Seventy Years" 1912; J. Brown 1914). An editorial for
the *Young Woman's Journal* argued that women should celebrate their abil-

ity to toil in public life alongside men ("'Woman's Day'" 1920, 285). Yet it concluded by hoping "that women will not forget in their race after new laurels that this new field is not so great nor important as the old, old one of wifehood, motherhood, homemaker" (286; for evidence of this continuing sentiment see A. W. Cannon 1923; and "The Swing of the Pendulum" 1930).

A report in the *Young Woman's Journal* on the American Woman Suffrage Association's 1920 national convention marked the Nineteenth Amendment's victory. It assumed that suffrage provided all the authority women needed: "[AWSA] members were called to rejoice that their struggle is over, their aim achieved and the women of the nation are about to enter into the enjoyment of their hard-earned political liberty. It is no longer necessary to fight for woman suffrage, the great work now is to prepare women to cast intelligent votes. To use, for the uplift of mankind, their power, brains, and consciences" (Kesler 1920, 271). The report exhibited complacency about Utah women's achievements. "One object in representing Utah at the convention was to insist that she be given her proper credit in the ranks of suffrage" (276). (Many national suffragists tended to forget that Utah women obtained suffrage first in 1870.[14]) The article implied that Utah women gained adequate social authority long ago. They attended women's conventions to credit early Utah women and support out-of-state sisters until they, too, had such authority. Sentiments that women ought continually to struggle ideologically for social authority were absent (see also R. W. Young 1919, 149).

Reassertion of Distinctions between Male and Female Spheres

Mormon women's decreasing ideological insistence on broad female social authority was intimately intertwined with strengthened distinctions between male and female spheres. Such distinctions always existed in LDS culture, but suffrage and greater female education blurred and called the distinctions into question. While most Mormon women defined their spheres (and had them defined for them) in terms of home and motherhood, women who took advantage of the new opportunities had the potential to present examples of broadly spread female authority. They might have helped break down the strong distinctions between male and female spheres. Even some LDS Church leaders, such as Joseph F. Smith, willingly questioned traditional spheres at times (Burgess-Olsen n.d., 8). For a few years, it appears, distinctions eroded. But socially ambitious LDS women gradually ceased to represent blurred gender spheres; instead their accomplishments and concerns helped reconstitute and separate these spheres. Regional women in

1920 operated within a larger sphere than in 1880, but distinctions between female and male spheres again solidified and became difficult to challenge.

The following words, probably written by Annie M. Romney, help define the issue: "Never before was [woman's] *field of labor and usefulness so broad and expansive;* never before has she been allowed to make her voice heard in public, as she can today; never before, except perhaps in a few instances, has she dared to step forward and use the talents with which nature has endowed her: and even at this time, there are only a few women in the world, (comparatively speaking,) who have dared to break the bands of conventionality . . ." ("Editorial" 1877, emphasis added). There were women whose unconventional and expansive view of women's public role provided a model for Utah women. Although 1877 role models were eastern non-Mormons,[15] some Mormon women soon took advantage of opportunities and also advocated an expanded female sphere. The 1890 *Young Woman's Journal* published a University of Michigan medical student's journal excerpts (Cactus 1890). Ten years later, an article pled with college women to maintain involvement with their local Young Ladies' Mutual Improvement Association. Such women could give other young women much, it suggested (Grover 1900, 360).

In the late nineteenth century, Latter-day Saint women debated conceptions of women's sphere and whether such a sphere should even exist. One article, simply signed "Skurlock" (1890), responded to a characterization of women as weak and dependent by arguing that although men and women possess different talents, no line divides manly and womanly attributes, only a gradation. Women should pursue all good attributes without regard to whether others think they are " 'mannish.' " Do not strive to be "womanish," the author admonished; rather, concern yourself only with being saintlike (Skurlock 1890, 445). Likewise, S. W. Richards argued that "there is no limit to [woman's] sphere within the circle of man's ultimate destiny;—that her intelligence, her moral obligations, her susceptibilities and sensibilities;—her place and power, and her appreciation, all render her competent to be a complete companion of man. . . . [W]e may cease to talk about woman's sphere as though it had a limit, other than the world in which she lives" (1894, 129–30; see also Clark 1896; and Cragan 1895, 255). Women's sphere should be questioned partly because many women had unconventional domestic situations. Rather than ask all women to create conventional homes, as became the twentieth-century norm, nineteenth-century Mormon women argued for accommodating women in their various circumstances ("Minutes" n.d.; Fox 1895, 41; E. Wells 1895b, 234).

Women of achievement thus had an uncommon opportunity. Although most women remained firmly rooted in the home, these women of achievement could have altered the definition of women's public sphere or erased notions of separate spheres altogether. Distinctions between men's and women's public roles in fact changed, but they also sharpened early in the twentieth century (see also Carver 2000).

The never-absent notion that women's societal participation derived directly from duties as mothers and wives gave twentieth-century women a tool with which to harden the distinctions. As Ruby Lamont, writing in the *Woman's Exponent,* put it, "[W]e *demand* the ballot as a *right* through which to express our will for all mutual good; and, above all things for the good, the moral protection, the education, the happiness of our children—the very thing to which the most radical anti-suffragist would point as our first and greatest duty" (1895, 7). While claiming broad-ranging social influence, LDS women regularly argued (perhaps partly to placate suffrage opponents) that they would use this influence to more capably raise morally upright children. They considered women a force for purity, compassion, and virtue (Cox 1893, 49). Women's duty to install such characteristics in the home extended to society, they argued. Women should use the ballot and increased influence to advance such qualities in society, among other things ("Women in Politics" 1896).

Soon, however, the "among other things" faded. Mormon women began to discuss duties of civic participation only in relation to "female" concerns. They suggested that women promote their "natural" attributes through a narrow range of social activities. Womanly characteristics no longer qualified them to deal with the broad spectrum of social issues, as it had before (A Mugwump 1898, 74). An article by Susa Young Gates, writing under the pseudonym of Homespun, exemplifies the transition. Despite celebrating women's right to choose their social role, she suggested that women properly operate only within certain limits in the public sphere. Women have received the "precious right of a voice at the ballot, and the no less precious power to choose her traditional place in society or to reject it if she will. When woman has achieved her perfect liberty, she will choose to be tender, gentle, intuitional, and, in a word, womanly; she will eschew too active public life, and she will esteem her natural sphere as godlike and perfect" (Homespun 1901, 71).

The LDS media encouraged women to promote political reform in specific areas. Medicine was a properly female activity. Not only could women adequately practice medicine, but also nature better fitted them to care for women and children ("Progress of Women in the Last Seventy Years" 1912; "Medical Colleges Open Doors to Women" 1917). Health and hygiene,[16] child labor, education, and minimum wages brought women's compassion into society, they argued. Women promoted virtue and purity on such issues as temperance, community cleanup, and prostitution. During World War I, Red Cross work perfectly represented how female domestic concerns extended into social contributions.[17]

Biographical portrayals of Mormon women of achievement represented this expanded but recodified sphere for female social authority. Whether because their collective efforts congregated around a few themes or because Mormon writers prioritized only certain accomplishments (or both), portrayals presented a limited image of public-sphere womanhood. Martha Hughes Cannon's legislative action, for example, was summarized as "secur[ing] the passage of a number of bills, relating to health and sanitation" (" 'Mormon' Women Physicians" 1915, 355). Jane W. K. Skofield was noted for championing a nine-hour-workday law and a minimum-wage law for working girls, in addition to her medical bills (" 'Mormon' Women Physicians" 1915, 356). Utah female politicians emphasized education, children, morals, labor, and corruption (Gates [1920a] and 1920b, 271–75). Women lobbying politicians also recognized a sharply delimited women's sphere. May Belle Thurman Davis, a member of the Utah House of Representatives, wrote:

> [I]t was my observation that the woman [lobbyists] were as a rule the advocates of measures characterized by the sympathetic or welfare element, as the teacher's pension bill, bill providing for the appointment of a state welfare commission, bills on health and sanitation, bill making a man who willfully refuses to support his wife and children guilty of a felony, and memorial bills. It was also my observation that the men who came . . . were as a rule advocates of measures characterized by the "economic" element, as bills pertaining to insurance, real estate, agencies, imitation milk, farming, taxation revenues. (Quoted in Gates [1920a], n.p.)

Davis found that women injected the same elements into the social body as in the home—human sympathy and social welfare. This strong equation between women's domestic and societal roles confined women's social influence. Church publications through 1920 noted educational, political, artistic, and professional opportunities for women, but they increasingly implied that women made only very specific contributions in these areas. Although Davis herself hoped women would expand their political expertise, most women heard from LDS culture that their potential "public" contributions derived directly from domestic duties. Mormon culture thus separated women's sphere from men's sphere just as strongly outside the home as within it.

Reassertion of Male Privilege

When B. H. Roberts opposed woman suffrage at the 1895 state constitutional convention, many people thought he had come down on the wrong side of history. To Mormon feminists, especially, his position was anachronistic. Faith in contemporary Mormonism implied faith in the progress of both the church and society (Whitney 1907; "Symposium" 1901). Just as (and because) the church would surely grow, society would encompass greater freedom and righteousness. Aided by Mormonism's spread, social progress inevitably included female liberty and development. Thus, Ruby Lamont confidently and bitingly told readers to "forget not the dramatic courage of a hero [Roberts] digging his political grave in defense of wrong and oppression!" (1895, 6).

Roberts lost the immediate battle over suffrage, but Lamont could not have been more wrong in another sense. Roberts's political ambitions suffered little from his opposition. In fact, Utahns elected him to the U.S. House of Representatives in 1898. His opposition to suffrage appealed to many, particularly non-Mormons (U.S. Congress 1906, 1:927). His political career failed not because of suffrage opposition but because he continued to live with his plural wives. Congress nullified his election. America continued to work to deny voices to anything or anybody associated with polygamy. However, Roberts's continued local popularity illustrates that male privilege (apart from polygamous male privilege) was more stubbornly and deeply embedded in Mormon (and non-Mormon) society than early LDS feminists believed. Feminists chipped away at the edifice of male privilege in the late nineteenth century but could not prevent its repair in the twentieth; it was less vulnerable in 1920 than in 1890. Van Wagenen argues that such male privilege quickly reestablished itself in formal politics: "Once it became clear to Utah's political parties that despite woman suffragists' successes in 1896, prejudices against women had not evaporated, Utah's male politicians became increasingly disinterested in soliciting women as candidates or tapping their skills for party leadership roles. . . . As Utah entered mainstream American politics, its men—unsurprisingly—grew less and less willing to veer from the norm" (1994, 474).

Male privilege relies on the assumption that regardless of whatever else they may do, women may not seriously challenge male wisdom, opportunity, or comfort. It assumes that men's advantages over women are naturally deserved rather than socially structured.[18] Such assumptions filled Roberts's arguments against suffrage. "I stated that such was the relationship of woman in the family that she was not capable of acting independently without the dictation or the suspicion of dictation from her husband. . . . Gentlemen will deny that there will be such dictation, but is that an argument? Do we not know from the great facts of human nature that it will be so?" (quoted in "Life Story of B. H. Roberts" n.d., 177). Male privilege may be recognized or unrecognized, even in the same person. Ruth M. Fox realized that she gave too much deference to the priesthood, especially to the leading brethren of the church (Fox n.d., 32). But when traveling with one of those leaders on Mutual Improvement Association business (she was the president of the Young Ladies' Mutual Improvement Association), she found nothing unusual about the assumption that when he needed his clothes washed, she would wash them (Fox n.d., 33). Male privilege implies that the category of male needs no explanation; its norms are taken for granted.[19] The numerous jokes about women's supposed quirkiness in the *Home Writer*, a Mormon paper for both young men and young women, depended on male privilege. Maleness represented normality, nonmaleness deviance. Emily P. Young's August 1880 diary entry also articulated this assumption: "Some men seem to think the more they can say to cast reproach upon woman's nature the more honor they heap upon their owen [*sic*] heads. They take pleasure in ridiculing her character *as God has made her*" (E. Young n.d., 4, emphasis added). Even though she thought men ought not to mock women's nature, the phrase "as God as made her" implies that female nature is something peculiar, something needing explanation.

Male privilege presents itself in many guises and is strongest when habitual. Mormon culture's dominant norms never drifted far from these habitual privileges. They consistently told women to put off selfishness and keep their worries to themselves. "Does husband hurry home with buoyant heart if he knows he will be met with complaints?" an article in *Young Woman's Journal* rhetorically asked ("Place Your Trials in God's Keeping" 1900, 380). When male privilege was recognized, the culture most often justified it in terms of male and female natures. Women were told to be shy and retiring, while men were to be assertive and bold (L. Smith 1890; "Home Builders" 1900, 376). Such doctrines as polygamy and a male priesthood combined with most Mormons' Anglo-American and northern European Victorian backgrounds to instill strong habits of male privilege.[20]

However, Mormons faced some unique obstacles in the perpetuation of male privilege. Mormons' toleration of a double standard on extramarital sex was low (though polygamy institutionalized different expectations of sexuality within marriage). They enjoined young men to possess the same virtue and purity as young women.[21] Mormon doctrine also made possible unusual challenges to male privilege. A Mormon interpretation of Adam and

Eve has feminist implications, for example. B. H. Roberts aligned himself with mainstream Christianity by deriving women's subservience from Eve's having eaten the forbidden fruit first, but other impulses existed in Mormonism. Adam's "fall" is not the disaster in LDS theology that it is to mainstream Christians. While the "fall" involved transgression, church leaders often held that members should thank Eve and not criticize her actions since God's children could come to earth and participate in the salvation process only through the "fall" (B. Young 1871, 145; 2 Nephi 2:25[22]). The LDS belief in a mother in heaven lent women a gender-specific dignity unavailable to mainstream Christians (Jorgensen 2001).[23]

The LDS doctrine of salvation also differed from mainstream beliefs. It insisted that men and women could not receive the highest glory without each other (Young Men's Mutual Improvement Association n.d.d, 48). This moderated—though did not obliterate—the sense that a woman was her husband's property. "When a man can say of his wife in spirit and in truth, 'mine forever,' and the woman can say of her husband 'forever his,' and he 'forever mine,' not only the expectation but the condition of eternal domesticity are with them both," Mormons were taught ("Lesson XV" 1920, 337). Since salvation occurred in families, Mormons often argued that women's domestic responsibilities placed them in positions of authority. As African American and Native American feminists teach, women's home-centered lives do not *necessarily* deprive them of authority; to think so is a Eurocentric conceit (Collins 1990, 44–47; hooks 1990, 41–49; P. Allen 1986).[24] Mormon women could and did (and continue to) use LDS theology to disrupt some types of male privilege. "No woman," Susa Young Gates contended, "could safely carry the triple burden of wifehood, motherhood and functioning in priestly orders. Yet her creative home labor ranks side by side with her husband's priestly responsibilities. . . . Moreover, in this Church, men can and do share faithfully the burdens of home-life, and women happily enter the market-place of public activity whenever or wherever she desires" ([1920a], n.p.).

Nevertheless, these peculiarly LDS doctrines existed uneasily beside American ideals in turn-of-the-century Mormon culture. Most Mormons were as eager to become Americanized as non-Mormons were to Americanize them (U.S. Congress 1906). American cultural norms dominated day-to-day activities, even if LDS doctrines sometimes modified their meanings. The Americanization of Utah helped reassert male privilege. The Smoot hearings, especially, reminded Mormons that they deviated from national norms and perhaps still merited surveillance when women gained too much social authority.[25] Reminders came in many forms. Senators gently mocked Angus M. Cannon upon learning that his plural wife (Martha Hughes Cannon) had defeated him in a state senatorial election (U.S. Congress 1906, 1:915). They listened soberly to reports that (male) church authority might have benefited particular political parties, but they laughed when Orlando W. Powers (a former Utah Territory supreme court justice who was not Mormon) testified that the Democratic Party believed the Relief Society recently canvassed on its behalf (U.S. Congress 1906, 1:867). The lawyer for Smoot's opponents asked a non-Mormon woman whether she participated in her community's politics "within, of course, proper limits or such limitations as would be put upon a woman who was interested in it" (U.S. Congress 1906, 3:171). Senators consistently asked male witnesses about family activities in terms that assumed males unquestionably ought to make family decisions.[26] Even Massachusetts senator George Frisbie Hoar's persistent (if seemingly innocuous) questioning of church president Joseph F. Smith about female ecclesiastical authority reinforced the fact that there were differences between Mormon and American norms (U.S. Congress 1906, 1:187–90).

One significant challenge to male privilege was in representation. Mormon female activities confronted male representational privileges in a number of ways (see also Morin and Guelke 1998). National suffrage alliances allowed Mormon women to represent themselves against their negative images. Publishing journals (the *Woman's Exponent* and the *Young Woman's Journal*) permitted them to shape LDS women's images of women (and LDS men's to some degree). Involvement in healings and spiritual gifts offered Mormon women female representation before their God. Women did not always need male mediators to deal with problems that strained their individual, mortal capacity. When they needed special access to God's beneficence, they could call on women, at least in certain circumstances (Young Ladies' Mutual Improvement Association n.d., 54). Women often offered their dreams or visions to guide their LDS sisters (Ella Campbell 1890; Homespun 1890; Price 1890). Each of these female privileges gradually eroded, however.

Representing themselves to women's rights groups became more difficult (though it continued to a diminished degree) when the church withdrew financial support for conference attendance. LDS women continued to edit journals, but the journals were less independent than they had been. The *Relief Society Magazine* replaced the *Woman's Exponent* as part of the church's process of institutional centralization and as the church incorporated the society as an auxiliary under priesthood direction. Instead of being privately owned, as the *Woman's Exponent* had been, the *Relief Society Magazine* was owned by the church. Its editorial content experienced a slow but sure increase in male authorship—about 10 percent of bylined articles by 1920 (Evans 1992, 62). Simultaneously, the church assumed central control over study in the Relief Society (and other church auxiliaries) (Alexander 1986, 134–35). Men's emphases, whether or not substantially different from women's, replaced women's editorial control. Finally, men increasingly mediated LDS women's engagement with spiritual representation and priesthood authority. Male church leaders gradually codified spiritual gifts and priesthood procedures into regularized male-centric patterns (Newell 1992a and 1992b). The privilege of women representing one another dwindled in each of these cases; male representation of females came to dominate.

Male privilege was never in serious danger in Mormon culture, but Mormon feminists for a brief time had begun to question it. Nevertheless this critique quickly retreated. Male privilege was reinstalled as a mostly unchallenged mode of life.

The Retreat to Victorian Ideals

Despite periods of separation from other Americans, Mormon women were always influenced by Victorian ideals of love. Expectations of deep spiritual communion permeated many polygamous relationships, making them more disappointing than they might otherwise have been. Still, these marital expectations were not the only ones for nineteenth-century Mormon women. Other, not entirely compatible, norms were also important. The shift to Victorian ideals must therefore be charted (see also Foster 1991). The shift is actually more of a spurt. Around 1900, LDS conceptions of love moved strongly toward Victorian ideals as the only viable, if not perfect, models for male-female relationships.

Nineteenth-century Mormon women most effectively countered the Victorian notion that women live fulfilling lives only to the extent that they cherish and are cherished by their husbands. Men, according to this notion, should adore wives for possessing attributes males lack: virtue, refinement, dependence, delicacy, vulnerability, and even weakness—"selfless abnegation" in Louis Kern's words (1981, 63). Mormons did not eliminate adoration as a lovers' norm, but they often argued that it should not dominate relationships. A member of the Young Ladies' Mutual Improvement Association wrote, "Woman, without having lost anything of her gentleness and grace, no longer accepts that once famous axiom, 'man should support woman.' She cares not for adoration alone, but wants to carry her intellect and activity into spheres suited to her" (L. Smith 1890, 175–76). While she later remarked that women are better (but not exclusively) suited to maintaining homes and lauded women who realize that their social status is not equal to men's, the writer implied that marriage relationships should place more importance on admiration and respect than on blind adoration. She rejected norms of vulnerability, weakness, and dependence in favor of male-female interdependence. An Ellen Jakeman story (1890) articulated similar views. Marital happiness, it implied, comes not from idealized notions of womanly virtue but from mutual understanding and respect for the different burdens men and women bear (see also Skurlock 1890; and Marie 1895).

Mormon women could use Victorian rhetoric to promote their political agenda. Dr. Ellis R. Shipp mobilized the discourse to protect Mormon women's dignity when it came under acute attack: "We are accused of being down-trodden and oppressed. *We deny the charge!* for we know there cannot be found a class of women upon the earth who occupy a more elevated position in the hearts of their husbands, or whose most delicate and refined feelings are so respected as here in Utah" (*"Mormon" Women's Protest* [1886], 37). Although Shipp wielded Victorian terminology, she implied that wives found greater worth in winning husbands' respect through independence and initiative than by being placed on a Victorian pedestal. As Michel Foucault argues, discourses cannot be completely monitored and do not always serve unified political agendas; hegemonic meanings can be inverted or turned on their heads (1990, 100–102). Dr. Romania Pratt's argument at the same 1886 mass meeting that Shipp attended evidences more inversion than reproduction of Victorian discourse: "[W]e do firmly believe . . . that this system [celestial marriage] conduces to the elevation and independence of women—that the men of this faith who are guided by the spirit of the Gospel have the highest regard for virtue and morality . . ." (*"Mormon" Women's Protest* [1886], 33). Male admiration of female virtue and morality would come not through dependence and vulnerability but through independence and strength.

Mormon culture taught that love ought to exist between marriage partners. Mormons shared with middle-class white Americans the sense that love meant unique identity with, by completely revealing oneself to, one's partner (Lystra 1989, 7–43; Seidman 1991, 39–61).[27] It meant that one partner (particularly the woman) gave himself or herself completely to the other's happiness. Each attempted to become the ideal the other had been taught to love (Kern 1981, 64). As Rhoda M. Young put it, "To be loved by her husband, and looking to him as her head and perfecter, is better than merely aiming to be his servant or plaything" (1878, n.p.). Mormon culture tended to idealize the husband-wife bond as qualitatively different from other relationships. This tendency paralleled broader norms of the age.

Mormon fiction (especially that not published in women's journals) borrowed freely from these Victorian ideals. Alfred Lambourne's love story captures the essence of these ideals:

> And Fiametta, too, why did she feel a strange stirring of the heart when Laurence was near? . . . The subtle poison of love . . . may be running in our every vein before we are aware. . . . How beautiful it is when two souls blend together in the harmony of perfect love! When each is all to each. . . . How precious, how necessary to the spiritual repose is that true adjustment of soul to soul. Without it we were ever incomplete; forever would be our highest longings unfulfilled, our highest endowments undeveloped. . . . How many a true and pure heart and mind have become aware at last, when too late, that friendship, respect, gratitude, even a certain kind of fondness, are not love; but resembles it only, when we hold them up to the searching gaze, as sleep resembles death!" (1890, 252–53).

Echoing Lambourne, another storyteller wrote that the words *husband, home,* and *motherhood* "are to true women the most expressive of affection and happiness of any to be found in the English language. . . . Every woman's nature calls for these three things, the longings of her soul can never be satisfied without them" (Amethyst 1890, 269–70).

But these Victorian/romantic tendencies continually ran into the Mormon impulse to prioritize earned respect above blind love, strength above vulnerability, and interdependence above dependence (Lula 1890). The ubiquitous stories about falling in love demonstrate these dueling impulses. "The Western Boom" story mentioned at the outset of this chapter is one example. In it, a husband's love grew for a woman only after she demonstrated strength, initiative, and resolve. In another story (N. Anderson 1890), the author portrayed the female protagonist as "beautiful," "good," "virtuous," one who "talked good sense," a hard worker, and a "heroine." She struggled over marrying her fiancé immediately or waiting until they could marry in a LDS temple.[28] "Would Oscar spurn her if she refused to yield to his request? Oh! it was hard; this battle betwen [*sic*] love and duty going on within the breast of this simple minded girl" (29). The story implied that independently following beliefs about right and wrong was better than immediate and complete submission to romance. This capacity to follow one's convictions could aid romance. In another story (Ella 1890), the heroine's selfless domestic sacrifices impressed an admirer. He "thought what a contrast there was between her and the selfish young ladies that he generally met in society. . . . He was very much surprised also to find how intelligently she could converse upon all subjects, and to find that she was perfectly refined and ladylike in all her words and ways. He regarded her with much interest during the day and decided, before they parted that evening, that she was the

one woman for him, providing he could win her" (171–72). Mormon female culture expected the non-Victorian impulses of womanly strength, independence, and intelligence to temper Victorian love. Blind adulation did
not take precedence.

These nineteenth-century norms changed, however. It appears that
change came easily and was scarcely noticed, perhaps because LDS female
culture already partially embraced Victorian ideals. The change was uneven
and never complete. Nevertheless, the balance of power in normative LDS
culture shifted to a Victorian ethos between 1890 and 1920; the modifying
impulses weakened. Writers admired biblical Sarah for strength and motherhood, for example, but her romance with Abraham demanded central attention (Done 1900; Freeze 1900).

Continuing efforts to differentiate Mormons from non-Mormons (now
morally more than socially) aided the shift. Young Mormons learned to beware of those outside the church. Many groups erect symbolic boundaries
between insiders and outsiders (Cohen 1986). In their rapidly changing social environment, Mormons attempted to refigure difference in many ways
(Alexander 1986; Flake 2000, 130–89). Redefinitions of LDS and non-LDS
lovers bolstered the project. The Mormon media separated LDS lovers from
non-LDS lovers and increasingly ascribed Victorian characteristics to the
former. Authors often did so by attributing purity and innocence to Utah
and its youth (Carroll 1920–21).

"What Happened in Dreamland" (1900), a very unsubtle play intended
to "illustrate the lesson in Ethics," exemplifies this point. Fred, a young
LDS man, sees in a dream the consequences of pursuing Marcia, an allur-
ing, urbane, and non-Mormon young woman. A subsequent dream con-
trasts this with his potential relationship with Rose, a sweet Mormon young
woman. Marcia is scheming, manipulative, and (significantly) eager to leave
Utah. In the first dream, she inverts preferred gender roles, aggressively trying to win Fred, while confiding to her sister, Ethelyn: " 'I am determined
to make this country beau bow to my will. He has much to thank me for,
now, in the freedom of thought and spirit which I have helped him to; he
shall have yet more gratitude, for I am quite resolved to make him so dis-
satisfied with his tame and stupid surroundings and friends that he will be
glad to escape' " (71). As Fred's dream continues, he marries Marcia, they
move to New York City, and she turns into a greedy, class-conscious ma-
nipulator. " 'I am sick of America; I want to live in England, where people
are put in their proper places and kept there. . . . I've taught him [Fred] to
break loose from his stupid Puritanical, Mormon notions . . . but he does
get so stupid and sentimental even now, at times. Talks about honor and

virtue and the family being the unit of society, and such silly nonsense'"
(72–73). Ethelyn, impressed by Fred's Utah innocence, plays her sister's foil.
Marcia, having grown tired of Fred, tells Ethelyn she should have married
Fred instead. Ethelyn responds, "'Indeed I wish he had asked me. Or his
fine old Uncle John; I never saw such strong, handsome men, and such good
men as I met in Utah.'" Marcia retorts, "'How many times must I ask you
not to repeat Utah or anything connected with it. I am so ashamed of ever
having seen the place that I cannot endure one word about it'" (73).

Still in the first dream, Fred predictably comes to his senses, asking Marcia what happened to his relationship and life. "'We have no home life. . . . I
left home, parents, the girl I was engaged to, and even my religion for you.
You have fascinated and enthralled me. . . . You soon wearied of my love
and tender devotion. . . . '" He mutters to himself, "'I have had no home. . . .
No love, no wife, no peace, nothing but sham. . . . Oh for my peaceful,
happy home in Utah!'" (74–75). Fred's subsequent dream spotlights the
potential love and happiness with faithful Rose in a Utah home. Fred tells
Rose, "'The thought of our pure and happy courtship comes to me at times
with such overflowing joy that I am moved to tears, almost. My wife, your
love and confidence are the most precious things I have. Our cottage home,
our friends and relatives all, our happy associations, and best of all, our religion—oh, Rose, we are blessed above mortals'" (76).

In this and similar stories, ideals of interdependence and respect still existed, but the balance shifted. Love no longer derived from interdependence
and respect; rather, interdependence and respect followed love. Loving the
single correct spiritual partner became the ultimate goal, almost the only
goal (N. Anderson 1898). Mormon culture assumed Victorian ideals with
a re-presented Utah symbolizing Victorian love—youth, beauty, innocence,
purity, a place to experience deepest reality, and a refuge from an uncom-
prehending world. Earlier LDS literature also used regionality to moralize
about taking non-Mormon spouses (Jakeman 1890–91; Mollie 1890).
What was new around the turn of the century were more explicit claims
about the necessity of romantic love and its impossibility outside Utah and
the Mormon-Mormon marriage relation. Movement away from the region
symbolized abandonment of both faith and the potential for true and
fulfilling love. The region alone, symbolized as either hilly, mountainous
terrain or rural villages, housed one's intimate confidant of the soul (A. M.
Cannon 1910; Loraine 1900). Benjamin Forest (1995) argues that narratives of morality can help constitute places. These love tales both reclaimed
the region for church members who felt its distinctiveness threatened and
eased Mormons into altered norms of love. The dual function has great

significance. Reconstituting region and remaking gender norms were not separate projects.

A desire to retain LDS values and establish a historical Mormonism while sliding toward Victorian ideals characterized turn-of-the-century Mormon literature. Perhaps the best example is Susa Young Gates's novel *John Stevens' Courtship* (1909). Gates sets this novel during the so-called Utah War, which occurred when federal troops occupied the Salt Lake Valley in the late 1850s to quell a supposed Mormon rebellion (Furniss 1960). No blood spilled during the "war," but tensions ran high for many months. Gates's story exemplifies themes that helped reestablish Mormon distinctiveness. It represents innocence as young LDS females face their greatest temptation in publicly gallant and sophisticated but ultimately debauched non-Mormon soldiers. The story served as a morality play. It portrays a slow, but virtuous courtship between two Mormon youths, and a young LDS woman's disgrace in falling for a soldier. Toward the conclusion of the story, the young woman who chose the right path warns her fallen friend: " 'I am beginning to see things as they are: the glamour and glory and romance which once so fascinated me is fading away—anyway as it relates to men who drink and carouse or who do wrong. And especially do I begin to see how unsafe we are associating with any man outside this Church and kingdom' " (306). Though a distinction between true love and inappropriate romantic fascination remains, the sense that love exerts an almost irresistible power appears. When this speaker's courtship culminates in marriage, she becomes a model of Victorian wifehood (370–77). Household duties are a pleasure because she does them for her husband. She loves to be called "wife," having entered into the special state of Victorian ownership. As her single, true companion, "[h]e was hers now, as perfectly as she was his" (371). Her husband says, " 'I think I have loved you, sweetheart, since we sang together with the morning stars and shouted in unison with our companions when the foundations of this earth were laid. . . . Ever since I saw you, a tiny, silver-haired tot of a girl, I felt that you were apart and separate from everything human for me, and I loved you' " (373). To Susa Young Gates, a highly influential figure in mainstream Mormonism,[29] male-female relationships were to follow this Victorian romantic ideal (see also the partially different analysis of this novel in G. T. Smith 1993, 119–84).

Stories with ideals of Victorian love appeared most frequently in the *Young Woman's Journal* around the turn of the century. Later issues contained fewer love stories, and those that did appear (for example, Greenwood 1920; and Carroll 1920–21) reopened more space for carefreeness and female independence in love. Finding one's proper partner, though still important, no longer needed be such a grave business. These stories slightly cynically embraced Victorian love. Like many in twentieth-century America (Seidman 1991, 65–118), they rejected Victorian love's serious nature and emphasized friendship somewhat more. But they found few alternatives to Victorian notions of unique and exclusive spiritual partnership. The turn-of-the-century flurry of Victorian tales thus installed a specific notion of love as mainstream Mormon culture's only viable option for male-female relationships. LDS literature no longer promoted the model as intensely after 1910,[30] perhaps because Mormons had started taking it for granted. In any case, there is little evidence of serious questioning of the model after 1910. Some older sentiments among women even became unthinkable. Elsie Faust could declare in 1897, "I can say as the most of you can say, that the best friend of my life has been a woman" (111), but in the twentieth century, to have anyone other than a husband occupy that position would be admitting failure. In this context, a Mormon feminist critique of monogamous relations grew ever more unlikely.

Codification of Gender Roles in the Family

Latter-day Saints always valued home and family. But the ways LDS culture operationalized Mormonism's teachings shifted over time. While late-nineteenth-century Mormon culture encompassed different family styles, by 1920 a single set of norms dominated and (perhaps more important) was virtually unchallenged. Families found gender roles more fixed and nonnegotiable. In particular, Mormon culture circumscribed the categories of husband and wife, father and mother, much more precisely.

Polygamy allowed LDS women to draw on Christian ideals but also to interpret these ideals in a feminist manner. Romania B. Pratt claimed that "the Christian idea of home, where one father and one mother, each the equal of the other . . . rear about the hearth-stone an intelligent and God fearing family" was more completely attained in Mormon plural families than anywhere else ("Mormon" Women's Protest [1886], 28). Her appeal to home and family utilizes a female-centered definition of the home. Multiple wives means multiple homes. The father may preside, but existence of this most important social unit depends on the mother. She defended polygamy in female-centered terms: "Has not every woman the undeniable right to be an honorable wife and mother—of fulfilling the end of her creation, and do not the circumstances of life and statistics prove this to be impossible under the monogamic system?" (29–30). She further noted that polygamous women have greater independence in the family than monogamous women do (31). Thus, while Mormon culture's defense of the family and home utilized hegemonic rhetoric, for a few years it contained various family norms, some of which potentially empowered women more than commonly realized.

An editorial in the *Equal Rights Banner,* the newsletter of the woman suffrage organization in Beaver, Utah, proposed blurring distinctions between husbandhood and wifehood. Women ought to take time to develop their God-given talents: "If it be verily true that we have not time, (which I believe is the case with the majority of wives and mothers) is it not because we willingly place ourselves on the altar of sacrifice, and bear heavy burdens that ought to be shared by husbands . . ." (Editorial 1894b, n.p.). The same issue contained a proverb encouraging women to "shake off a portion of the useless burdens" of home duties. It suggested that women should not "tamely submit" to husbands' expectations of wifely sacrifice for male comfort ("A Picture" 1894, n.p.). Men, according to this vision, should take responsibility for part of their own domestic comfort. Husbandhood might confer the privilege of a wife's domestic labor, but these voices suggested that the imperative of female personal development placed limits on such privileges. To be sure, women prioritizing housework, children, and male comfort continued to speak alongside the more critical voices ("Woman's Sphere" 1894; L. Smith 1890). But for some years competing voices existed. Lost or shut out in later years were these nonconventional desires to blur distinctions between husband and wife. Articulating or even imagining alternative models of husbandhood and wifehood became more difficult.

Increasing emphasis on formalized methods of domestic labor facilitated the shift. Such strong formalization began near the turn of the century. A 1900 Young Ladies' Mutual Improvement Association study manual suggested home management lessons, but it also incorporated older, less codified norms. Instead of recommending books for further home management study, as it did for other topics, it asserted that "practical counsel from mothers and grandmothers, experienced cooks, and housekeepers, with plenty of home experiments and labors will furnish all the material necessary in this study" (Young Ladies' Mutual Improvement Association n.d., 13). The same year, the editors of the *Young Woman's Journal* decided it was necessary to have a regular column instructing readers on domestic affairs, "including art in the home, clothing and fashions, as well as cooking and kitchen matters" ("In the Home" 1900, 84); the number of articles on such subjects increased thereafter. Likewise, the *Relief Society Magazine* addressed domestic management much more seriously than the *Exponent* ever had. As this formalization of housework began, Susa Young Gates argued that women and society would advance through increased emphasis on domestic science. It would lighten women's toil and drudgery and allow women to promote civilization's advance more effectively (1901). Whatever the benefits of new methods and implements were, instead of liberating women from housework, the new emphasis more tightly defined women by domestic duties.[31] Young Mormon women learned to attract a desirable husband through quality domestic labor (Peay 1910).

The male-oriented *Contributor* and *Improvement Era* used stories from eastern syndicates and other outside sources more than the *Young Woman's Journal* did. These invariably presented images of husbandhood and wifehood in which a woman sacrificed her own interests and desires for her husband's aspirations. A story on Thomas Carlyle and his wife is typical (Lancaster 1910). It noted her many disappointments, from being childless to performing domestic duties from lack of money to hire servants. Yet, the article suggested, "she should not have regarded her marriage as a failure." After all she was "pre-eminently the companion of the man she had married. . . . She was 'the true and loving helpmeet' of her husband, and, knowing his greatness, . . . she aided his greatness by insuring daily peace and order, even in dusting, or darning his socks" (415). A successful wife facilitated her husband's success. According to this model, a man is a successful husband when he turns from masculine affairs long enough to notice his spouse's discouragements and concerns and to express love and appreciation (see also Amethyst 1890; "Mother and Home" 1890; and "Lesson XV" 1920, 338).

Like husbandhood and wifehood, motherhood was also subject to multiple interpretations. While Romania Pratt emphasized female independence and spiritual glory, others promoted male comfort and glory. Wilby Dougall used nearly the same terms as Pratt—the ideal woman should think that "one of the greatest honors in this life is to become a 'mother in Israel,' and fill the measure of her creation" ("The Perfect Woman" 1890, 454)—but the context makes it clear that he considered the husband's success to be a wife's primary orientation. The *Young Woman's Journal*'s request to a few church leaders and "honorable" young men to describe the perfect woman provoked Dougall's statement. In this "symposium," the older men emphasized companionship, while the younger men's concerns lay in a wife's ability to comfort her husband and complement his aspirations. This generational difference in answers parallels the generational shift in discourses about motherhood and wifehood.

Domestic self-sacrifice more completely dominated women's roles. By 1920, LDS culture told women that motherhood and home duties not only should take top priority but also should, except for a few exceptional women, become virtually the only priority ("'Woman's Day'" 1920). Lifelong female development fell by the wayside. Increasing emphasis on motherhood in LDS general conference messages during the 1910s reinforced this point.[32] Having studied four generations of Mormon women, Maureen Ursenbach Beecher argues that the Americanization of Utah carried "overwhelming shifts in lifestyle for individual Latter-day Saint women" (1993, 132). Women shifted their devotion from other women to their husbands, she suggests.

Mothers' contribution to society came to depend more completely on their sons' achievement. Early arguments about motherhood's social importance centered on a woman's capacity to rear children as good, virtuous people (*"Mormon" Women's Protest* [1886], 76–77; M. Cannon 1894, 114; Done 1900, 363). Articles about rearing children did not often categorize mothers' contributions according to the children's sex ("Home Builders" 1900, 377; Whalen 1900, 366–67). However, focus increasingly shifted to male achievement. A son's involvement in economic, church, political, or social leadership began to overshadow the general virtue of one's children as the sign of a mother's success (Frost 1920; "What Women Will Do with the Suffrage" 1920, 294).

While Mormon culture traditionally separated women's and men's roles, women in LDS culture threw motherhood open to additional possibilities and meanings early in the period under study. They blurred distinctions between wifehood and husbandhood. Gender norms did not follow this trajectory for long. After the turn of the century, distinctions between husbands' and wives' roles hardened. Mormon culture more narrowly defined motherhood. It offered fewer domestic models to women and men. Susa Young Gates's contention that LDS men allowed wives to pursue interests outside the home may be accurate, but young LDS men increasingly learned that their domestic responsibilities covered a narrow range of activities. These activities became increasingly male focused—the kind of activities recent white feminists identify when they mark the home as a site of oppression (Rose 1993, 53–56). Mormon culture increasingly trained young LDS women to accept this situation. Codifying family roles helped Mormons claim that they were defenders of the home. Mormons used this claim to assert membership in the larger society. Although this shift may have aided (or even been necessary for) LDS Americanization, it made a strong LDS critique of dominant norms more difficult.

Conclusion

A regional debate over gender authority existed in the struggle over the fate of Mormon polygamy. A critique of the nation's gender structure welled up from a number of early Mormon women. From about the late 1870s to the early 1890s, they argued that American society devalued women in comparison to men. This critique was not a completely independent critique. While the views held by many Mormon women in these matters were strong and genuine, they were linked to their support of Mormon polygamy and their belief in Mormonism. This Mormon critique of gender authority did not question all elements of gender as a category, though it sought greater equality between genders. There is debate about whether these Mormon women were true feminists. Scholars calling them feminist point to their strong support of woman suffrage, their critique of the lack of female privilege in American society, and their development of independent female networks. Those who deny that Mormon women were feminist note that those women did not criticize the strongly patriarchal authority structure of their own church, did not effectively challenge the notion that women's most important responsibility was in the home, and performed few acts of defiance against male authority.

To the latter set of scholars, the debate turns on the issue of whether Mormon women were more deeply Mormon or more deeply feminist; the two categories are assumed, ultimately, to be mutually exclusive. I believe this search for true feminists is misguided. One of the main lessons history teaches is that people usually operate with multiple, not wholly compatible identities and loyalties. Most of the time, people function without needing to subordinate one identity to another. In some cases, however, people are forced to choose one over others. The identity subordinated depends on the situation as much as on the strength of the identity. In such cases, it is not altogether fair to question the reality of that subordinated identity. Feminists of color teach a similar lesson. Being asked to choose between ethnic or racial culture and feminism is a choice they should not be asked to make, they argue, even when their culture contains strongly patriarchal elements. Rather, they should be allowed to create their own feminist strategies in their own cultures. They should not be asked to conform to mainstream feminism when their culture is under attack from mainstream society. At times feminists of color make alliances with other women (and upset nonfeminists in their ethnic culture), while at other times they join with males of their own culture (and upset white feminists). Their action depends on what they feel is the greatest need.

This was the situation Mormon women faced. They enunciated a critique of patriarchal society that was valid as far as it went. They helped women of the territory gain opportunities and privileges they had never had (and that few women elsewhere possessed). They were beginning to raise the status of women in Mormonism itself (although how much more they could have done remains an open, probably unanswerable question). The late-nineteenth-century attack on Mormonism forced them to choose either their feminism or their Mormon identity. It should come as no surprise that most Mormon feminists calculated that the latter was most vulnerable and defended Mormonism more strongly than feminism. They probably had little reason to expect that their defense of Mormonism would result in a blunting of the socially critical edge of their feminism by 1920, but that seems to have happened.

In the 1880s and the 1890s, Mormon feminists questioned the authority women held in America compared with that held by men. They argued that the ideal of romantic love and the dominance of monogamous marital relations left women too emotionally and socially dependent on (usually unreliable) men. These Mormon women believed that there were significant differences between men and women. Like some of their contemporary feminists, they believed women were naturally more pure and nurturing than men, and they had little trouble translating these beliefs into the notion that women ought to be the ones raising the children. Yet they believed that these special qualities of women did not confine them to only that sphere. Women were every bit as capable as men of excellence in professions, academics, and leadership. Like most feminists of the day, they trusted the institution of marriage but believed Mormon doctrine placed women higher in the marriage relationship than did mainstream Christian doctrine. Theirs was a feminism that thought of men and women as necessary partners, but more equal and autonomous partners than they had hitherto been. This feminism made a distinction between equality and sameness regarding men and women. Because of their equality *and* their unique qualities, women ought to be much more involved in almost all areas of "public" life than they had been.[33]

Those on the other side of the polygamy debate also claimed to be working to benefit women. Various representatives of the federal government and mainstream Christianity allied with regional citizens who despised Mormon power and numerous people worried about how civilized society could continue to exist with such a "barbarism" as polygamy in its midst. Although most of these people saw few problems with mainstream American gender structures, they argued that LDS women and men were being unequally yoked through polygamous marriage. Women in such marriages could never be equal to men (nor could they be placed on a Victorian pedestal). This critique of polygamy combined with the work of Mormon feminists to produce a region in which dominant gender structures were frequently questioned and debated.

By 1920, neither Mormons nor non-Mormons were quite so critical of gender relationships (this is not to say that there were not women pursuing "women's issues"). A new conception of gender authority had hardened into a regionalized moral order. According to this moral order, women were not to be concerned with the whole of the "public sphere" but were to worry about children's issues, family issues, or issues of morality. Even as some women tried to expand this sphere, they were limited by its definitional confines (Carver 2000). Many women operated with more freedom than they had in 1880, yet men's authority was paradoxically once again repositioned ideologically as superior to women's authority, especially in Mormon culture. Here social and cultural pressures worked in opposite directions.

The years from 1880 to 1920 constituted a period unlike any other for the Mormon culture region. The rapid social changes and accommodations that both Mormons and non-Mormons experienced opened up various possibilities. These possibilities included a strong and more fully regionalized critique of American gender norms. Such a critique depended on Mormon women continuing to criticize mainstream monogamy, even while inhabiting it. This was no easy task. Males both inside and outside the church happily enforced rigid, "traditional" gender norms. Mormon women themselves wanted acceptance as Americans. Continuing criticism of Mormonism gave them strong reason to seek unity with LDS men. Mormon feminists' retreat from fundamentally transformative critique is therefore not surprising. Strong pressures pushed them toward conformity.

I found little evidence suggesting that LDS women thought their viewpoints and attitudes changed significantly from 1880 to 1920. In an important sense, little in fact changed. In 1920, most Mormon women held attitudes extant for decades in Mormon culture. Even the leading edge of Mormon feminism in 1890 had espoused 1920 attitudes in one form or another. Yet in another sense, everything changed. Mormon women, as a group, no longer participated in the leading edge of what earlier generations called female progress. Instead of advocating fundamental change, they stood for reform, if not the status quo. In today's political terminology, Mormon women shifted from being radicals and liberals to being liberals and conservatives. Many still worked for the progressive movement's causes. Some still claimed solidarity with the women's movement (even with some nonconventional elements of it). But most Mormon women (and men) distanced themselves from the leading edges of gender critique.

Mormons felt that they held true to principles that their parents lived. Mormon culture, like other cultural systems, was (and is) multifarious. It contained numerous not entirely consistent elements. Dominant cultural trends may appear, such as this movement toward the American mainstream, but elements always exist that strain dominant meanings. In Mormon culture, elements that threaten the status quo sit beside elements that fortify it (as well as those that fall somewhere in between).[34] In historical analysis, negotiations and struggles over the contrasting elements demand attention to see why certain inflections dominate at specific historical moments. Inflections are crucial. Early-twentieth-century Mormons did not lose or forget cultural elements that an earlier generation used to critique American norms; these discourses (women's eternal value, motherhood, natural difference between sexes, eternal marriage) remained central to LDS culture. But these discourses gradually lost their critical inflections. Mormons instead increasingly used them to maintain dominant gender structures.

In the late nineteenth century and early twentieth, Mormon women won increased authority in society. A combination of doctrinal, social, and cultural elements aided their cause. But the contextual terrain quickly shifted. Since Utah quickly became a suffrage state after the Manifesto and since many women were taking advantage of unprecedented opportunities, continued progress seemed assured; many women no longer regarded gender issues to be as vital as they had earlier. Actors demanding Utah's economic and political Americanization strongly enforced conventional monogamous gender structures. By 1920, Mormon culture's norms shifted to conventional patriarchy.

Possibilities for a potentially transformative regional postsuffrage feminism foundered without a radical Mormon presence. Non-LDS feminism's blind spot was monogamy. Lack of a willingness to critique monogamy did not always characterize non-LDS feminism; both before 1880 and after 1920, strong elements in the American women's movement criticized romantic monogamy. But during the crucial years of the transformation of the Mormon culture region, the antipolygamy campaign helped maintain the dominance of mainstream gender moral orders (Iversen 1997), especially within the region. LDS women could have drawn on critiques by their earlier polygamist sisters, but they ultimately did not do so. This is not to say that female and even mild feminist alliances did not develop. Indeed, many alliances between Mormon and non-Mormon women blossomed, especially after 1890. These alliances appealed particularly to women with the education, inclination, and means to devote to literary clubs, temperance organizations, and patriotic groups (Carver 2000). Women in the region increasingly divided along class lines. In this climate of the ascendance of class culture, regionalized concerns to Americanize and to prevent and forget polygamy strengthened conventional gender norms. By the time the American women's movement was prepared to question the power and moral relationships involved in contemporary monogamy, LDS women had become strong advocates of the American status quo.

CHAPTER THREE

Privatizing Mormon Communitarianism

Near the end of Leonard J. Arrington's classic work on the nineteenth-century Mormon economy, he noted that between 1901 and 1906 Joseph F. Smith, president of the Church of Jesus Christ of Latter-day Saints, took the church out of a number of businesses (1958, 406–9). It divested itself of many interests in utilities, sugar, resorts, and mining. "With these [changes] the self-sufficient Kingdom may be said to have been brought to an end. A more acceptable adjustment between spiritual and secular interests was attained. And with this adjustment, the church no longer offered a geographic and institutional alternative to Babylon. Faith became increasingly separated from community policy, and religion from society. Individualism, speculation, and inequality—once thought to be characteristics of Babylon—were woven into the fabric of Mormon life" (409). This story's general outline is well known. The theme here, like much of turn-of-the-century Utah/Mormon experience, is Americanization. Nineteenth-century Mormons attempted in various ways to establish communitarian economic patterns, but pressure from outside the church and church members' own problems in instituting these patterns led the Saints to abandon them by the 1880s and 1890s. Thereafter, Mormons adopted American economic practices and norms.

This story has become nearly axiomatic; its accuracy and utility can hardly be disputed. Nevertheless, it takes too much for granted. It is a story based primarily on the experiences of corporations, church leaders, and economic elites. It privileges the Mormon church as an economic entity and assumes that the actions of the institutional church and of church leaders as individuals represent the Mormon experience. It assumes too easily that the new LDS norms were those shared by most Americans. It also fails to take into account the continued economic debates between Mormons and non-Mormons and the persistent memory of Mormon communitarianism when describing the twentieth century's emergent economic order. It generally represents the shift from "Mormon" to "American" norms as a rapid conversion from one clear-cut set of practices to another, not as a somewhat messy transition between two different but not entirely stable or internally consistent systems of moral claims.

Part of the problem is that scholars seldom seriously treat the economy as having a cultural constitution, as constituting a system of meaning. Too often, the culturally specific drive for capitalist maximization of profit and material wealth is regarded as temporally and geographically constant, not particular to specific regional social structures (Saxenian 1994). Seldom do analyses of the Mormon/regional economy consider the economy as a moral order or a set of conventions that strongly convey and fundamentally depend on notions of right and wrong and responsibility to one another (Scott 1976; Wuthnow 1987, 79–96). The regional economy, as a moral order, was a fundamental terrain of contest between Mormons and non-Mormons, as each group jockeyed to reestablish itself as the producer of regional morality and propriety after the rapid weakening of the LDS Church. Americanization of the region meant more than simply Mormons becoming like, and interacting with, non-Mormons economically, though this well-known story is surely important. The debates and compromises between Mormons and non-Mormons also helped create a regionally specific economic culture.

This chapter examines turn-of-the-century economic shifts. It regards the economy as sets of cultural norms conveying strong senses of social responsibility and propriety. Others have more closely examined Utah economy's changing industrial structure (see, for example, May 1974). The policies of the Mormon church as an economic agent are also addressed elsewhere (Mangum and Blumell 1993, 52–92; Alexander 1986, 180–211). Investigating the regional production of moral orders gives this chapter a somewhat different focus. I am not mainly concerned with Utah or the Mormon church per se. Instead, I show how particular norms came to dominate most people's economic thinking in a geographically specific area. Nor do I provide a complete economic history of the area. Rather, I center debates and trends in cultural meaning. My goal is to illuminate justifications, ideologies, and discourses that accompanied (by both shaping and being shaped by) the changing practices.

This chapter lays out the central regional economic debate of the late nineteenth century—the question of Mormon communitarianism—and then outlines key forces changing norms and practices by the early decades of the twentieth century. The bulk of the chapter is a close examination of the concepts through which regional citizens produced norms of economic responsibility. The first part explores two such concepts—those of wage labor and wealth—and the second part takes up concepts of self-sufficiency and communitarianism.

The Labor of Wealth

The Communitarian Context

In 1874, Brigham Young and other LDS Church leaders established communal economic systems, known collectively as the United Order, in most regional LDS communities. The previous year's economic panic provided the immediate impetus for establishing these orders, but something else weighed heavily on Mormon leaders. Joseph Smith had told the early Saints that they would have to be more materially egalitarian if they wanted to progress spiritually. Through the Law of Consecration, he gave them methods and principles by which they could achieve economic equality. The Mormon community never practiced these principles very successfully during Smith's lifetime, but Brigham Young sought to carry on Smith's legacy in economic matters. He led Utah Mormons in various attempts to place the Saints on a more equitable footing. The United Order was the last and most ambitious of Young's experiments (Arrington 1958). The United Order operated in a variety of ways in different communities but generally encompassed the goals of providing for all members' needs and eradicating the means of private accumulation (Arrington, Fox, and May 1992).

Other objectives besides establishing (or perhaps in order to establish) material equality characterized the United Order and other LDS economic strategies. These included minimizing economic contact with non-Mormons (especially outside the region), assisting new converts and immigrants in gaining economic viability, establishing economically successful colonies throughout the region, creating a culture in which simplicity—not fashion—was the dominant norm, and creating industries to produce wealth and comfort for the region (Arrington 1958). Mormon economic communitarianism served the Latter-day Saints well in building themselves up materially in a challenging environment. It helped them accommodate a steady stream of immigrants,[1] create scores of settlements and colonies in the area, and construct an unusually varied economy (for a nineteenth-century territory in the American West). An English visitor passing through Utah in the late 1870s or early 1880s was very critical of the Mormons but did comment favorably on the way they had made the desert blossom and had created neat, vibrant towns and villages (Marshall 1881, 144–235). The Mormons' separatist communitarianism led to what Dean May (1987) calls two

Utahs. Farming, light industry, and mining for industrial metals characterized Mormon Utah. Non-Mormon Utah prioritized gold and silver pros-
pecting, as well as mercantilism. The two Utahs, May argues (perhaps a bit
too strongly), rarely met outside the major cities of Salt Lake City and Ogden
(May 1987, 113–33).

None of the communitarian experiments were long-term successes. A few,
such as the Brigham City cooperative, accomplished the general objectives
church leaders had for them (Arrington, Fox, and May 1992, 111–33), but
most faced significant resistance from church members and disapproval from
nonmembers and therefore fell far short of their ultimate objectives. By 1877,
the United Order movement was no longer active as a result of Brigham
Young's death and an improved economy. Many orders in individual communities had collapsed by this time, though some functioned into the 1880s.
With less enthusiasm for strong forms of communalism but some desire to
maintain a cooperative Mormon economy, Young's successor, John Taylor,
let the orders die peacefully and established Zion's Central Board of Trade
in 1878 as an alternative. This board focused on creating regional economic
growth instead of local self-sufficiency. Rather than retreat from capitalism,
the board sought to moderate capitalism by stabilizing the relationship between supply and demand, fixing certain prices, aiding home industries, and
obtaining fair prices for producers of goods (mostly agricultural at this
point). Although protecting the economic "freedom" of business concerned
Taylor more than it ever did Young, Taylor envisioned Zion's Central Board
of Trade as preliminary to full industrial cooperation and an eventual fully
cooperative society (Arrington, Fox, and May 1992, 315–32). In spite of a
promising beginning, however, within half a decade the board fell victim to
the raids on polygamists. Continued coordination of economic priorities
proved impossible.

Taylor was also more open to trading with non-Mormons than Young
had been. The Gentile boycott ended in 1882 after straining economic relations between Mormons and non-Mormons for nearly a decade and a
half (Arrington 1958, 384–86). Mormons in 1880 constituted nearly four-
fifths of Utah's population, according to one estimate (May 1992, 125). By
this time, regional non-Mormons, fighting a full-fledged war on Mormon
institutions, knew well their main complaints against LDS economics.[2] The
economy ought to operate in a religiously neutral manner, they argued. That
is, they wanted no boycotts of business along religious lines, a local market for their products, freedom to join forces with Mormon entrepreneurs,
and greater development of Utah's natural resources through speculation
(Brigham Young had proclaimed speculation immoral). These demands had

been enunciated for years by (military-based) prospectors, dissident Mormons (Walker 1998), and urban merchants. These goals implied nothing
less than a full unleashing of American capitalist markets on the regional
economy. Non-Mormons, by and large, wanted the same opportunities to
make fortunes in Utah as existed elsewhere throughout the American West.

Forces of Cultural Change

The 1880s raids on polygamists greatly weakened Mormon enforcement
of communitarian economics by sending many Mormon leaders into prison
and most of the rest into hiding. Progressively stronger legislation enabled
the confiscation of church property and forced the church out of many economic activities. Tithing receipts fell during the 1880s to the degree that the
church faced substantial debt throughout the 1890s (Alexander 1986, 5).

The decades following 1880 also witnessed profound social change affecting regional cultural norms. The composition of Utah's population was
in great flux. The proportion of Mormons fell from four-fifths to roughly
two-thirds by 1890, remained about the same during the following decade,
and thereafter continued falling to its low point of 55 percent in 1920 (May
1992, 125). The state rapidly urbanized. Utah shifted from a 65 percent rural
and 35 percent urban mix in 1890 to a virtually even mix by 1910 (Dyal
1989, 19). Salt Lake City was a major destination of both Mormons and
non-Mormons during the period and more than doubled its population (to
nearly 45,000) between 1880 and 1890 (Alexander 1995a, 8). Utah's population became more centralized. The four major contiguous Wasatch Front
counties (Salt Lake, Weber, Utah, and Davis) increased from about 45 percent to 55 percent of the state's total population between 1880 and 1920
(see also Bennion 1980). While some Chinese immigrants had remained in
Utah after working on the railroad, few other non-Mormon immigrants lived
in Utah before the Manifesto. In the 1890s, Italians began to be a presence
in the railroad industry, in mining, and elsewhere. Austro-Hungarians, Slavs,
Greeks, Japanese, and Mexicans followed (May 1987, 135–55).

In such an environment, capitalist forces greatly increased (see also Berry
1992). Mormon capitalists, though nurtured by Brigham Young's preferen-
tial treatment during the communitarian era, now found themselves free to
compete and grow as they desired. Many prospered. Regional non-Mormons
opened new markets among the Mormons. By 1892, economic elites in Salt
Lake City practiced cross-religious cooperation (Alexander and Allen 1984,
87–123). Social and economic differences often assumed as much significance
as religious differences. In the following decades, these economic elites began
to link Utah enterprises with national monopolistic corporations (Alexander

and Allen 1984, 87–123, 134). Although Utah boasted the highest percentage (around 90 percent) of owner-operated farms in the country between 1890 and 1910 (Arrington 1974, 16), the pattern was set. Capitalism was taking control of the regional economic practices that the LDS Church had previously dominated.[3] Utah's industries decreased their focus on local markets and instead assumed a growing national orientation; staple exports gained greater significance (Arrington 1974, 7).

Forces beyond demographic change and the expansion of industrial capitalism in Utah also affected economic morality. The whole American West experienced demographic change and capitalist expansion. But elements specific to the region combined with these forces to produce results not found elsewhere. The peculiar nature of these elements stemmed from debates over the place of the LDS Church and Mormon culture in twentieth-century America. On the one hand, the LDS Church remained convinced that part of its mission and ability to attract converts lay in the success of the regional economy. On the other hand, many regional non-Mormons were equally certain their fortunes depended on regional integration with the national economy. The decades surrounding the turn of the century decided such questions as could the LDS Church function as an economic actor and if so how, on what bases could Mormons and non-Mormons cooperate and compete in an expanding capitalist system, and what were appropriate connections between economic morality and religious morality? Each of these questions had geographical content. Their answers helped produce a geographically distinctive set of economic moral orders that, together with similar moral orders of gender and national loyalty, effected a reconfigured but still distinctive culture region.

The most immediate economic question stemming from conflicts between Mormons and non-Mormons in the late nineteenth century concerned the survival of the LDS Church. Many opposing church power during this time would have cheered the church's disintegration, but their LDS counterparts fought vigorously to ensure that the church endured institutionally with some modicum of loyalty to its nineteenth-century legacy. By the early twentieth century, both groups were able to claim victory of some sort, and both had made concessions. Non-Mormons won in the sense that regional economic patterns mirrored American economic patterns much more closely than they had earlier. Mormons could boast that the institutional church survived and continued to exercise great influence on the area's economy. The regional economy even today continues to be marked by regard for certain forms of communitarian welfare, presumably because of the presence of the LDS Church, yet the LDS Church itself developed capitalist savvy. Concessions are also centrally important. Scholars have identified Mormon concessions to Americanization, but there has not been careful enough exploration of the implications of these concessions. Mormon and non-Mormon concessions combined to produce something not quite equating with standard conceptualizations of Americanization.

A set of moral orders emerged by 1920 whose accompanying economic actions seemed consistent with national norms but whose momentum later accounted for regionally distinctive trends of particularly individualist capitalism. Change occurred within the context of both the rapidly growing American West and continuing debates over Mormonism's place in the United States. The new norms had both connection to and distinctiveness from the trajectory of Americanism.

Wage Labor: Young Men's Mutual Improvement Association and LDS Leaders

When the LDS Church, under the direction of President John Taylor, initiated Zion's Central Board of Trade in 1878, labor was not represented. Since the board aimed to strengthen and solidify the regional economy, it included mostly representatives of industry and business (Arrington, Fox, and May 1992, 317–27). At the time, however, labor's lack of representation may not have signaled total LDS capitulation to capital. From very early on, the church strove toward a Jeffersonian ideal of yeoman farmers. The church encouraged members to obtain a piece of land and work it for their own sustenance. Brigham Young strongly discouraged church members from taking part in mining (at that time in the American West, the mining industry harbored the greatest laboring class consciousness). By 1878, few Mormons regarded themselves as part of the laboring class. Most owned property or realistically saw themselves as potential property owners. Most depended on more than wages for maintenance (Arrington, Fox, and May 1992, 326–27).

This practical lack of reliance on wages paralleled worries in LDS culture over wage dependence. A poem in the *Home Writer,* a newspaper produced by the mutual improvement associations in Manti, Utah, warned farm boys not to be enticed by the city and its promise of quick profits. Rather, it suggested, boys should stay attached to the farm with its sureness and reliability. On the farm, "[y]ou are as free as the air of the mountains, [a]nd the monarch of all you survey" (14 August 1882, 4). Although by the end of the nineteenth century, many could not own and live off their own land, Mormon culture expected wage labor relations to be temporary and members to exit such relations as quickly as possible. The 1899 sentiments of Abraham Woodruff, a church leader, are typical. He maintained that the younger generation was too wont to seek a "life of ease" in the city rather than bring its muscles into conflict with the soil. "It is my firm belief that if this spirit prevails . . . it will only be a matter of a generation or two until our people will be the employed and not the employers," he declared (1899, 6). Parents, he argued, should furnish their children with farms so that they would not go off to the city for employment. Recently arrived converts to "Zion" were also a problem when they went directly to the cities and became employees. The culture held that wages corrupted by not allowing people to develop the same love for God that the farmer had and by placing people in a dependent relation to others who ought to have been their equals (A. O. Woodruff 1899, 6–7). In an important sense, LDS culture considered wage labor the antithesis of personal self-sufficiency.

This conception of wage labor changed around the turn of the century because of the rapidly increasing population, the dearth of new arable land, and the enforced separation of economic and religious activity. Church leaders' increasing personal capitalist orientations also played a role. Wage labor's opposite shifted from personal self-sufficiency to idleness. The norms and conventions of wage labor gained acceptability and then predominance. Within Mormonism, wage labor shifted from being a option to accommodate those on the economy's "margins" (young men, converts, women) when other means failed to being part of the natural economic order that reflected innate differences in capabilities and inclinations. Different agendas between capital and labor began to appear inevitable. LDS culture increasingly justified wage laborers' lack of social power. As a result, pleas for church members to avoid wage labor (especially by staying on the farm) were increasingly anachronistic and impotent. The Mormon culture region no longer incorporated much resistance to a wage labor economy because Mormonism itself did not. Two shifts, in particular, helped change wage labor's connotation from negative to positive: regularization of economic roles within the family (see chapter 2) and increased training for wage labor and indoctrination of company loyalty.

The Young Men's Mutual Improvement Association (YMMIA) played a fundamental role in regularizing economic roles in the family. Throughout the early twentieth century, it instructed young LDS men on economic duties. A 1902–3 YMMIA manual naturalized the LDS scriptural assertion that women and children have claim on men for maintenance (Young Men's Mutual Improvement Association n.d.a, 108). This naturalization of different roles for men and women provided an important basis upon which the concept of wage labor could change but, by itself, had little direct connection to such changing norms; it only perpetuated nineteenth-century Mormon approaches to gender. The YMMIA some years later began to spell out how husbands' obligations translated into practices.

A manual for YMMIA classes eight years later used differing men's and women's roles to shift some of the value previously assigned to yeoman self-sufficiency toward wage labor (Young Men's Mutual Improvement Association n.d.b). In a section on cooperation and business organization, it suggested that "men" could accomplish more working together than they could working separately. One established type of division, it noted, was that "men do the outdoor and women the indoor work" (35). Although it suggested that some disadvantages resulted from labor too finely divided (37), its general argument was that assigning one or two manufacturing processes to each individual honed skills, saved time, stimulated invention, and effected economic progress (29). The manual later argued that there was nothing unnatural about the employment of women,[4] but it implied that female laborers did not engage as fully in the public economy as men did and that this fact should cause no concern. Most women, it claimed, did not acquire the same level of skill as men, did not expect to stay employed because they anticipated getting married, required less money on which to live, and therefore received lower wages (93–94). Since the manual claimed that at least some of the increase created by capitalist production went into the pockets of laborers as wages (87), the following statement should not be read in a gender-neutral manner: "The way is open to the laborer to work for himself if he chooses. Many of them do this, as a matter of fact, and gradually become employers of labor" (87). This statement functioned in the manual's argument to justify the system that featured wage labor. Such a system was morally acceptable, the manual implied, because it offered fluidity of position to individuals. But it also implied that women did not have the same chances to find their own place in the economy; the economy relegated them to low wages. A wage labor economic system that shunted women to increasingly narrow forms of participation was regarded as morally acceptable, because it provided opportunity for male advancement and fluid labor roles.

Likewise, women who worked at home were marginalized from the "progress" the wage labor system seemed to embody. A later YMMIA manual suggested that primitive societies valued the ability to do all kinds of work (Young Men's Mutual Improvement Association n.d.f, 5). While the manual claimed that "there is danger of dividing work up to such an extent that men become mere machines" and that such a threat especially inheres with manufacturing (7), it made it clear that the necessity of divided labor fundamentally separated modern society from both primitive and "less civilized" societies (5–7). The manual quoted the journalist Charles Dana whose words echoed the manual's attitude toward the changing economy: "Above all, believe and know that humanity is advancing; that there is progress in human life and human affairs, and that as sure as God lives the future will be greater and better than the past or present" (75–76).

The YMMIA held that boys must prepare for the duties of manhood. These responsibilities included choosing a vocation in which they could become expert and training in an industry (Young Men's Mutual Improvement Association n.d.e, 10–18; see also Roberts 1913). Young men were to take part in the economy's progress through their specialization. Women who worked at home, of course, could have no direct participation or influence in this part of progress that divided manual labor into ever smaller and more rationalized elements. "In many of the less civilized countries of the world [little division of labor] is found today. There is little difference in the work done by the various members of an Indian village existing in the native state. About the only division of labor is based on sex or age," the manual observed (Young Men's Mutual Improvement Association n.d.f, 5). While men had "progressed," much of women's work remained remarkably similar to the situation in "less civilized" societies. Women who worked at home increasingly bore an ahistorical economic nature. Women's options included temporary and marginal participation in the "progressive" aspects of the economy, with no real opportunities for advancement, or no direct participation at all. Wage labor's valorization in normative Mormon culture thus accompanied the regularization of gender roles in the economy.

Two important and not entirely consistent connotations of wage labor had existed in nineteenth-century Mormon culture. On the one hand, wage labor allowed some people to gain control over others' lives. A laborer's efforts were subordinate to and dependent on the employer's profit motives. In this sense, a stigma attached to both parties in the wage-labor relation. Yet a host of religiously based expectations constrained employers' dealings with employees. While not preventing capitalist exploitation and accumulation of wealth, these expectations encouraged greater efforts to make employees the economic equals of employers than existed in much of American capitalism. On the other hand, wage labor provided people with needed opportunities to work when other avenues failed. It gave men, in particular, the ability to fulfill religious responsibilities by providing for their family. The balance between these two connotations shifted during the decades surrounding the twentieth century from the first to the second.

By the early twentieth century, wage labor implied very little shame. A husband's duty could be honorably filled through wage labor; social inequality took a backseat to family structure, as is reflected in a 1913–14 YMMIA manual:

> Perhaps there is not a more pitiable sight than a father who, though strong and well, fails to provide sufficient for his family to keep them in respectable decency. *We Americans* have this idea deeply grounded in our constitutional make-up. Whatever qualities a man may have, the failure on this one score causes us to look with scorn at the wasted endowment of strength. . . . When once a young man leaves home, his first responsibility is to provide for himself the natural and legitimate wants of respectability. Should he become a family man, or when he becomes one, as he doubtless will, then other lives have a claim upon his manhood. . . . This group and personal responsibility is not merely a society form; it is a basal law of nature—to care for the weak until they grow strong. (Young Men's Mutual Improvement Association n.d.e, 48, emphasis added).

The family had a single, preordained set of roles available to men and women. Women might work outside the home in unusual circumstances, but generally—and increasingly as this period progressed—the culture expected them to run household affairs with little hope of reaping monetary rewards. Men provided the sustenance, which increasingly meant money. Moral focus shifted away from social relations of male (and female) labor to its monetary potential. A YMMIA manual argued that a man's vocation ought to ensure not self-sufficiency or independence but adequate income. It claimed that since unskilled laborers' incomes were usually not sufficient (and implied that this state of affairs was entirely appropriate), young LDS men should become specialists (Young Men's Mutual Improvement Association n.d.k, 10–20).

By the late 1910s, neither YMMIA manuals nor general Mormon culture seriously questioned some people's subordination to others through wage labor. Instead, Mormons trained men and women for the disciplines of wage labor and inculcated the importance of company loyalty. The increasingly naturalized subordination of women to men in Mormon culture (especially wife to husband), I would argue, allowed increasing economic subordination of one man to another to obtain without protest (and with declining notice).[5] The two types of subordination operated in a complementary manner. The wife's increasingly clear household management labors allowed the husband to assume the characteristics of a capitalist laborer. On different occasions, each subordination was naturalized and served as a model and justification for the other. Economic peace came to be seen as possible through acceptance of the roles society offered rather than through struggles for equality. As Stephen L. Richards, one of the church leaders, put it, "If the gospel conception of wealth were prevalent in the world there would be no . . . estrangement between rich and poor, between so-called capital and labor, as we see today. . . . The gospel points out that the foundation of society is the home and the marital relation." This relationship is "the basis of all social order" (1920a, 97).

Nineteenth-century Mormon concern about concentration of capitalists' power over laborers carried over into the twentieth century among a few. B. H. Roberts, the anti–woman suffrage champion, was one of the church leaders most concerned. In a 1903 general conference, he noted that the question of labor and capital increasingly affected LDS youth, particularly those entering the mechanical arts or trades. In the contemporary environment, he argued, labor and capital increasingly organized against each other. While he understood why many Latter-day Saints despised labor unions,[6] he argued that labor's organization was simply a response "to hold its own against the growing force and greed and power of combined capital; and whatever the excesses may be, and however much we may regret them, nevertheless organization and union on the part of labor became an absolute necessity to the working masses" (Roberts 1903, 14). Nevertheless, Roberts increasingly stuck out as the exception to the majority of church leaders, who easily accommodated capitalism. Analyses presenting the wage labor relation as devoid of power differentials were more common. A YMMIA manual argued that "[t]he moral rights of individuals in all relations are based upon the rule, 'Do by others as you would have them do by you.' The employer has a right to the employee's time, strength and skill, according to the terms of the contract expressed and understood. . . . The employee has the right to courteous treatment from the employer" (Young Men's Mutual Improvement Association n.d.d, 26). The legal contract between employer and employed was figured as morally neutral. The social context permitting such contracts was no longer the problem; instead, social danger lay in not acting courteously within the confines of the contract.

Concern about the capital-labor relation also came in the form of a back-to-the-farm movement around 1910. John Henry Smith was the chief advocate of this position among church leaders: "People who crowd into cities and live in rented homes, who are . . . in great measure, the slaves of their fellow-men, can not be fully patriotic and devoted to their country. The man who lays his foundation upon the basis of the soil . . . soon finds himself among the independent ones of the world" (1910a, 36; see also Lund 1911, 13–14). This perspective similarly had little ultimate impact. Most church leaders recognized the necessary limits of future regional agricultural development and realized yeoman independence was no longer a viable option for many. They approached the problem (inasmuch as they viewed it as a problem) through accommodation and by training young LDS men to succeed in the emerging system.

LDS culture taught its youth how to best succeed in the system. A 1913–14 YMMIA manual told of the importance of boys' choosing a vocation and training for their life's work (Young Men's Mutual Improvement Association n.d.e, 3). It attempted to instill devotion to a calling, constant industry, and work efficiency. Later manuals emphasized dependability, marriage (firms preferred married men), perseverance, honesty, order, and punctuality (Young Men's Mutual Improvement Association n.d.g, 35–37, 58; and n.d.l, 17–59).

Mormon culture thus conceptualized idleness as the opposite of wage labor. While idleness had always been paired against labor in LDS culture, wage labor held a much more problematic position than labor itself in the late nineteenth century. Wage labor implied a loss of personal freedom and represented the rotten nature of the "Gentile" economy. Now wage labor was equated with labor; no longer was the wage relation critiqued. Focus shifted to enjoining the individual to avoid idleness and to perform tasks within that unquestioned relation (Young Men's Mutual Improvement Association n.d.k, 14–16). LDS leaders and Mormon business people led the shift.[7] Church leaders likely had little choice. Pressuring the LDS Church to reconcile itself to American norms, non-Mormons would have tolerated little principled opposition to the wage labor system.[8] Although Mormons could possibly have quietly resisted capitalist norms, they could not have safely organized opposition to the increasingly powerful capitalist economy. Non-Mormons (including organized labor) were watching at every turn.

Wealth: Colonizing Competition and God's Favor

Turn-of-the-century regional non-Mormons watched to make sure LDS communitarian principles did not get put into practice once again. One occasion for vigilance was the 1905 opening of the Uintah Indian Reservation to white settlement. Non-Mormons worried Mormons would organize and gain unfair advantage in settling the area. They worried that a particularly Mormon form of wealth generation would dominate. While these non-Mormons had less to be concerned about than they realized, the controversy reveals much about the changing regional conceptualization of wealth. Profit generation took center stage from the ideal of widespread welfare. The LDS discourse about regional wealth indicating that God favored the Mormons also reveals this shift.

Wealth had been a double-edged sword in Mormonism. Mormonism from early on conceived of itself as a means to both material and spiritual improvement. Brigham Young insisted that the two aspects could not be separated. Early Mormonism thus represented a drive to prosperity. But LDS leaders moderated this trajectory with warnings against the complacency and social divisiveness wealth brought. George Q. Cannon, the first counselor to the president, told Saints in 1882 (in the midst of growing antipolygamy legislation) to "watch the effect of wealth. . . . Communities get wealthy and they begin to think about their wealth. Where their treasure is there is their heart also. Especially is this the case if they are divided into classes. . . . If we are nearly alike temporally we feel alike. In this has consisted much of our strength in the past. We were not divided into classes, with interests diverse one from the other. . . . The increase of wealth, therefore, and the consequent increase of fashions are more to be dreaded than hostile legislation" (1884, 46–47). Mormons feared the effects of poverty in the midst of wealth. Conceptions of wealth, both in positive and negative senses, were inextricably tied to welfare. Latter-day Saints hoped for material increase, but material increase that benefited all and did not divide the community.

Around the turn of the century, this welfare emphasis began eroding in favor of concern for individual and corporate freedom to accumulate as much wealth as possible. An argument by Joseph F. Smith, who was soon to become president of the church, signals the shift (1898, 23–24). He suggested that no man should have more than another, but since some people had greater capacities, their inheritances ought to be greater. Neither element of the argument was new in Mormonism. But the argument's second part (that people possessed differing capacities that their inheritances ought to reflect) could only mean something different in the capitalist context of 1898 than it did in the communitarian context of the Brigham Young era. The church no longer assigned or even sought to influence inheritances (usually the land and goods a family utilized). Capitalism solely, with its accumulation ethic, now measured differing capacities. Smith suggested that those with wealth should not take advantage of those without wealth, but this nod toward a welfare ethic would have little impact with capitalism as the yardstick to measure personal capacity. The controversies surrounding the opening of the Uintah Indian Reservation demonstrate the rising prioritization of individual wealth in LDS culture. They also reflect the mediation of mistrust between Mormons and non-Mormons. The controversies were legitimized by, and simultaneously obscured, genocidal colonialist norms of regional whites, both Mormon and non-Mormon.

On 13 July 1905, the *Eastern Utah Advocate* reported two rumors concerning the imminent opening of the Uintah Indian Reservation (the newspaper was headquartered in Price, Utah, and represented a non-LDS per-spective). Government townsites had already been sanctioned on land reserved for the Indians, one rumor suggested. A second rumor, perhaps re-lated, held that LDS officials were trying to carry out a reservation colo-nization scheme through connections with the U.S. government's land office (*Eastern Utah Advocate*, 6 July 1905; see earlier hints of this non-Mormon worry about Mormons' gaining unfair colonization advantage in the *Ver-nal Express*, 5 September 1903; and Kearns 1905b and 1905c). Apparently the rumor started in or was given credence by the *Salt Lake Tribune* (an-other non-LDS, and at times anti-Mormon, paper). The LDS hierarchy re-portedly wanted a lottery method of registration to flood registration offices with Mormons and shut Gentiles out of settlement. That land office officials decided to use a lottery was evidence to both the *Tribune* and the *Advocate* of LDS leaders' influence. While the same issue of the *Advocate* reported land officials' denials of Mormon advantage, non-Mormons in eastern Utah and elsewhere in Utah and Colorado clearly worried that LDS organiza-tional power would unfairly hamper individualistic non-Mormon settle-ment.

A letter written by the presidency of the Wasatch Stake (a geographical division of the LDS Church headquartered at Heber City) stirred up the rumor. The stake presidency wrote that the presidency's members "have land office connections" that could be of some use to LDS settlers (*Eastern Utah Advocate*, 13 July 1905). Non-Mormons regarded LDS colonization schemes as part of the nineteenth-century oligarchic Mormonism they were trying to bury; intimation of continuing Mormon territorial expansion set off shouts of protest. Mormon interests immediately responded that while the letter may have contained ambiguous wording, the church did not in-tend to gain unfair settlement advantage. The pro-Mormon *Wasatch Wave* gave this interpretation:

> [Stake presidency members] were acquainting themselves with tracts of land on the reservation through the medium of public documents distributed by the gov-ernment and people familiar with the country . . . though [*sic*] connections they were forming with land attorneys, they expected to be able to furnish valuable information to parties wishing to locate upon the reservation lands . . . it has al-ways been the policy of the church to look after the welfare of the people in tem-poral as well as spiritual affairs. . . . This cry of intrigue and conspiracy to vio-late the laws of the land we believe to be purely imaginary. (*Wasatch Wave* [Heber City, Utah], 14 July 1905)

This controversy over LDS colonization schemes quickly diminished to a smolder in eastern Utah, but its initial rapid and bright flare-up bears testimony to the explosive mistrust between Mormons and non-Mormons still apparent two decades after Mormons ostensibly gave up separatist economics.[9]

An element of controversy continued outside of eastern Utah. In Salt Lake City, where the newly created American Party (a revival of the nineteenth-century non-Mormon Liberal Party) was gaining political capital with its anti-LDS agenda, the *Salt Lake Tribune* was convinced Mormons had colluded with the government to grab reservation land. The *Tribune* claimed that the land commissioner's decision to make (heavily LDS) Provo a registration site instead of Salt Lake City was evidence that Mormons, especially through Senator Reed Smoot (a Provo native), were trying to discourage non-Mormon settlement. The land commissioner tried to counteract this impression by adding a registration site at Grand Junction, Colorado, but rumors persisted that land officials deliberately downplayed the quality of land to accommodate an LDS agenda. Long after the local eastern Utah newspapers reconciled themselves to the fact that the land could not support many people, non-Mormon Salt Lake City and Grand Junction interests continued to suspect deliberate understatement of the land's value (*Eastern Utah Advocate*, 20 July 1905; *Emery County Progress*, 22 July 1905).

The controversy points to an important means of social differentiation between Mormons and non-Mormons. Both LDS and non-LDS desired wealth through the opening of the reservation, but their regional debates suggested to those involved that the groups sought different kinds of wealth. The Mormons, in particular, prioritized community and long-lasting wealth,[10] whereas many non-Mormons went after more exploitative forms of wealth (see also Peterson 1974; and Wright 1993). Debate between Mormons and non-Mormons over the moral high ground, however, allowed both groups to add another level of conceit to their justifications for continued policies of extermination of the Ute.

Mormons held Native Americans to be a remnant of the house of Israel.[11] In the final days, Indians were to receive lost blessings. At certain times and places Mormons attempted to relate more sympathetically with Native American groups than did most other Americans, but, for various reasons, this was not one of those times and places. In most practical ways, white Mormons and non-Mormons of the region strongly believed Indians to be an inferior people that had to give way to white civilization. Such notions justified forced removal from lands whites wanted, elimination of Indian means of survival, lack of concern for dwindling numbers of Indians, and expectations that the only hope for Indian people was in rejecting their culture (their very peoplehood) in favor of assimilation into white society.

White America's manifest destiny was never seriously questioned by either Mormon or non-Mormon whites. Mormons, like early English Protestant colonizers of America, added religious justification to the doctrine of manifest destiny that was elsewhere justified in increasingly secular terms (see Stannard 1992, especially 231–46). The early white colonists of the region held that the region was essentially empty; their challenge was to remove Indians from "productive" lands. By the time of the period under study, Indians had mostly been relocated to reservations, but whites still coveted additional lands and wanted to remove Indians from the reservation by destroying their ways of life. Debates between Mormons and non-Mormons over the morality of reservation settlement obscured even further the morality that countenanced cultural destruction.

A newspaper report of an LDS quarterly conference held in Vernal, Utah (near the reservation) illustrates a Mormon view: "[Apostle Abraham O. Woodruff s]poke of the richness of this valley and felt that there was a great future for it. There are millions of dollars worth of mineral in the surrounding hills. Advised the people to secure the water right, power and reservoir sites legally and not let other men come in and get them while we wait. Hold your land. It's valuable" (*Vernal Express,* 30 May 1903). This address did not directly concern the reservation itself, but it relied on common Mormon attitudes toward eastern Utah. Mormons, though less often criticizing social divisions, still emphasized community development and long-term residence when discussing wealth. The LDS-oriented *Wasatch Wave* echoed these sentiments just months before the reservation opened:

> [The opening] means that in a few years time Wasatch County will have a population of 50,000, instead of 5,000 as it now has and a proportionate increase in wealth. . . . Heber City will be transformed from its present status of an important frontier town, to the highly important position of chief broker between the producer and the consumer. . . . There has not been a reservation opened in a quarter of a century past, which offers as many advantages to the home seeker, the capitalist, the merchant, the artisan and all the various trades and avocations which make up a prosperous, producing, community, as this great empire. . . . (19 May 1905)

Mormons thought the event promised wealth, but achievement of wealth came through the hard work of a community. They expected those who gained wealth to spread its benefits in the community. However, they, much like most people throughout U.S. history, thought only through their own conceptual prisms (Deloria 1999). They exhibited few qualms about sacrificing Native American communal wealth at the altar of their own Zion. They did not understand, nor did they particularly care to understand, that the Indians' land loss had deeper implications than their own expulsion from the Midwest. While Mormons always knew that they could move on, to Native Americans land transfer was, in the words of P. Jane Hafen, a "loss of ontological wholeness" because of the importance of sacred places in creating identity and communal relationships over multiple generations (1998, 37; see also Deloria 1999). In creating their new world, Mormons, like many others, felt authorized to build communities on the lands of those they evicted (Parry 1985; Stannard 1992, 240, 249).

Non-Mormon visions of wealth resulting from opening the reservation were more individualistically oriented and encompassed a more temporary scope. The *Eastern Utah Advocate* editorialized, "The drawing [for reservation claims] offers wonderful possibilities. Out of fifty thousand persons who will register, in the neighborhood of eleven thousand will make small fortunes of from $1500 to $25,000 each" (29 June 1905). Letters to the reservation's Indian agent show many (especially out-of-state) non-Mormons were not particularly attached to amassing wealth *there*. For example, "I am somewhat anxious to learn all I can . . . as I might make some investments and . . . I would be in a better position to decide whether I like the country and know what chance existed" (Meyer 1905). Editorials in the *Vernal Express* suggest a get-rich-quick mentality:

> It makes no difference whether the Indians are willing or not, the reservation will be opened just the same. . . . When the reservation is opened for settlement, there will be thousands of acres that are valuable for agricultural purposes and most of the balance of it is good for grazing land. Prospectors and miners will open up many rich mines in the mountains where they are not allowed to do anything at the present time. It will take but a short time to let the world know what we have in this country after the reservation is opened and a railroad is built through. . . . (16 May 1903; see also 7 February 1903)

Settlement did not match popular expectations—as land officers had predicted—after the reservation opened. Many who registered intended only to prospect, not to homestead (*Eastern Utah Advocate*, 24 August 1905). Even many homeseekers went away disappointed after finding promises of wealth in the Uintah Basin greatly exaggerated (*Emery County Progress*, 2 September 1905; *Eastern Utah Advocate*, 7 September 1905). Much of the arid West, including this portion, required communal efforts, further encroachment on Indian lands, and heavy governmental involvement even to secure subsistence (Committee of Homesteaders 1905; Harmston 1905; Worster 1985). The Mormon-influenced *Wasatch Wave* simultaneously gloated about its own accurate predictions and proclaimed the superiority of slow and steady LDS paths to wealth: "Many of those who drew numbers entitling them to enter land on the reservation are not farmers and never will be. . . . Such entrymen will never aid much in building up a new country. . . . Their places will be filled by real homeseekers in a few years and the reservation will, in our opinion, become one of the richest agricultural districts in the state of Utah" (8 September 1905; see also *Eastern Utah Advocate,* 31 August 1905).

The posturing between Mormons and non-Mormons accompanying the reservation's opening made no real difference to the continued assault on Ute culture and lands. Much like the insignificant differences between British, Spanish, and French colonization of the Americas (Berkhofer 1978, 116–34), or the similar effects of Christian and U.S. governmental institutions' treatment of Native Americans (Deloria 1999, 174), Mormon and non-Mormons ideals of colonization tended to the same rending of the Ute people.[12] However, the presumed differences allowed Mormons to maintain an identity separate from non-Mormons; Mormons compared LDS and non-LDS norms and found themselves to be a steadier, less greedy people.[13] The constant quarrels also permitted Mormons to think that their values had changed little since Brigham Young's day. If non-Mormons still complained about Mormon practice, little must have changed.[14] Little had changed in LDS relations with Native Americans, but the forms of wealth accepted in Mormon culture were changing rapidly. Mormon priorities were switching from communal wealth to individual and corporate wealth. In the months leading up to the reservation's opening, for example, the *Wasatch Wave* prioritized development through capitalist business and boosterism (see, for example, 19 May 1905). It attributed hope for increased county wealth to a company—the Wasatch Development Company (25 August 1905).[15]

The LDS discourse of Mormon regional success as God's favor demonstrates these changes even more clearly. An assumption that Mormon success evidenced divine favor lay behind the *Wasatch Wave*'s criticism of reservation wealth seekers: "Had the sturdy pioneers who first entered this state . . . become so easily discouraged . . . , we would never be enjoying the advantages we do today. . . . But they were real homeseekers and, bending steadily to their work, accomplished what they sought" (1 September 1905). Latter-day Saints believed their diligence and God's blessing combined to produce economic success. In 1880, Wilford Woodruff, future president of the church, told the Saints, "When I . . . contemplate the work of this people in these valleys and in the surrounding Territories; when I perceive how this desert is occupied, how the Latter-day Saints are progressing, how they are cultivating the earth, building temples, halls, tabernacles, schoolhouses, towns and villages, I marvel at the work of the Lord" (1880, 10). Mormons made this a consistent discourse in subsequent decades (see, for example, Crosby 1902; A. Ivins 1910, 14–15; and H. Cannon 1913, 82–83). God had helped them utilize correct application of natural principles and turn a difficult land into a prospering region.[16] They thought, based on earlier progress, that they were destined to achieve greater wealth, independence, and prosperity than any other people (J. H. Smith 1899, 34–35; Jenson 1914, 77–78).

Although this discourse remained remarkably strong during these decades, the LDS approach to wealth shifted. In 1899, Abraham Woodruff argued that LDS history showed that when people settle on their own, not under the direction of leaders, they become disunited and fail. When they follow leaders, they become "a wealthy and industrious people" (1899, 8). Early expressions of the discourse emphasized church unity as well as community and regional success. George Q. Cannon said a young man was better off employing himself than seeking employment from others:[17] "There is no need to go to California, Montana, or to the mines; go to some place in the State and build the State up, build up Zion, and take example from those who have preceded us, who have shown what can be done in building up a commonwealth and making a rich people" (1898b, 4). Seymour B. Young spoke of colony building when he said the Lord brought Mormons to the Great Basin to redeem the barren waste through his power (1899, 58).

This communitarian emphasis on using the land to produce wealth became weaker over time, though it did not entirely disappear. Instead, private wealth assumed priority. In the twentieth century, Seymour B. Young again found that LDS material success proved that God remained with the Saints (1906a, 12–13; and 1906b, 92). But he also sensed a lack of loyalty to the communitarian ethic through which their early success came, specifically loyalty to home industries. Had the Saints been loyal, he speculated, the industries would have been "sources of wealth . . . and great benefit to all the people in this region" (1906a, 13). Francis M. Lyman moved responsibility for creating wealth from the church to private initiative while simultaneously prioritizing living upright religious lives as the Saints' key goal over any economic objectives (1907, 17; see also L. Young 1915, 403). John Henry Smith's counsel also shifted to private wealth. He talked, as he had in previous years, about colonizing and commonwealth building in a 1909 conference address (1909, 22–23), but he also pointed to more individualistic notions of embracing thrift and shunning idleness (23–24). He suggested that Mormons ought to involve themselves more in the "development of business interests, [to] secure themselves a part in the coming tide of prosperity" (25). A year later, he touted what was almost surely the Uintah Indian Reservation as one of the finest sections of the world, "a place where . . . industrious men, in the course of a few years, can stand in the possession of opulence and wealth" (1910b, 12). Focus shifted from community wealth to individual accumulation and individual disposal of such wealth (see also "Lesson III" 1920).

In the following decade, private wealth continued to assume priority over wealth for the welfare of the community. Apostle Reed Smoot told the Saints, "I believe that God intends that as the people grow in the spiritual things of life, so shall they be blessed with the temporal things of life. We have heard many testimonies during this conference of the wonderful prosperity of the people of Utah" (1915, 131). Although here he emphasized regional wealth, his remaining comments made it clear that such wealth stemmed from individual efforts (of both labor and accumulation) more than from collective work. Thriftiness makes better men, women, children, and nations, he claimed: "It means more than the mere saving of money. It means prosperity, good husbandry, good farming, economical management, frugality. It means individual efficiency. It means order and system" (132).

In LDS cultural logic, wealth increasingly resulted from individual initiative and individual deservedness. To be sure, church leaders and others who regarded themselves as leaders (politicians and capitalists, for example) continued to speak of regional and sometimes communitarian ethics,[18] but these leaders gave ordinary church members little reason to share such an ethic. Besides, the leaders wanted wealth for building productive capacity within communities and the region as much as for bettering people's lives.

Wealth no longer provoked much worry, and disparity of wealth posed no necessary problems. In 1899, Rudger Clawson, an apostle of the church, extolled the Saints' material accomplishments but told them that riches carry the danger of class distinctions (1899, 3). Eleven years later, he spoke again on the dangers of wealth but framed potential damage in terms of an individual's character (1910). Similarly, Andrew Kimball, president of the stake in St. Joseph, Arizona, warned of the pitfalls of wealth (1911, 82). While he mentioned that wealth could lead to inequality, he insisted that wealth itself was not the problem; rather it was people who flaunted their possessions (see also Alexander 1986, 182; and "Lesson V" 1920). Charity became the dominant theme of welfare rather than equality (Lund 1910, 10). Here, as with gender norms, inflections were important. LDS culture had earlier emphasized thriftiness and charity, for example, and calls for equality did not entirely vanish by 1920. But the relationship between the norms had changed, with emphasis shifting to thriftiness and charity. By 1920, a church leader found no reason why poor and rich should regard themselves as separate. While he said that the rich should think not just of themselves, the Bolshevik Revolution apparently led him to believe the sin of the age was that the poor envied the rich (Ballard 1920, 79–80; see also A. Ivins 1919, 83).

That same year, another Mormon leader uttered words with which a Brigham Young–era Mormon would have agreed. By 1920, however, they connoted something different. In LDS colonization schemes, he said, one would find "orderly communities containing meetinghouses, schoolhouses, amusement halls. . . . If that one hundred years had been spent by the 'Mormon' people in Mexico and the people of Mexico at the end of the one hundred years were as degraded and wretched and superstitious and in so many ways undesirable as we see them today, then you might know that 'Mormonism' could not be from God" (S. L. Richards 1920b, 126–27). "The gospel," he stated, "teaches the fundamental laws of wealth—its acquisition and proper use. It teaches industry, thrift and economy; honesty in business and unselfishness. It points out that all means and substances are gifts from God, committed to the care of men as stewards or trustees, to be used for the benefit and advancement of the people of the world" (1920a, 97). The sentiments accommodated both the nineteenth-century focus on community initiative and welfare and the twentieth-century prioritization of private wealth, but it masked the changes in inflection that had taken place (see also Young Men's Mutual Improvement Association n.d.m, 83–85). By 1920, the individual and the company, not the community and region, were the key producers and consumers of wealth.

The Discourses of Self-Sufficiency and Communitarianism

Self-Sufficiency: A Shift toward the Individual

Self-sufficiency was as important to Brigham Young as any economic objective. Nineteenth-century Saints regarded the church not simply as a new religious organization but also as the agent to bring about a new society (Hansen 1981; Shipps 1985; Stryker 1992). Their millenarian convictions held that their Zion society would eventually supplant Protestant American society, just as they believed Christianity had replaced Judaism, Protestantism had superseded Catholicism, and American society had eclipsed British society.[19] To achieve these aspirations, Mormon leaders, particularly Brigham Young, consistently told the Saints that Zion must be self-sufficient and independent of the rest of the world. Independence was a communal concept, even in the 1880s (*Home Writer*, 24 February 1882, 2–3). The Mormon sense that enemies everywhere sought to destroy the church strengthened teleologically motivated visions of a separate society. In 1852, Brigham Young stated that "our true interest is . . . in domestic manufacturing to the exclusion of almost every article of imported goods. Our clothing of every description, sugar, candles, soap, leather, . . . and many other articles, for which our merchants continually drain the country of money, might be manufactured just as well at home, within our limits, . . . and form the basis of a free and independent state" (quoted in Hunter 1973, 179).

These separatist visions eroded throughout the second half of the nineteenth century for understandable reasons. Zion, while growing in strength, never came close to matching the might of the United States. The United States showed few signs of decline after the Civil War. Instead, the country increased its influence in the Mormon realm. Nevertheless, emphasis on communal self-sufficiency persisted in Mormonism during the 1860s and 1870s. During the decades surrounding the turn of the century, however, Mormons reconfigured the concept. Self-sufficiency, like wealth, acquired a much more individualistic cast. Except for the most nostalgic longings for a church with power to enforce its economic will, Mormon pleas to be self-sufficient lost most of their regional and communitarian implications. Its mercantilist notions gained ascendancy with increased associations with capitalism. Self-sufficiency started to mean private economic independence instead of implying community well-being.

The shifting meaning of self-sufficiency and a devaluation of region in Mormon culture reinforced each another. Mormon regionalism always derived from the sense that the Saints were creating a latter-day Zion. Zion referred to the territory in which they were the dominant group.[20] This Zion region, in Mormon thought during the Brigham Young era, was to be self-sufficient and independent from the rest of the world. An 1880 Wilford Woodruff speech (quoted more briefly above) described Zion in such terms: "When I . . . contemplate the work of this people in these valleys and in the surrounding Territories; when I perceive how this desert is occupied, how the Latter-day Saints are progressing, how they are cultivating the earth, building temples, halls, tabernacles, schoolhouses, towns and villages, I marvel at the work of the Lord. . . . We are approaching an important day and time. We are approaching a period when there must be a change in Babylon, a change in our nation, and a change in Zion" (1880, 10).

This passage highlights key elements in church leaders' conceptualization of the Zion region. First, they claimed that Utah and the surrounding areas constituted a promised land, set aside by God for gathering the Saints together. Second, Mormons' material success evidenced God's involvement in creating this Zion. Third, they distinctly separated the nation from Zion. Zion, though part of a larger nation, possessed interests different from those of the nation (see also Cowley 1899a, 59). Fourth, Zion had a specific destiny in church leaders' views.

Despite profound changes during the 1880s and 1890s, turn-of-the-century Mormon leaders still emphasized building up Zion. They told members that they had a duty to come into the area to build up Zion (Lund 1897, 3; A. O. Woodruff 1902, 33); that church members belonged in Utah to form communities in which members associated with one another and looked after one another's temporal welfare (J. F. Smith 1898, 22–26; and 1901, 2–3); that members were obligated to build up the state of Utah and need not leave Utah to provide for their families (G. Cannon 1898b, 4–5; and 1897, 42); that Zion was still given specifically to Mormons by God (S. Young 1899, 58); that young and new church members ought to settle the vast (and supposedly empty) tracts of land in the area so that they would not find themselves surrounded by people unlike them (A. O. Woodruff 1899, 7); that members should consider the good of community and neighbors rather than their own potential wealth when going into business (A. O. Woodruff 1898, 21–22); and that members ought to value regional independence (J. F. Smith 1900, 48–49; U.S. Congress 1906, 2:396).

But other elements of Zion's conceptualization had begun to change. Zion's separation from the world weakened, as is reflected in George Q. Cannon's declaration: "It is our duty to build up [Utah]. Not for Mormons alone but for every man and woman that wants to live an honest and upright life and be a good citizen. . . . We are in the world, and a part of the world" (1897, 42). The destiny of Zion as an entity also received less attention by the turn of the century; instead, church leaders prioritized the destiny of the people constituting Zion. "I believe," Rudger Clawson asserted, "that it is the purpose of the Lord to make this people rich. See what a vast multitude inhabit these valleys of the mountains. . . . [T]heir characteristics . . . are such as will make any people wealthy" (1899, 3).

Still, this shift from Zion as an abstract entity to the people of Zion was not complete, as Apostle Anthon H. Lund made clear: "[The Lord] says that the people should work for Zion. That should be the object of their coming together, the one aim and purpose of their lives—to work for Zion, and not to make anything else the object of their lives. If they make money their object, He says they shall perish" (1897, 3). A sense still existed that the good of the community or the welfare of all community members was as important as the success of individuals. The least well-off members' welfare took precedence over any individual's financial prowess. Even Joseph F. Smith, who championed individual economic independence, told members that independence comes only after fairly distributing the means to independence; he recommended that those who had more land than they could cultivate give it to others to help them stay in Utah and be independent (1898, 22–24; and 1901, 3). Self-sufficiency, to turn-of-the-century church leaders, was still a geographical notion. All inhabitants of Zion and the region's communities were to support home industries, as well as employing immigrants and the poor and providing them with means to become self-supporting (Lund 1899; Merrill 1899, 14–15; J. F. Smith 1899, 41–42; G. A. Smith 1906, 52).

Yet the objectives for which church leaders stressed self-sufficiency and independence continued changing after the turn of the century. Mormon leaders spoke of a regional Zion as important in and of itself less forcefully and less often. Feminist analyses of gender codings suggest a useful way to explicate this point. Feminists (especially poststructuralists and ecofeminists) argue that in Western thought gender has been defined through and associated with a set of seemingly opposed characteristics (Merchant 1980, 1–42; Merchant 1989; Griffin 1978). Binaristic thought is a dominant motif, even if, as poststructuralists argue, the binaries are never completely consistent, settled, and unchallenged. A few such gender binaries include:

Female	Male
Feminine	Masculine
Passive	Active
Dependent	Independent
Natural	Cultural
Context	Actor
Ahistorical	Historical
Containing	Penetrating
Reproductive	Productive
Maternal	Paternal

Feminists argue that objects described with terms on the left have been devalued compared with those described by terms on the right, along with women's devaluation relative to men. This argument should not be taken to mean that the codes accurately describe real women and men. In fact, as Susan Griffin argues, the illusion of male independence can exist only by rendering female labor (and male dependence on it) invisible (1995, 75–76). Rather, the point is that throughout Western history this conceptual structure powerfully affected ideas (from the mundane to the philosophical) of what women and men ought to be. Mormon doctrine offered a potential critique of these codes by suggesting an equality and unity between male and female principles, much as gnosticism had in the early Christian era (Merchant 1980, 16–19). But—as the fact that Mormon feminism never acquired fully dominant status in Mormonism would suggest—this critique never had full purchase in Mormon culture. Mormonism was never so separate from Western society that these broad conceptualizations of gender, strongly ensconced in uses of the English language, disappeared.

My argument here is that Mormon leaders increasingly coded the local region in "feminine" terms and thus devalued it. This is not to claim that region was once coded in completely "masculine" terms and then became coded in totally "feminine" terms. Use of both types of codes always existed. Rather, the balance shifted to terms on the left, or "feminine" characteristics, while the nation and individual more often received "masculine" codings.[21] Nation and individuals came to be seen as active, independent, and historical, while region was increasingly characterized as a passive container of the action of individuals, as dependent on the nation for its destiny, and as ahistorical.[22] In the process, the focus of Mormon efforts to achieve self-sufficiency devolved from Zion as regionally or communally conceived toward the private individual or nation.

William H. Smart's exhortation on staying in the Mormon region is only the most obvious example of gender codes at work: "We have hundreds of acres in the valley still covered with sagebrush—virgin soil which has not yet known the plow—and our hearts are going out in loving sympathy to these untilled acres. Our hearts are also going out to our young men who are going to Park City, delving in the mines for gold and silver, and being led astray by the vices of the world, when there are still hundred of acres yet uncultivated at home" (1902, 31–32). A feminized region (through its land, in this case) plays Other to the masculine (and male) individual.[23]

Other sermons reached similar conclusions. Church leaders continued to prioritize a Mormon region through such suggestions as buying from home manufacturers and staying in Zion for self-sufficiency and independence.[24] But teachings about self-sufficiency and independence increasingly described individuals rather than the region as an interrelated whole. The colonizers of the Uintah area "will find that they are in the line of independence," John Henry Smith declared (1910a, 37; see also Smoot 1910, 70). This is "a place where good homes can be built, where ample water, by labor can be secured, and where industrious men, in the course of a few years, can stand in the possession of opulence and wealth," John Henry Smith later elaborated (1910b, 12). Regional welfare of all inhabitants (or even all church members) was growing less important than opportunities for individual success. Church members were no longer responsible as members of a community or region for making sure all people's temporal welfare was secure; rather, this responsibility passed to the poor themselves or to wealthy or influential individuals.

Anthon H. Lund, who became a counselor to the president of the church in 1901, was known for his sensitivity to recent immigrant converts' plight; he himself had migrated from Denmark to Utah in his youth. At various general conferences, he pled with Saints to recall the situation new immigrants faced upon arriving in Utah. Even these pleas, similar over time in many respects, reveal a gradual shift of emphasis from community to individual. In 1899, he told Saints to look after the converts: "They may not be able to find the kind of work they have been used to, and we may not be able to provide that for them, but we should try to give them an opportunity to earn their livelihood" (1899, 11; see also Merrill 1899, 14–15). Former missionaries ought to look after these people, he continued. The Saints should encourage immigrants to avoid cities and instead go to Mormon settlements where social and educational advantages were available. In 1907, much of his message remained the same, yet there was an increased sense that specific individuals, rather than the community as a whole, should help. In addition, the admonition weakened. Instead of urging people to find something for the new converts to do, he suggested merely trying to help them if possible. He said that former missionaries ought to remember the people they worked with, take them into their homes, and try to find a place for them to work (1907, 12). In 1911, he again noted converts' difficulty in finding employment in cities and suggested they go to the settlements. But instead of the communitarian advantages mentioned in 1899, the reason was that "they will be more likely to get a home of their own and in some degree become independent" (1911, 13).[25] By 1920, Mormon leaders essentially equated the communal cooperation of the LDS past with individualistic charity of the LDS present (McKay 1920; "Lesson VI" 1920, 588).

Individuals were eclipsing communities as economic agents of most importance. Zion referred increasingly to a home or context in which individuals lived out their destinies and sought their independence. The region or state was described as "a pleasant abode" (Jenson 1908b, 22); a place of prosperity, security, and protection (C. Hart 1913, 41); and a haven from anarchy (Whitney 1916a, 68). The back-to-the-farm movement and some lingering attention to colonization suggest that some in the church longed for the early, more communally self-sufficient days. But these sentiments relied on ever more idealistic and ever less practical sentiment. They appeared nostalgic and removed from contemporary norms and realities. They, too, were inevitably caught up in individualist discourse.[26]

Increasingly, as well, church leaders spoke of the nation, rather than the region, as a social actor. During World War I, cultivation of the soil and ability to help one's neighbors described not regional but national citizenship and progress (Austin 1917a; Nibley 1917, 73–74). Church leaders still valued the region, but now more for its capacity to raise quality sons and daughters (especially sons [on nationalism's gendering, see Sharp 1996]) as paragons of American citizens than for its self-sufficiency or independent destiny (McKay 1912, 55–56; Nibley 1916, 132–34; S. L. Richards 1917, 139–40). It became a repository of unchanging values, raising citizens up to support the nation's active work. Church leaders partially removed the region from the realm of history while simultaneously elevating the nation.[27]

The move from communitarian self-sufficiency to individual self-sufficiency and from regional independence to national participation registered in other contexts as well. Mormon public memory erased or minimized the importance of communitarianism in LDS history. A YMMIA manual, for example, suggested that Brigham Young promoted youth retrenchment societies to help families make ends meet, but it failed to mention the broader communitarian/social goal of retaining independence from the American economy (Young Men's Mutual Improvement Association n.d.a, 109). A YLMIA manual claimed that Mormons welcomed the transcontinental railroad to better participate in national social and economic life, but it did not note LDS leaders' ambivalence toward its effects on communitarian bonds. The manual explained the formation of Zion's Cooperative Mercantile Institution as a means to prevent price gouging by merchants, but it mentioned no communitarian ambitions (Young Ladies' Mutual Improvement Association n.d., 37). A YMMIA manual during the World War I period claimed Brigham Young taught that "it is false policy to feed men in idleness when work can be provided. He provided labor, and insisted that there should be no idlers among the people" (Young Men's Mutual Improvement Association n.d.j, 71). The manual used the quote to warn against individual idleness, but it elaborated little on community responsibilities to provide labor. YMMIA manuals, despite efforts to situate individuals sociologically, gave young men the impression that individual, manly work and individual and family development were what would ultimately produce lasting progress.[28] Similarly, Apostle John Henry Smith suggested that the impetus for providing work for young people should lie with family rather than community (1909, 23).

In spite of the shifting cultural emphasis away from region and community, the Mormon homeland retained an economic capacity for regional self-sufficiency. It was not yet what Thomas Alexander (1974) and Leonard Arrington (1974) call a dependent commonwealth, at least not all at once. Brigham Young had concerned himself with regional capacity to produce what was consumed. To evaluate this regional characteristic, I computed a "vulnerability index" from census data to compare states' ability to produce their consumption needs (see figure 1). The higher a state's vulnerability index, the greater the mismatch between what it was able to produce and what it consumed. A high vulnerability index identifies a state that could not have been self-sufficient, while a low vulnerability index indicates that a state could have been self-sufficient if needed.

The vulnerability index (VI) is calculated according to the following formula:

$$\text{VI} = \sum_{i=1}^{v} P_i \, (1 - LQ_i)^2$$

  LQ = locational quotient—the proportion of state's workforce engaged
    in sector divided by proportion of the country's workforce engaged
    in that sector.
  v = set of sectors for a state in which LQ is less than 1.0. These consti-
    tute the sectors in which a state is "vulnerable" (the proportion of
    the state's workforce engaged in that sector is lower than the national
    average for that sector).
  P = percentage of the country's workforce engaged in sector (12 per-
    cent = 12, not 0.12).

This index is based on a simple, standard locational quotient, such as that used by Leonard Arrington (1974). A locational quotient compares the proportion of workers in a state engaged in any particular economic sector with the national proportion of workers engaged in that sector. If, for example, a state had 18 percent of its workforce engaged in agriculture while the nation had 24 percent of the workforce involved in that sector, the locational quotient for agriculture in that state would be 0.75.

Agriculture for that state would then fall within v, the set of sectors for a state in which the locational quotient was less than one. This set, v, constitutes the sectors where a state was likely to be unable to produce its consumption needs. Sectors include such categories as agriculture, forestry/fishing, mining, manufacturing, transportation, trade, public services, professional services,

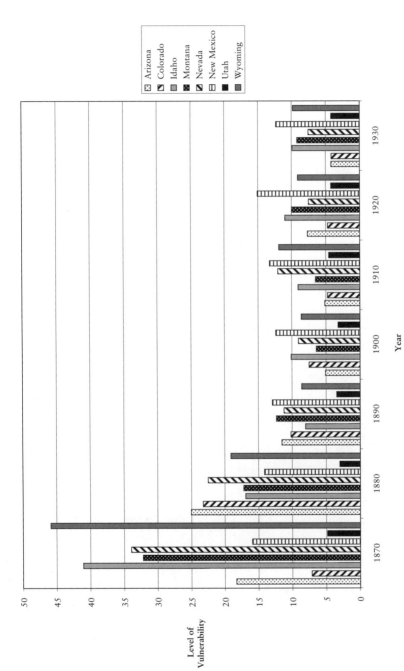

Figure 1. Mountain West States' Level of Vulnerability, 1870–1930. (*Source:* U.S. Census, 1870–1930)

domestic services, and clerical occupations. To calculate the vulnerability index, I made the assumption that a state's "vulnerability" is greater with one or a few large sectoral divergences from the national average than it is with several small deviations. Instead of adding the total divergences from the national average (based on the locational quotients) within the set v, the squares of the divergences are added, after being multiplied by P to reflect the sector's importance in the country's economy as a whole.[29]

According to this index, Utah's productive capacity remained well balanced and suited the needs of Utah's consumption at least through 1930. Utah—with a lower index—was potentially more self-sufficient than most of its neighbors from 1870 to 1930.[30] Other intermountain states first approached Utah's capacity for balanced production only around the turn of the century. Compared with the rest of the country, Utah had a low vulnerability index; typically it was in the lowest quartile of states (even though low population states—such as Utah—are more prone to "distortions" between productive capacity and consumption requirements).

Other signs of regional distinctiveness remained as well. Although Mormon leaders clearly embraced capitalism (and suggested that church membership do likewise), Thomas Alexander rightly identifies leaders' ambivalence about this process (1986, 180–211). They remained concerned about the region's self-sufficiency and employment opportunities in communities, particularly when they periodically returned to the issue of home manufacturing.[31] Church leaders withstood accusations of personal profiteering and church monopolies in the Smoot hearings.[32] They responded that church and church-leader influence in (or promotion of) various industries was intended not so much to ensure private profits as to secure the region's balanced productive capacity and promote employment (to the extent that the goals were seen as separate—and they often were not [Lund n.d.; Smoot 1997]). But even this emphasis on home industry accommodated a growing acceptance of private, concentrated wealth, as long as such wealth remained in the community.[33] Church leaders also lauded the benefits of non-Mormon capitalist activity (F. Lyman 1909b, 20; Lambert 1921, 51).

Concepts of regional and community self-sufficiency thus underwent substantial and complex change between 1880 and 1920. The concept of region was important to Mormon leaders in attempting to retain church authority and integrity in the face of profound change. Leaders sought to keep Mormons in the region to influence members' lives. But as the individual and the nation gained more prominence in Mormon thought, the region was gradually devalued. Its sense of independence and destiny flowed toward the individual and the nation. Region and community represented contexts in which individuals sought their own self-sufficiency rather than institutions seeking self-sufficiency to guarantee the welfare of all inhabitants. Regional self-sufficiency came to be an objective in the service of private wealth.

Thomas Alexander (1986) and Susan Stryker (1992) correctly suggest that norms of regional and communitarian self-sufficiency did not completely disappear in Mormonism. Although LDS culture made great accommodations to capitalism, the norms of regional and communitarian self-sufficiency remained institutional church objectives. The church continued to be economically creative, even resistant to dominant norms, and even today the church retains many egalitarian norms (Arrington, Fox, and May 1992, 337–58; Mangum and Blumell 1993). But Mormon culture only partially consists of institutional church action. In much of Mormon culture—the Mormon culture of members' everyday lives—new norms emerged. Members internalized capitalism's messages from both leaders and non-Mormons to such an extent that regional and communitarian self-sufficiency diminished in collective Mormon memory and consciousness. This sublimation worked hand in hand with a regional rejection of the possibility of a communitarian society.

Communitarianism: Smoot, Natives, and Socialists

The Smoot hearings helped crystallize the meanings of Mormon history. Beginning fourteen years after the Manifesto and eight years after Utah statehood, they came when Mormons and non-Mormons had had time to search for consensus with each other on how to build a regional society. In many respects, they had already achieved remarkable cooperation, but some dissatisfaction remained among non-Mormons. The Smoot hearings focused on and prompted a public airing of these lingering issues. The hearings brought Utah national attention again and reminded Mormons that the potential for further anti-LDS legislation still existed. In essence, the hearings further disciplined the church and its members regarding acceptable American practices.

Although Mormon communitarianism was not the major concern (polygamy and ecclesiastic control of politics were the major issues [Flake 2000]), it did garner some attention. E. B. Critchlow, a Salt Lake City lawyer, testified at the hearings that it was not Smoot himself as a politician that bothered most opponents; rather, it was "the fact that the entry of an apostle into the political arena, clothed . . . with such tremendous power in the State of Utah, a power which extends into the most minute details of religion and business and politics, was such as could not be tolerated under our system of government" (U.S. Congress 1906, 1:590). Smoot's opponents thought the church should not be directly involved in business and the economic sphere generally.[34] The church might indirectly discuss how people were to treat one another, but it was not to reapply communitarian pressure. The original petition protesting Smoot's seating expressed fear that though Mormons had temporarily suspended the United Order in deference to the laws of the land, it had not been repealed and church leaders planned to return to it after they gained enough public favor (U.S. Congress 1906, 1:8–9). Critchlow claimed that a member of the church daring to cross a church leader's stated will would essentially be "disfellowshipped from the church and ostracized from the society of those who were formerly his coreligionists" (1:594). He reported a rumor suggesting that a Brigham City stake president tried members before the stake high council for their membership after they disagreed with his recommendations on how to electrify the city. He also claimed that in Brigham City members were disfellowshipped for attending a different dance hall from one church authorities supported (1:596–97; see also 3:324–34, 436–37).

These arguments that Mormonism's communitarian elements, its hierarchical organization, and its capacity to pressure nonconformers had not entirely disappeared were no idle concerns. The Mormon boycotts in the 1870s and 1880s had greatly damaged many non-Mormon businesses, and many local leaders and members continued to feel that their religion required them to do business with those friendly to the church (Dawson 1993). Even in the 1890s, church leaders' influence could still make or break an industry (Van Wagoner 1991, 190–95). In the early years of the twentieth century, many non-Mormons felt that Mormonism still exerted communitarian pressures on its members (under a more capitalist cover). Such influence, they felt, was subtle enough that obvious examples could not easily be found but also widespread enough that it was a matter of common community knowledge (U.S. Congress 1906, 1:691). A woman who described secret LDS temple rituals testified at the hearings that although she did not expect physical violence for revealing Mormon secrets, she worried about her business (2:196). Some Idaho Democrats claimed that the church controlled the Idaho Sugar Company and that the church improperly influenced passage of an act providing a bounty on sugar raised in the state (2:197). An Ogden businessman suggested that the church (through businesses in which its leaders owned stock) unfairly prevented competition (4:78–83, 240–54; see also 4:416). Other Utahns told of a land dispute in Sevier County, where the church claimed jurisdiction and made a binding decision (2:321–44).

Senate committee members hearing the charges worried that Utah lacked commercial independence and that the church exerted too much power in commercial industries (3:154–58, 284–85). Henry W. Lawrence, a former member of the church, feared that Mormons had quit their communitarian practices only temporarily, as a strategy to gain acceptability: "The teaching is that there is the kingdom of God here upon the earth, which is a temporal and spiritual kingdom combined. Their leader said at one time in public, it was hard to tell where one left off and the other commenced" (4:107; he could accurately have been referring to J. F. Smith [1898, 22]). Lawrence believed the doctrine remained, although "[t]hey can not carry out their purpose now like they used to. It is not politic to do it" (4:107; on Lawrence, see also McCormick and Sillito 1994, 223–24).

Smoot's side responded to the charges in two basic ways. At times they justified the apparent communitarianism in terms they thought the Senate committee would find agreeable. James Talmage offered the most direct defense. He claimed that no separation existed between spiritual and temporal work, that the church ought to be able to advise members to support institutions it owned, that the church had always supported institutions that brought people employment, and that Mormons ought to feel obligated to support local industries (3:133–43). John Henry Smith was more equivocal. When asked about church colonization and care for foreign converts, he located communitarianism in the past: "We are not colonizing in any State, only as people drift there. . . . In former days, when there were little chances of employment and all that sort of thing, we used to look after them very carefully and place them in a neighborhood where they could provide for themselves" (2:319).[35] He used what has become a dominant Mormon strategy since then: acknowledging communitarianism in the early Mormon economy but arguing that such was installed only to facilitate frontier settlement (see also Alexander 1986, 76). Smoot himself used a slightly different strategy. He denied that communitarian or any other church economic institutions (such as tithing) affected members' standing in the church community (3:250). He said that church courts should not have tried the Sevier County property case (mentioned above) and that the presidency's involvement was probably inadvertent (3:256–58).[36] He also argued that the worth of church-controlled industries was a pittance (3:284–85). Smoot's lawyers reminded the committee that churches had certain rights to enforce policies within their membership, but they simultaneously claimed charges against the church were exaggerated (4:448–49).[37]

But more often than justifying LDS communitarianism, Smoot's lawyers found witnesses who claimed that for all intents and purposes it no longer existed. Both Mormons and non-Mormons insisted that twentieth-century Latter-day Saints stood economically independent of the church and that individual economic action had assumed preeminence. The memory of Mormon communitarianism was just that—a memory, never to be returned to again. Orlando W. Powers, a non-Mormon lawyer and a former Utah Territory supreme court judge, claimed that Mormon and Gentile capitalists had united and formed the usual regional promotion alliances (1:925; see also 3:347). He vouched for Utah's class culture: "[W]e have there in Utah just as good and just as exclusive society as there is anywhere" (1:936). Similarly, Smoot's lawyers argued that Gentiles played an important, sometimes even controlling, role in supposedly Mormon businesses (4:258–61, 374–98). Mormon leaders suggested that their business actions were only the actions of individuals and had nothing to do with the church as an institution and that these actions did not put ecclesiastical pressure on members (2:292–93, 297). Provo's postmaster testified that Gentiles owned a majority of businesses in the city (which he estimated was 85 percent Mormon) and that it made "absolutely no difference" whether business owners were Mormon or non-Mormon: "People trade at where they get the best prices" (4:325–30, quotes on 330). To Smoot's lawyers and apparently to many younger Mormons, communitarianism ranged from an unfortunate episode to a contextually appropriate ethic of the past; it had no twentieth-century role. Smoot's supporters and opponents shared the same economic ideals; they differed only on whether these ideals had yet come to pass.

The treatment of Native American communalism also bears witness to the removal of a communitarian ethic from regional possibility. Both Mormons and non-Mormons defined Indians against their own "civilized" cultures.[38] White regional inhabitants disparaged many aspects of Native American culture, including communalism.[39] Communalism suggested, to most white regional inhabitants, a society in the thrall of unredeemed traditionalism.

Mormons, like other white Americans but with a more direct theological motivation, hoped to remake Native Americans in their own image. In spite of their belief that Indians were descendants of the house of Israel, Mormons found it difficult to overcome their Euroamerican heritage (T. Murphy 1999). Much like other Americans, they eagerly grabbed land during the nineteenth century and maintained a mostly separate existence from Indians. A YLMIA manual admitted that unfortunate aspects of Mormon-Indian relationships had arisen historically, but it insisted that the Saints were not to blame. Instead, the problem rested with either the Indians themselves or the Spanish (Young Ladies' Mutual Improvement Association n.d.,

34). Why were the Mormons not to blame? A *Deseret Evening News* editorial gave a hint: "There are valuable lands and mineral deposits within the boundaries of the reservation, which ought not to be excluded from occupation, cultivation, and development. . . . The time appears to be rapidly passing when large tracts of arable or mineral lands shall be kept as hunting ground for roving bands of semi-savages" (23 January 1902, quoted in Malanson 1985, 14). In other words, since the Indians could not develop the land, according to Mormons, it properly fell into white hands. Mormon custom held that through disobedience the Israelite Indians became a cursed and degenerate race;[40] they would therefore be trampled by the Gentile (European) nations. Through the Mormon gospel's influence, they would eventually be redeemed and civilized (R. Pratt 1913). If Mormon-Indian relations were unfortunate at times, Mormons were not to blame because God had decreed that the Indians would suffer before being redeemed and that the Saints needed a homeland (McKay 1909, 65; Young Men's Mutual Improvement Association n.d.m, 83).[41] Besides, the Saints (selectively) argued, Mormons had primarily kind feelings toward the Indians. Had not Brigham Young taught it was better to feed Indians than to fight them (Young Ladies' Mutual Improvement Association n.d., 34)?[42] And did not Mormon Indian fighters, such as Jacob Hamblin, approach battles reluctantly, without thirsting for blood (Young Men's Mutual Improvement Association n.d.h, 39–46)?

George Brimhall, an officer in the YMMIA, quoted in his diary an 1895 address by a commissioner of education to the Indians: "The indian [*sic*] must be taught to work to aspire to something higher, to be clean, to form [habits?]—of decorum and kindness, before literary attainments can be hoped for. Reservation tribal life does not meet these ends, the development of individuality is neglected and students returning from college often under reservation environment fall back into semi-savagery" (Brimhall n.d., 69). Brimhall responded not by claiming that tribal life offers sufficient individuality but by suggesting that taking tribal attributes (apparently including communalism) out of Indians should be done slowly; to do as the commissioner suggested would rupture the Indian personality too quickly (70). By agreeing that Native American society was too communalistic, Mormons asserted membership in white America.

Regional non-Mormons also rejected, often less subtly, any hint that Native American communalism possessed something upon which regional society could build. The *Salt Lake Tribune*, which often assumed a frontier voice, is a case in point. After suggesting that Uncompahgre Indian Reservation police acted unfairly on behalf of eastern interests during that reservation's opening at the expense of "bona-fide" Utah citizens wishing to make mineral claims, it argued that "[c]ertain sentimentalists have said that it was a shame to rob the redman out of what the Government had set aside for his benefit. . . . Tell me how a man who has located a gilsonite claim has robbed an Indian? Why, the loafer never was known to dig for anything, and can never be taught to" (12 March 1897; see also *Vernal Express*, 7 February 1903). Indians lacked individual initiative, most whites thought (Leech 1967). The *Eastern Utah Advocate* put it this way: "The Indians will be compelled to take agricultural lands. Indians who have taken land along the Duchesne river, as has been asserted, as would stand in the way of the establishment of townsites will not be permitted to retard the advance of the homemaker and homeseeker" (6 April 1905). Much as for Mormons, many non-Mormons saw the reservation's opening and the destruction of communal Indian society as the inevitable course of progress (*Eastern Utah Advocate*, 17 August 1905). They could not see the Ute had use for more than a small allotment (*Eastern Utah Advocate*, 24 August 1905). Here, as elsewhere, many actively tried to remake communal hunters and gatherers into soil-cultivating, atomistic economic agents.[43]

Although the rare non-Mormon saw value in communal Indian cultures (Hoy n.d.;[44] Strongwil 1912), most whites, Mormon and non-Mormon, used Native American societies to define their own society by reminding themselves of what they did not want to become (as another example, see the socialist comparison of Native American female labor to child labor in the *Ogden Morning Examiner*, 23 April 1905). Both groups viewed individualism as superior to Native American communalism.[45] Whiteness gave regional Mormons and non-Mormons common cause in preventing a communal ethic from competing with an individualist one.

Mormons and non-Mormons parted ways only over the lingering worry that whites might have asserted control over Native American peoples and lands in unwarranted ways. Each side asserted innocence in these matters and blamed the other side. The *Eastern Utah Advocate*, reporting Ute grievances during the opening of the reservation, suggested that the Ute distinguished between Mormons and other whites: "In relating their grievances the Indians refer to the inhuman slaughter of their people in the early days of Utah, and to the wrongs they suffered at the hands of the acquisitive Latter-day Saints. . . . These [stories] and numerous other instances the Indians relate with much seriousness, and it is not a characteristic of the Utes to invent such things . . ." (21 September 1905). Mormons used similar rhetoric to make the opposite claim. In 1880, Wilford Woodruff contended that Mormons had done more than anyone else to foster peace among these "wandering, warlike" people (1880, 12). Nearly forty years later, a similar claim emerged from the same pulpit. The church, but not America, should congratulate itself because "no indictment has ever been framed, or could be formulated against the 'Mormon' people for their attitude or treatment of the aborigines of this continent. We have always treated them fairly and squarely, as of course they should have been treated" (R. W. Young 1919, 149).

Robert Berkhofer Jr. (1978) argues that whites use a dual image to place an unbridgable gap between Indian and white ways and to constitute Indians as timeless objects, incapable of contributing (or even adapting) to a changing society. When explaining naked land grabs and racial/cultural genocide, whites call on ideas of Indian savagery and indolence (the latter encompasses a critique of communalism). Both Mormons and non-Mormons produced such images to justify the Uintah reservation's opening and the destruction of Indian culture.

Nevertheless, colonialism's atrocities are not easily erased from the perpetrator's culture. Glimmers of a sense that the colonizer might have illegitimately usurped often return (Memmi 1965). In such cases, Berkhofer argues, a more "positive" image of Indians as a simple, innocent, and liberty-loving people emerges. The image says more about white society than about Native American societies. Such images help whites critique the failings of white society, not assist in returning power to or seriously communicating with Native American groups. To the degree that whites can see their own culpability in relations with Indians, they typically transform a sense of Indian innocence in political and cultural struggles against whites into a notion that Indians possess character traits of childlike innocence. Paternalism and maternalism thus become the dominant attitudes in trying to "improve" the Indian's lot (Memmi 1965; Donaldson 1992, 66–87). In the regional case under study, whites called on these "positive" Indian images without even seriously critiquing their own group. Instead, both Mormons and non-Mormons used the images to criticize each other. Both groups still felt white civilization and gospel must inevitably conquer Native American ways. They (perhaps Mormons more strongly than non-Mormons) boasted of paternalism toward Indians. Both groups assumed the legitimacy of their power vis-à-vis the Indians but quarreled over who had obtained such relations more benevolently. In such a climate, learning from Indian communalism to help reconstitute regional society appealed to neither Mormons nor non-Mormons.

There is no reason to suppose that either Mormons or non-Mormons would have sought alliance with Native Americans on anything but paternalistic terms. Both white groups imbibed deeply in racial ideologies. One might have anticipated closer ties between Mormons and socialists, however. After all, early socialist and Mormon critiques of wealth and class shared a number of similarities. But no significant alliance emerged. This space for potential alliance, as much as anywhere else, illuminates why a regional communitarian ethic did not develop.

Within Mormonism itself, in addition to church efforts to retain an egalitarian ethic and a few lingering attempts to ameliorate capitalism's harshness (Alexander 1986, 180–211; Mangum and Blumell 1993), reference to more thoroughgoing efforts at communitarianism occasionally appeared. Although church leaders began speaking less of gathering and geographical concentration to build Mormon communities, these themes were not entirely absent. As noted earlier, many leaders advised young Mormons to stay at home or move to newly opened Mormon settlements. Those who spoke of gathering did so with less vigor than pre-Manifesto leaders had, however. The assistant church historian Andrew Jenson presented the strongest case. The whole history of the world, Jenson argued, showed that God wanted his people to gather in certain designated localities (1908a, 45–46). Church history demonstrated this claim, he said (1914, 73–79). Utah history showed that when Mormons were left to themselves, they produced model communities; when outside influences entered, even those that strengthened economy and culture, they inevitably weakened those communities' moral quality (1915, 26–29; and 1908b, 21–22). But even amid renewed emphasis on community, Jenson shifted the emphasis from egalitarian economics to a narrower moral unity.

Few others went even this far on the importance of gathering a community. Gathering had lost one of its functions. While it retained its value to missionary work (Underwood 1993, 24–41), it lost the sense that spatial propinquity promoted needed economic equality. Some framed the doctrine of gathering in terms of wealth creation (Ballard 1913b, 125–26). Orson Whitney reminded the Saints that theirs was a gathering, not a scattering, dispensation; he said the Saints' scattering defeated God's purposes (1910, 86). But he implied that God's purpose was to create a community strong enough to be noticed by the rest of the world (a missionary objective) while saying little about how gathering furthered God's economic purposes (although see Whitney [1916b, 52] for an interpretation of gathering that retains older notions along with newer elements). Similarly, Joseph McMurrin said nothing about community or economics when he contended that the purpose of gathering was to assist people who were "thirsting for the word of God, thirsting for information concerning the purposes of the

Almighty" (1905, 86). Although Benjamin Goddard spoke of gathering to promote community, he meant a vaguely defined spiritual community, not an economic community (1915, 64). Another Mormon leader, Asahel Woodruff, articulated what was to become the increasingly dominant interpretation of gathering (1902, 16–17). Members gathered, he suggested, primarily to facilitate temple attendance. Otherwise, gathering weakened the church outside of Zion and was not to be desired. The notion of gathering thus no longer carried the economically egalitarian ethic it had earlier. Even those who remembered the fuller economic implications of gathering implied that such objectives served little purpose in the twentieth century (Roberts 1914, 107–9), except where land remained to be settled (Robinson 1915, 106–7).

Similarly, the United Order was periodically emphasized as an ultimate goal for the Saints. Soon-to-be church president Lorenzo Snow called on a long-held desire by Mormons to return to Jackson County, Missouri, which Joseph Smith had designated as the original land of Zion. Snow predicted at an 1898 general conference that many people he addressed would return to Jackson County and live the United Order if they kept God's commandments: "There will be no poverty in that day. There will be plenty of food, clothing and other necessaries of life; and the father who has a family, if called suddenly to depart this life, will know that his wife and children will be taken care of, that provision will be made for their sustenance and comfort. But this is the United Order that we sometimes hear mentioned, but the time perhaps has not yet come to establish it" (1898, 14). Snow repeated the common refrain that it was not yet time to "redeem Zion" (though it might soon be) or to reestablish the United Order, yet he insisted more strongly than other leaders that the Saints' ultimate goal was life in the United Order.[46]

Matthias Cowley (who resigned from the Quorum of Twelve Apostles at the church's request in 1905 because he continued to promote plural marriages) also addressed this last point: "The trouble with us is to a certain extent, we are Latter-day Saints religiously, but Gentiles financially" (1899b, 9). He said that though the church no longer formally practiced the United Order, its principles still applied. Weaker messages about the United Order also appeared. In 1880, Wilford Woodruff praised the orders that had not yet dissolved and in a very general sense suggested that the Saints' duty was to unite and cooperate (1880, 11). Three decades later, Charles W. Penrose mentioned individual commitments (but not communitarian obligations, other than to promote home manufacturers) made by those who had joined the United Order (1913, 23). His object, apparently, was to call the Saints to live lives of personal purity without chasing after the latest trends and fashions. Nevertheless, general conference references to the United Order were noteworthy most of all for their paucity.

Relations between LDS economics and other egalitarian visions took time to sort out. Some LDS writers and speakers found reason to compare Mormon economic principles with contemporarily debated ideas. Susa Young Gates, for example, argued that the LDS gospel "is interwoven closely with mingled threads of democratic and republican principles; or, rather, it is carefully constructed of the best elements of individualism and communism" (1911, 29). Without explaining what she meant by communism, Gates used the statement to introduce the YLMIA's early history (when Brigham Young created retrenchment societies for young women to help keep the region, communities, and families self-sufficient). She followed with examples of community centeredness. A YMMIA manual specified the relationship between LDS and secular visions more clearly than Gates had (Young Men's Mutual Improvement Association n.d.b). A chapter on cooperative economics mentioned the socialistic ideal of state ownership of capital (39–41). It noted that it was not easy to criticize the socialistic system philosophically, although it brought up questions of practicability. Directly after differentiating between socialism and communism (the latter seeks an equal division of consumption), it stated that "in this connection the teachings of 'Mormonism' in what is known as the United Order, are worthy of serious attention" (41). It claimed the United Order attempted to establish economic homogeneity and explained the method by which it bound its members to one another (41). Though not a ringing endorsement to ally Mormonism and socialism, the manual's treatment at least suggested that some Mormons found similarities worthy of serious investigation.[47] John Sillito and John McCormick found that many LDS members of Utah's Socialist Party regarded socialist goals an extension of their loyalty to cooperative Mormon principles (1985, 123–28).

A message apparently presented by John Wells (1914) to a local class of LDS high priests examined similarities even more closely. Entitled "Thoughts on the United Order," Wells's notes begin with the history of European communism: "The ideas of these communities were the equality of wealth, the common eating table, the standard dress, property held in common by all" (1). Wells followed this statement by summarizing the scriptural bases of the United Order. These scriptural communitarian societies were characterized by "[e]quality in wealth, no rich, no poor, ample for everybody, no poverty, ample funds to build up Zion. [They] dignified labor, there were to be no idlers . . ." (1). He succinctly described the purpose of establishing the Utah orders: "The purpose being to benefit the whole community, to stop the

transfer of land to gentiles, to retrench the extravagance of the younger people, to economize and to do away with useless wants" (2). After detailing
the Utah orders' failures, Wells more explicitly connected secular socialism
to the Mormon United Order:

> Ther [sic] German, French and English socialism is an attempt to apply the United
> Order without religion. The more complex such a system becomes, the more the
> individual loses his individual liberty. . . . The observance of the United Order by
> the Latterday Saints means the equality of wealth, and individuality in personal
> matters. Insurance against poverty or want. Excess wealth to be placed in the
> hands of the Church and would be used to aid weaker communities. . . . The con-
> veyance and ownership of large improvements such as canals, railroads, trans-
> mission lines, reservoirs, etc. and would prevent the chance of these facilities being
> placed in the hands of a few, the Church would have the service, which would
> be the operating source of the enterprise. In fact there [is] no end to what the
> United Order could do if the Latterday Saints would overcome their selfishness
> and enter into the Spirit and meaning of this great revelation. (3)

Some Latter-day Saints saw substantial similarities between LDS economics and other egalitarian ideals. But Wells's notes hint at increasingly pervasive LDS criticisms of secular egalitarianisms: lack of the LDS religion
and loss of individuality.

LDS leaders gradually carved out a critique of socialism (see also Sillito
and McCormick 1985, 129–30). At first they worried that socialism was
somebody else's project, not the Saints'. Matthias Cowley told of meeting
a man who started a socialistic party, ostensibly to make reestablishing the
United Order easier when the time came to do so:

> I had to ask him if he was so blind as to believe that after God has revealed the
> principles of the United Order, and the people are not prepared to carry them
> out, you can go to some institution of the world and find those principles and
> exemplify them for the benefit of mankind. I told him that no matter how near
> the world comes to the theories of the Gospel, no matter how much they try to
> establish them, without the Spirit of the Gospel, and the authority of the Holy
> Priesthood they can never carry them out. . . . Humanity is too selfish to carry
> out these great laws of God. (1903, 52–53)[48]

Cowley believed socialism was the devil's counterfeit of the United Order
(Lund n.d., 22:25). Lorenzo Snow suggested that egalitarian efforts could
not succeed without God's direction. Snow claimed that "the Latter-day
Saints will never be satisfied with any other arrangement [than the United
Order] that might be proposed. The nations of the earth have for a long
time been trying to establish some principle by which they can be financially sustained, united and live in peace, but have not succeeded. But the

Lord has revealed a principle clearly and definitely . . . The system will bring financial union to the Latter-day Saints . . ." (1898, 14).

Other church leaders were not quite so pessimistic about the role of non-Mormons, as is clear in Charles Nibley's statement at a general conference:

> I know people think that we are advancing, and we are advancing, until ultimately the United Order will be realized. There are at work influences in the world—and they are appointed of the Lord, I believe,—which are making for righteousness, and which will make for a communism, for a building up of a society that will make it easier for the Lord's plan to be established, namely the United Order. We are not ready for that yet, but it will come. . . . The United Order when it does come, I think, will mean individuality, personal effort, personal salvation, with you in your stewardship and me in mine. . . . Then the surplus will go for those who are not so well situated and who need help. (1914, 121–22)

Nibley went on to criticize the (presumably what he considered socialist) principle of dividing products evenly among people. Although he retained hope in some communitarian economic system, he assumed that ultimately the individual is solely responsible for economic attainments. He downplayed the early Mormon critique of economic power and wealth. He said in spiritual, rather than material, terms that the gospel satisfies socialist yearnings: "All that men struggle for in socialism—that is, all that is best in what they call socialism—is to be found [in the church], a perfect equality, the same ordinances, blessings, and gifts of the Gospel for rich and poor alike. Men and women are equal in it" (1906, 62; see also Gates 1918). Nevertheless, as Thomas Alexander argues, church leaders grew wary of socialism. At first they merely suggested that members not conflate the United Order and socialism and that socialist church members not recruit other Saints to socialism through ecclesiastical arguments. Alexander reports that later, in the 1910s, the First Presidency wrote to the church in Thatcher, Arizona, where an active socialist campaign had emerged, urging church members to join only the Republican Party or the Democratic Party (1986, 184–85).

Silences between Mormons and those espousing some form of socialism were as important as rejection that grounds for discussion existed. Growing silence on the United Order spoke loudly about changing LDS norms. Collective Mormon memory developed amnesia on the United Order and its original purposes. A 1900 YLMIA manual, for example, recited major elements of Utah church history. It mentioned the United Order but said nothing about what it was or why it existed (Young Ladies' Mutual Improvement Association n.d., 39). Similarly, a YMMIA manual covering church history through

the Missouri period made no mention of the United Order's Missouri an-
tecedents (Young Men's Mutual Improvement Association 1899). Another
YMMIA manual referred to the principle of cooperation but said little about
specific LDS attempts to create a cooperative system (Young Men's Mutual
Improvement Association 1895, 30). Similarly, a church leader discussed
gathering and tithing but made no mention of the communitarian link between the two (D. Cannon 1913). Another suggested, without specifying the
principles upon which such achievements were based, that the church did
more than others to help the poor: "there are no more advanced conceptions
of social justice anywhere in the world" (R. W. Young 1919, 149). Few Mormons explored nineteenth-century communitarianism's implications for
twentieth-century life. It was as if the "new era of peace and prosperity" that
Utah entered after the Manifesto could be achieved only through LDS silence
on peculiar Mormon practices (Young Ladies' Mutual Improvement Association n.d., 40; see also Flake 2000, 164–75).

Even when Mormons discussed communitarianism, they rejected the idea
that it could be a basis on which to rebuild regional society. Their memories of the United Order relegated it to history, something appropriate for
its time but no longer influential (Young Men's Mutual Improvement Association n.d.i, 101). By 1920, although many Mormons still espoused what
is today called welfare liberalism (almost all YMMIA manuals in the 1910s;
Alexander 1986, 180–211; Gardener and Bowler 1993), LDS culture,
broadly defined, no longer represented an alternative to the American economic status quo.[49]

Blame for a possible egalitarian regional ethic's demise rests just as much
with the socialists as with the Mormons. Silences on the relationship between the United Order/Mormon communitarianism and socialism were
just as loud from the socialist quarter. Reasons for these silences mirror
those for Mormon silences. Socialists seemed certain that they had unlocked
the key to knowledge and that those participating in progress could do so
only through socialist thought (*Ogden Morning Examiner*, 27 May 1906
and 12 August 1906).[50] Most non-Mormon socialists saw egalitarianism as
something to be imported into, not partially indigenous to, the Mormon
culture region. They would form no alliances with those espousing other
egalitarian visions, particularly those relying on different epistemologies.
Socialism nationally was not then the rigid ideological movement it became
within a few decades. Strong distinctions between socialism and communitarianism or between religious and secular utopian visions did not fully
exist (Pitzer 1997; Fogarty 1990; Cort 1988; J. Green 1978). Yet while regional socialism desperately needed the support of some Mormons to coun-

teract the strongly capitalist orientation of most non-Mormons, non-Mormon socialists took no effective steps to build such coalitions.

Non-Mormon socialists approached the need for economic cooperation from a different angle. They were much more strongly engaged in the intensely individualistic capitalist sectors of western mining and commerce than Mormons were (May 1987). Most non-Mormon residents of the region migrated there as adults, and many had gained socialist perspectives from earlier extraregional experiences. By contrast, Mormon migration into the region had slowed greatly by the early twentieth century; the LDS population was increasingly born and reared in the region. Mormons' socialistic leanings derived more from LDS communitarian experiences and the weaker capitalist influences on agriculture. Differing discourses of socialism thus emerged disjunctively in the region (on disjunctures within local cultures, see Appadurai 1990). Non-Mormons more often led Utah's socialist movement, however, and their concerns silenced conversation with Mormons.

Silences in the *Ogden Morning Examiner*'s weekly column called the "Socialist Department" were particularly acute. Kate Hilliard—an ally of Mormon women in the battle for suffrage and the most active writer for the paper's socialist column—often wrote on socialism's relation to religion. But she invariably wrote on Christian socialism; she had almost nothing to say about Mormonism or Mormon economics. In one such column, she explained why many socialists were not Christian and yet why so many people thought socialism functioned as a religion. She suggested that socialism ultimately says little about religion. Socialism is a political movement, she claimed, and it makes no more sense for people to call themselves Christian socialists than to call themselves Christian chemists. Religion and politics, she suggested, echoing the ontology being forced on Mormons by mainstream America, are radically distinct projects with different epistemologies (5 February 1905). While the *Morning Examiner*'s socialist column backed away from this complete separation of religion and politics at times (12 March 1905, for one example), it made no direct effort to compare socialism with Mormonism.[51] The column's reports of Utah speeches by traveling socialists similarly show that while speakers often discussed Christianity's relation to socialism, they did not favorably refer to Mormonism or local history.[52]

In fact, the only mention of Brigham Young in the weekly column's four-year run was written by an Englishman:

> For hundreds of ages we have been imprisoning, murdering, persecuting and starving our Brunos, our Pauls, our Socrates, our Raleighs, our Joans of Arc, and we have heaped rewards and honors on our Alexanders, our Bonapartes, our Jay

Goulds, our Rothschilds. Are we to go on forever in the worship of Usury and slaughter and intrigue? Are we still to make the basest, the fittest to survive? To bless power above benevolence? Shall we never have done admiring and obeying our Brigham Youngs, nor crucifying our Christs, nor scorning those who follow Him and such as He? (2 June 1907)

Clearly such a statement could not have promoted careful comparison between Mormonism and socialism, and it would not have facilitated any broad-based egalitarian regional ethic encompassing Mormons and non-Mormons.

The only other place the column lowered the volume of its silence on Mormon communitarianism was in its few denunciations of communalist utopias. Even here, the "Socialist Department" made no mention of anything uniquely Mormon. Rather, one gets the impression that socialists hoped some very broad statements would sufficiently discount the LDS legacy. An article reprinted from the *New York Daily People* was the most direct:

> The numerous "Socialist" colonies and "co-operative" schemes exploited in the past generation have been fore doomed to miserable failure and he who lends even passive support to any of these pleasant delusions Plays into the Hands of the Enemy. How many men and women have lost their money, time and, alas! their faith in "human nature," as a result of dabbling in "Brotherhoods of the Co-operative Commonwealth,"[53] "Co-operative Stores" and other mixtures of book-keeping and misapprehension of natural phenomena. . . . To the revolutionists these scarecrows are a warning to keep "the straight and narrow path". . . . (23 July 1905)

Similarly, Hilliard responded to a writer criticizing socialism as hopelessly utopian: "Socialists are not Utopians, but scientists. The Utopian is one who draws up a plan and claims that it will solve everything. The socialist forms no plan, but goes directly to the facts for his solution, and finds it there ready to his hand. . . . Socialism is not a scheme, nor a dream. It is the scientific philosophy of government, having its origin in the industrial and economic system that has developed and evolved from past conditions" (1 October 1905). Surely socialists were no less confident than Mormons that they possessed the only true gospel. While the Mormon gospel came from on high, the socialists' was transmitted from afar. Unlike in Britain where the Chartist movement emerged (Howell 1995), there seemed to be no space for socialist cultural philosophy to spring from local sources. The regional result was silence and rejection rather than conversation between the two groups.

The *Morning Examiner*'s socialist column is noteworthy not only for its silence on Mormonism but also for its general neglect of regional life.[54] To

be sure, it evaluated locally debated issues on occasion, particularly just before elections.[55] In addition, local crimes sometimes came to its attention.
The column discussed child labor, opportunities for the young, and morality. It pointed to failings of the local juvenile court and educational systems.
It discussed Ogden's billboards and Sunday closing laws, and it commented
on the adventures of William (Big Bill) Haywood, a former local labor ag-
itator, and his Industrial Workers of the World battles.[56] But far more commonly, it produced universalistic arguments. Its pages discussed events in
New York, Denver, and Chicago as much as those in Utah.[57] It made such
claims as, "[W]hat's the difference between German Socialism and American Socialism[?] Exactly the same difference that there is between the multiplication table printed in German and the multiplication table printed in
English" (19 February 1905). And, "The following definition of Socialism
is . . . clipped from a socialist paper, *Justice,* published in London. Since Socialism is an international movement and is working for the same results
in all countries the definition is just as good in this country as in England"
(19 January 1908). Most important, even when writing on local issues, the
columnists made almost no attempt to analyze local systems of production.[58] The editors seemingly assumed that analysis of the country's major
captains of industry would turn Utahns into socialists. The column argued,
in fact, that very little could be done locally. Only the national level—with
the power of the state—mattered (19 March 1905). Step-by-step improvement (encompassing local action) was futile (7 January 1906).

Other socialists were not always as antiregional as those editing the
Morning Examiner's column (Hilliard herself—influenced by the increasingly radical International movement—moved left of Utah's Socialist Party
and its political emphasis, and the column itself split in two about halfway
through its four-year run). Just as elsewhere in the country, socialism in
Utah encompassed a huge variety of sometimes overlapping, sometimes antagonistic movements and agendas, including syndicalism, industrial union-
ism, and Christian socialism. In Utah, Christian socialism and moderate,
reform-minded agendas were strongest (McCormick 1982; Weinstein
1984). Still, a religious split seriously hampered Utah's Socialist Party (Sillito and McCormick 1985). Some non-Mormons, such as the Christian socialist William Thurston Brown, found the church to be nothing except an
obstacle to progress. While some non-Mormons were more conciliatory,
LDS and non-LDS Socialists too often had strained relations. Too many regional socialists possessed more clearly defined national visions than local
ideas (Strongwil 1912; State Committee of the Socialist Party 1908; *Socialist State Ticket* 1914), had too few ideas on establishing socialism lo-

cally (McCormick and Sillito 1994), and did not effectively bring the memory of Mormon egalitarianism into conversation with socialist aspirations.

The Salt Lake City Episcopal bishop Franklin Spalding makes a good case in point for the last claim, despite his admiration for nineteenth-century Mormon communitarianism and despite perhaps being the region's best hope to support such a conversation. One of the country's strongest Christian socialists, Spalding began embracing socialism when he was a parish priest in Erie, Pennsylvania (Cort 1988; *Chicago Christian Socialist,* November 1914). He was one of the most active workers in Utah for socialist and working-class causes, constantly provoking those in his church who wanted to make peace with capitalism and capitalists when he contended that giving charity to the poor could never compensate for the immorality involved in capitalist accumulation (*Chicago Christian Socialist,* November 1914; *Salt Lake City Intermountain Worker,* 3 October 1914). Spalding claimed to be a thoroughgoing Marxist in all but Marx's antireligious sentiments (understandable to him because of Marx's nineteenth-century Europe).

Despite his ability to critique mainstream society in some fundamental ways, he remained locked in the Americanist ideology of progress. He therefore never brought his own egalitarian ethic into very productive conversation with other alternative visions regionally (Spalding n.d.). Progress, he thought, occurred only by following Western civilization's most profound thinkers; Mormons and Native Americans (to different degrees and for somewhat different reasons) had nothing to contribute to the conversation unless they gave up traditional notions and joined civilization (Spalding 1905a and 1905b). Education would lead Mormons out of their errors (Sillito and Bradley 1985; Smoot 1997, 138).

Spalding eventually came to see Mormons as people with whom he could sympathize. He replaced their early radical otherness in his mind and constantly struggled against those, both inside and outside of Utah, who failed to do the same. Nonetheless, he continued to view destroying Mormon truth claims as a central part of his mission (Sillito and Bradley 1985). He was still too much a Protestant of his era to let those revelatory claims go unchallenged (Spalding 1912). A statement from fellow Episcopal bishops seems accurate: "Going to Utah he immediately took such a grasp on the MORMON problem as made him . . . at once the worst foe of Mormonism and the best friend of the Mormons. He was, in other words, as keen to see good as evil, and was ready to learn from the lowly as well as the highly placed" (*Chicago Christian Socialist,* November 1914).

Spalding acknowledged errors, unfortunate alliances, and unethical uses of power by leaders and members of the Christian church. Despite such problems, he felt Christian principles should not be discarded and could—through alliance with socialism—still generate social revolution (see also the socialist column in the *Vernal Express*, 28 March 1903). While he expressed some admiration for Mormonism's early social vision, he was not simply agnostic but instead openly antagonistic toward the revelatory basis upon which Mormons felt this social vision was based. He was convinced that the LDS Church had recently sold out to capitalist interests, but in saying so he brought Americanized Protestant criticisms into his critique: the Mormon church was now acting more like a business than a church (Sillito and Bradley 1985).[59] In effect, Spalding wanted Mormons to join civilization, but when Mormons attempted to join American civilization (which to almost all other Americanizers meant Protestant capitalist civilization), he criticized them for making peace with capitalism. He did not reconcile how the church was to perpetuate its nineteenth-century values without being subject to the critique that it was exceeding its authority as a church. Mormon history, to Spalding, was not simply a tale of delusion and misfortune, as it was to many other non-Mormon socialists (Philippe 1906); but his insistence on the need for Mormon enlightenment undercut his valorization of Mormon egalitarianism.

Spalding said the following about socialists, but it also accurately describes socialist-Mormon relations: "I have been about forced to the conclusion that Socialists are a great deal fonder of hearing themselves talk than of hearing anybody else talk" (*Chicago Christian Socialist*, November 1914). In such a climate, with both regional non-Mormon socialists and Mormons leaders rejecting or undercutting common cause between Mormonism and socialism (see also Flake 2000, 89), it is a wonder only that so many Mormons—more than 40 percent of Utah Socialist Party activists (McCormick 1982, 232)—became socialists. While shifting wage ratios between different types of labor may have led to socialism's downfall nationally (Earle 1992, 400–445), cultural struggles placed an additional burden on the movement regionally.

Eventually the moment passed for progressive conversation between those holding differing egalitarian visions. Mormon leaders' opposition to organized labor and its socialist allies hardened.[60] Spalding—respected in the Mormon community despite his opposition to Mormonism—might have eventually helped such a conversation proceed, but he died in a tragic accident in 1914. The perception of syndicalist anarchy and violence manifested itself in the 1915 trial of Joe Hill, a member of the Industrial Workers of the World accused of murder and executed in Utah (G. M. Smith 1969), and the Russian Revolution tainted socialism itself (Ballard 1920,

80; Hunt 1993). A regionalized structure of antipathy between Mormons and radicals thus fully emerged (on regionalized expectations, see Paasi 1991, 249; and Pred 1990, 3–40). Some progressives and socialists found Utah's political climate too difficult and left the state (Sillito 1981 and 1992). Communitarian aspirations became internal provenances of organizations (churches, labor organizations, the socialist parties) and were removed from more general regional discussions.[61] A regional egalitarian ethic was thus the casualty of Americans who sought to eradicate lingering traces of Mormon communitarianism; of regional Mormons and non-Mormons who refused to consider (and in fact reacted against) Native American communalism; of Mormons whose Americanization caused them to neglect, compartmentalize, and deny the social application of their communitarian heritage; and of regional non-Mormons who held egalitarian aspirations but failed to regionalize such aspirations, especially by denying that the LDS legacy had anything to offer.

Conclusion

Like norms of gender authority, norms of economic responsibility underwent significant change between 1880 and 1920. Again the direction was from significant and substantial debate to general agreement and little desire to change the status quo. And again the crux of early debates revolved around "un-American" Mormon practices. None of the LDS communitarian systems attempted between 1830 and 1880 were long-term successes, and many Mormons proved themselves to be adept capitalists between attempts. But the attempts kept the regional economy more separate and self-sufficient than it would otherwise have been. Basing the Mormon economy on principles different from those of the national economy always remained an ideal. Though enjoined to make themselves financially independent as households, Mormons also possessed strong norms to look after those who were not succeeding. Mormon leaders taught that regional economic success, opportunity, and equality would prove the church's glory. God expected members to work for regional success as much as for individual success. Many non-Mormons who migrated for capitalist opportunity despised such practices, of course, especially their separatist manifestations.

The major turn-of-the-century change was not that Mormons suddenly became capitalists. Many church members had already successfully embraced such principles. Rather, the key transformation was further acceptance of capitalist cultural logic. The normative responsibilities economic actors had toward one another shifted. Less discussion remained of people sharing responsibility for one another's welfare on a community scale. Moral strictures by 1920 centered on a person's (a man's) responsibility to provide for his family and a general suggestion that he ought to willingly donate to the poor. The sense that people were responsible as members of a community or a region to help one another succeed weakened. Regional inhabitants denied possible bases for a regionalized egalitarian ethic, and the moral moderators of capitalist individualism and social indifference retreated.

During this period, the region increasingly tied itself to the national and world economy. Leonard Arrington (1974) argues that Utah's economy underwent two important trends. First, it became much less bifurcated after statehood. After 1896, the self-sufficient LDS agricultural economy and the eastern-financed non-Mormon mining economy started to come together, organized around the emergence of the business sector and the newly important copper industry. Leadership of the regional economy shifted, he argues, from agricultural valleys and scattered mining districts to business and industrial communities in Salt Lake City and Ogden. Second, producers in the state produced increasingly for consumers outside of the state. Utah's economy moved toward production based on comparative advantage rather than on regional needs. Still, nineteenth-century Mormon communitarianism had residual effects. Utah's economy remained anomalous in the Intermountain West for its diversification, its capacity to produce for itself, and its high percentage of owner-operated agricultural enterprises. By the end of World War I, Utah's economy had moved in the direction of an urban-industrial economy, though it had not quite become that. Agriculture still led the way, even if wealth centered in Salt Lake City, Ogden, or eastern cities directed production (Alexander 1974).

In such a context, four particularly important shifts helped create new norms for the Mormon culture region. Within Mormon culture itself, wage labor shifted from signifying unwanted dependence on others to representing skills and habits needed for economic progress. Second, the Mormon conception of wealth was shorn of most negative connotations. Instead of wealth being a mixed blessing, easily promoting dangerous social divisions, wealth rightly separated the industrious from the idle. Third, the communitarian and regional nuances of self-sufficiency weakened, while individualistic connotations increased. Fourth, and most important, an egalitarian ethic dissipated in Mormonism and was removed by both Mormons and non-Mormons as a possible basis for regional life.

The decades surrounding the turn of the twentieth century clearly constituted a period of Americanization for Utah and the Mormons. The Latter-day Saints found that they could, indeed must, find common economic cause with regional non-Mormons. Mormons, for the most part, no longer heard church instructions on specific economic activities. Regional economic activity came to be conducted, if not on a completely religion-blind basis, on a mostly religion-blind one. Class assumed higher priority. Few people mourned the loss of religious separation. In many important ways, Mormons became American economic actors. Yet this descriptive framework of Americanization misleads in at least one important sense. The notion of Americanization implies that regional uniqueness disappeared, yet regional culture remained important. Even though capitalism expanded, the Mormon–non-Mormon dynamic produced regionally distinct cultural accommodations; the struggle between Mormons and non-Mormons merely took a different form. Most important, it persisted in collective regional memory, part of an emergent regional habitus (Bourdieu 1977; Elias 1996). The memory of Mormon communitarianism and past struggles negatively affected possibilities for egalitarian regional economic norms.

Mormons' capitulation to capitalism came at a price, though perhaps a price many did not perceive paying. In their efforts to Americanize, they embraced, at least in nonchurch-related economic practices, particularly individualistic notions of right and wrong. While they may still have dreamt of someday living the United Order, such dreams had little practical effect on their everyday lives. They seemed to internalize the values of their "oppressors." Regional non-Mormons likewise lost something in the emergent norms. Although most had long embraced and promoted capitalist values, they found themselves insisting on a particularly individualistic version of these values. To show Mormons the way to Americanization, they set a communitarian ethic up as the antithesis of Americanism. Non-Mormons foreclosed on being regionally able to participate in debates about egalitarianism still open to those in other parts of the country. Even those who rejected many capitalist norms, such as the socialists, figured Mormon communitarianism as an irredeemable legacy.

On the regional scale, egalitarianism came be signified by "uncivilized" Native Americans, "fanatical" Mormons, or "anarchic" and "violent" radicals. The region was removed from possibly encompassing fundamentally different visions of American economic life. Mormons and non-Mormons increasingly centered regional economic priorities on capitalist boosterism. Conceptions of economic responsibility shifted from respect for those with less power to support for those already dominant; so did conceptions of national loyalty.

CHAPTER FOUR

RE-PRESENTING AMERICA

"As the people of the city awoke to the light of Independence Day they saw from the chief centers of Mormon power the American flag drooping at half-mast. It was a startling sight. Everyone wondered what it meant, and many were the surmises. But no one hit at first on the true reason—that it was the Mormon method of expressing their hatred of this Nation, and their contempt for its power." The non-Mormon *Salt Lake Tribune* thus explained a provocative LDS protest of mistreatment by the U.S. government (5 July 1885). Many buildings associated with Mormonism, including Zion's Cooperative Mercantile Institution, the Tithing House, the Gardo House (President John Taylor's residence), and even city hall and the county courthouse, flew American flags at half-mast on the Fourth of July in 1885 to publicize complaints against the territorial justice system. Many non-Mormons tried to force the flags to be raised but at best had mixed success persuading either police or military forces to aid their cause. The two sides exchanged threats, and non-Mormons held meetings and passed resolutions condemning the act. Word even reached President Grover Cleveland, who put the military occupying Utah on alert. While Mormons argued that they were simply protesting legislation against the church, the incident confirmed to non-Mormons their long-held suspicions: that Mormons truly were not loyal to the nation (Larson 1971, 139–42). As with gender and economy, debates over national loyalty broke along Mormon–non-Mormon lines during the 1880s. Regional norms of national loyalty went from being heavily questioned and debated in 1880 to being virtually settled by 1920.

Early debates revolved around the question of whether Mormons could be loyal to the nation, given their loyalty to the church and obedience to its leaders. National loyalty, many non-Mormons argued, was weak and secondary to Mormons, far beneath their primary allegiance to the church. Non-Mormons pointed to the LDS teaching that church authority covered all aspects of life. Mormons' political and economic practices, non-Mormons claimed, were extensions of their faith. Mormons responded, almost incomprehensibly to many non-Mormons, that they were the true patriots. Mormons felt that their struggles to live their religion in a hostile environment and establish a good, decent society made them more loyal to the principles of the nation than non-Mormons were. To Mormons, non-Mormons denied them the freedom to practice their religion and govern their own society. To Mormons of the 1880s, national loyalty implied loyalty to the Constitution and the principles upon which they felt the country had been created (especially religious freedom). They felt little compulsion to conform to national sociocultural norms or to follow the federal government in bad policies. They thought that protesting unwise policies and practices demonstrated loyalty. Non-Mormons argued that the essence of national loyalty lay in conforming to national social and cultural norms and federal policies and prioritizing national loyalty above all other loyalties. They felt true national loyalty could result only from individual political independence from churches or other organizations. While a regional consensus always existed about the desirability and necessity of national loyalty, in 1880 Mormons and non-Mormons debated what that loyalty meant.

By 1920, most Mormons and non-Mormons agreed that national loyalty implied obedience to and support for the federal government. It also implied conformance to nationally dominant cultural and social practices. The nation had assumed a virtually unquestionable image as an agent of progress. National loyalty now meant jumping on the national bandwagon more than feeling responsible for criticizing the nation's direction or defending the rights of those who did. In the first part of this chapter, these shifts are examined primarily through discourses of rights and responsibility, while the second part addresses political, cultural, and ideological conformance.

Many factors facilitated the changes. Perhaps most important was the separation of religion from other forms of social activity so that religion no longer challenged norms and values in those other areas. The status of religion was a key battleground between Mormons and non-Mormons; non-Mormons won perhaps their most significant "victory" here. Non-Mormons complained throughout the period that the LDS Church overstepped its authority—that it acted as a religion ought not to. They insisted that the church should not influence members politically or economically, other than through inculcating general Christian values. Churches were to have no direct role in politics and economics. Mormons started to believe and then eventually embraced the message, partly because of the church's vulnerability, partly because of the never-entirely-absent patriotism of Mormons, and partly because of the frequency with which the message was heard. Another ingredient of altered norms of national loyalty included LDS and non-LDS adherence to the ideology of progress and the sense that national progress drove world progress. Mormon church leaders also realized that being perceived as nationally loyal would benefit the church more than LDS resistance would. Whatever the causes, the Mormon church carved out a niche in the American religious system, and the Mormon culture region found legitimacy in the American system of political regions.

Peter S. Onuf (1996) argues that political competition between regions (what he calls sectionalism) has been endemic since American independence. Unlike most scholars, he maintains that sectionalism resulted neither from fundamentally different social systems nor from geographically distinctive systems of morality or character. Instead, he suggests, American regionalism and the political conflict resulting from it were "integral to the original conception and construction of the federal system" (12). The American system therefore institutionalized a method for resolving differences in geographical terms: "Union and section were thus inextricably paired: it was impossible to think or talk about one without suggesting the other" (21).

The Mormon culture region existed in anomalous terms in the 1800s. Its unique social system did not arise from the exigencies of sectionally based politics; rather, its social distinctiveness preceded any sense that it possessed a firm and legitimate place in the American regional system. In this way, the Americanization of Mormonism was fundamentally also the regionalization of Utah and Mormons. The Mormon culture region found a place in the American regional system by 1920. Most important, it joined the American West. As such, it represented the same progress and American development the West represented. Ideas of regional progress and virtue came to coincide with those of national progress and virtue. Although this project was generally quite successful, residual distinctiveness remained. The Mormon culture region may have joined the American West, but it still uniquely reflected controversies between Mormons and non-Mormons. By 1920, its dominant moral order contained an unusually strong sense that national loyalty required conformity. To use Edward Ayers and Peter Onuf's (1996) terminology, regional identity was not completely subsumed under nationhood during the Americanization of Utah, but this identity was transformed. Shifting norms of national loyalty shaped this transformed regional identity.

The Meaning of National Loyalty

Mormons and National Loyalty

Questions regarding their national loyalty hovered over Mormons since Joseph Smith's day. In efforts to curtail Mormonism, Smith's opponents used the charge of treason to bring him to "justice." Once in the Great Basin, non-Mormons continued to accuse the Saints of not possessing national loyalty; the federal government itself also grew more interested in the issue. A decade after the LDS exodus, President James Buchanan sent U.S. troops to suppress a supposed rebellion (Furniss 1960). Though this "Utah War" turned out to be bloodless, the government stationed permanent troops in Utah and continued to watch the Mormons for the remainder of the century to ensure that they did not foment rebellion. The government charged territorial officials with bringing Mormons into conformance with American political norms. Statehood—dearly sought by Mormon leaders—was withheld until officials felt that Mormonism's "un-American" ambitions were sufficiently broken (Larson 1971; E. Lyman 1986).

The nineteenth-century church had essentially parlayed its ecclesiastical power into political power. Mormons had their own political party and encouraged unanimous voting for church-nominated candidates (often church leaders themselves). Utah non-Mormons, always a minority, felt their franchise worthless in a theocratic dictatorship. They perceived themselves as cultural strangers in a land of polygamy, illegitimately powerless to enforce nationally dominant norms. Non-Mormons feared that Mormons sought to establish a kingdom within, but relatively autonomous from, the United States. Though Mormons expressed loyalty to U.S. institutions, they used sufficiently ambiguous rhetoric to worry the government that they were trying to establish a state independent of the United States (Eugene Campbell 1987).[1] The "Mormon problem" therefore garnered much attention from non-Mormons regionally and nationally. This attention only strengthened the Saints' sense of being a persecuted people. They resented that they were not free to create communities as independently as other Americans had.

These elements of mutual mistrust help account for regionally shifting meanings of national loyalty. The Mormons' relationship with the federal government changed greatly between 1880 and 1920. Legislation, particularly the Edmunds-Tucker Act of 1887, curtailed LDS power by making it easier to crack down on polygamists, disfranchising Mormons, disqualifying Mormons from authority within the judicial system, and confiscating church property. This legislation forced the church to make significant changes at the end of the nineteenth century. Most significant, the church ended the official practice of polygamy in 1890 and disbanded its political party in 1891, thereby ending voting dictates.[2] Mormons thereafter joined national political parties and sought common political cause with regional non-Mormons for the first time. By 1896, Utah's normalized politics convinced the federal government to withdraw territorial officials; that year the territory became a state.

As the federal government gradually withdrew from the "Mormon problem," Mormons switched from a rhetoric of rights to almost its opposite— a bandwagon mentality. By 1920, Mormons criticized resistance to the federal government's extension of power and cultural norms almost as readily as non-Mormons had insisted on federal discipline for the LDS Church in the late nineteenth century. Institutional viability explains part of the shift (the church felt profoundly threatened in 1880 but not in 1920). Just as important, Mormon culture lost much of its capacity to view national loyalty in multiple senses. National loyalty can encompass the constructive (even if harsh) critic, as well as the obedient, jingoistic citizen (O'Leary 1999); yet some always work to deny the critic's legitimacy. In their regional relationship, non-Mormon culture and LDS culture lost the sense that national loyalty allows for concerned criticism and differing visions of America's destiny. Instead, conformance became a nearly hegemonic standard.

American Rights

The late nineteenth century featured strong appeals by both Mormons and non-Mormons to rights they thought were being denied to them. Of course the groups differed strongly on which rights were most important and how regional life withheld them. Mormons found continuity between the persecution they experienced in New York, Missouri, and Illinois and their contemporary troubles with the federal government and non-Mormons. They claimed they were being deprived of freedom of religion and conscience. Non-Mormons saw themselves as a powerless minority, oppressed by a majority culture, and they claimed individual rights to be free from such smothering influence. Both sides repeated the arguments throughout the 1880s, often through inflammatory rhetoric.

LDS Church president John Taylor, for example, painted a seamless history of persecution in a speech commemorating Pioneer Day on 24 July 1880: "Robbed, pillaged, houseless and homeless, they wandered forth into the wilderness, with President Young as their leader and God as their only help, to seek that protection among the savages of the desert which was denied them within the haunts of so-called civilization. . . . Congress, goaded by religious zealots and political adventurers and demagogues, have passed inimical legislation against us, and . . . the courts, under the same influence have been as partial and hostile in their rulings" (quoted in *Salt Lake City Deseret Evening News*, 26 July 1880). The *Deseret Evening News*, for another example, decried an Independence Day speech given by the non-Mormon territorial governor Eli H. Murray in 1880:

> Utah, under the name of Deseret will truly yet be free![3] Free from officials who use their position to insult and browbeat the people! Free from imported autocrats forced upon them without their consent! Free from the superstitions of apostate Christendom. . . . Free from courts and officers that encourage licentiousness and put a premium on vice! Free from misrepresentation, abuse and calumny! Free to worship God as her citizens desire and to magnify and maintain the principles of the glorious Constitution which they have always reverenced . . . but which are now denied by those who shout themselves hoarse over lip liberty, and cover that independence which consists but in Fourth of July froth and spread-eagle orations! (6 July 1880)

Examples are easily multiplied.[4] Mormons felt government officials infringed on many rights: freedom of religion by forbidding polygamy, freedom to represent themselves and control their own destiny by withholding statehood and territorially elected officials, and freedom for Mormon women by disfranchising them. Frustration translated into strong appeals to restore rights. Mormons distinguished between principles set forth in the Constitution (which they regarded as inspired) and the conduct of officials who deprived them of rights. To the Saints, religious bigotry had led to their problems, so freedom of religion and freedom of conscience had priority in the Saints' constellation of fundamental liberties. As the *Deseret Evening News* put it, "Freedom of faith, freedom of worship, freedom to live and pursue happiness in our own way, so long as we do not infringe on the freedom and happiness of others. This government was founded to secure this liberty to all its citizens, and to be an encouragement to the oppressed of all nations in their efforts to become free" (3 July 1890).

Mormons used the rhetoric of individual liberty, but they clearly had more collective forms of individual liberty in mind than did most Americans. Mormon individualism paralleled Puritan individualism. Michael Hughey's description of Puritan individualism describes nineteenth-century Mormons just as well: "[I]ndividualism as conceived by the Puritans makes sense only within a collective context. Once voluntary choice was exercised and a bargain with God was struck, the individual was free only to follow the Lord's ways, and those ways emphasized social as well as personal duties. Although the rights and dignity of the individual were sincerely respected by Puritan opinion, their strong sense of common purpose, collective obligations, and joint accountability to God committed each person to serving the community as best he or she could" (1983, 74–75).

Non-Mormons saw matters differently. They cherished rights they thought lacking in a Mormon-dominated region—such rights as the freedom to buy and sell without church market control and the freedom to have their individual votes count without facing an insurmountable, religiously defined bloc of votes. Governor Murray's speech that the *Deseret Evening News* lambasted argued:

> Those who believe in the divine right of kings, those who would keep their fellowmen in ignorance and in bondage, those who would rob the fruits of honest toil, those who would subordinate State to any church, grumblers and traitors do not and cannot enjoy Freedom's Day. . . . [N]o new state will be formed, no new star placed upon the folds of our flag, until the people it represents come with the badge of freedom upon their breasts. Free to think for themselves. Free to act for themselves. Free from all kingly and priestly dictation in civil affairs. . . . (quoted in *Deseret Evening News*, 6 July 1880)

Rather than freedom of conscience and collective liberty, non-Mormons focused on individual political and economic liberty—freedom from controlling groups. The non-Mormon *Salt Lake Tribune* yearned for a land "where all opportunities are opened to all men, where under the laws all citizens are equal and where the laws press so lightly that every man has a right to do anything he may please to do so that he perpetrates no wrong upon his neighbor" (4 July 1880). Individual opportunity, non-Mormons argued, was what the nation-state owed its people. While Mormons and non-Mormons emphasized different rights, they both found a significant element of national loyalty was claiming rights that oppressive others withheld from them. Both groups, each with partial validity, claimed victimhood and held that their rights had to be safeguarded.

Clearly the issues changed in the 1890s with the end of polygamy and the Mormon political party.[5] The volume of rhetoric on rights decreased with growing cooperation and understanding between Mormons and non-Mormons. Yet change did not occur all at once. Two issues, in particular, motivated a revived 1880s-style rhetoric. Woman suffrage, as an unfinished piece of business, was the major "rights" issue of the 1890s. To Franklin Richards, for example, the fight to include woman suffrage in the state constitution "means that men and women [are] equally members of society, equally answerable to law, equally responsible in taxes for the support of the State, equally creators and consumers of wealth . . ." (1895, 5). God created men and women equal, he claimed, and he was probably referring to

LDS doctrinal influence in Utah when he argued, "Here we have the same Divine Image for both; they have the same blood, the same nature, the same intelligence, the same moral law, the same responsibility, the same destiny" (7). Thus the consent of all governed must be gained.

Renewed distrust between some Mormons and non-Mormons in the twentieth century's first decade disrupted the more amiable relations of the 1890s and also brought claims about violations of rights. Early in the twentieth century, some regional non-Mormons grew impatient with Mormon Americanization. They worried, with some justification, that Mormons made changes for public consumption only and that the church retained too much power and was simply biding its time until it could reclaim control of regional social and political life.[6] Non-Mormons particularly feared that polygamy would return and that the church would again instruct its members in voting and practicing commerce.[7] The 1904 formation of the American Party, largely a rejuvenation of the old non-Mormon Liberal Party, and the Smoot hearings were important expressions of these concerns (Alexander 1986, 16–36). The *Salt Lake Tribune* documented the concerns of some non-Mormons.[8] A 1907 Fourth of July editorial argued:

> [Non-Mormon] Americans who came [to Utah], in pursuance of their rights as citizens, were considered intruders, "Outsiders," and every possible obstruction, menace, and often violence, was employed to drive them away. . . . They were deprived of their constitutional rights in many ways, by biased laws, and by snap judgments under those laws.
>
> They were compelled to support an alien and treasonable officialdom [the LDS Church] that sought their injury instead of their benefit. . . .
>
> They were taxed without representation, and their objection to this has been hissed down with scorn. . . .
>
> . . . This intentional injustice to fellow-citizens of the Republic, the nation and the people at large have generously and wisely interposed barriers to prevent, but a ruling, law-defying, theocratic oligarchy in unmanly bad faith, breaking its pledges of submission to law, has been incited to virulent and pernicious activity in defying the law. . . .
>
> And so, we say, liberty is coming even to Utah. The day of freedom, and the sheen of the glory of the fathers is penetrating even the theocratic gloom and freedom is sure to win. (4 July 1907)

Church leaders hid behind the rhetoric of rights to perpetuate illegal activity (continued polygamy), the *Tribune* claimed (5 July 1907).

The rhetoric of rights from both sides was mutually reinforcing. In the Smoot hearings, Smoot's side often returned to the right of individuals to believe what they wanted as long as such beliefs did not lead to unwelcome practices (U.S. Congress 1906, 4:503–5). The *Deseret Evening News* argued that the Mormon pioneers came to the area seeking rights, only after having been deprived of them in previous locations:

> That the first settlers here were as enthusiastic for liberty as their descendants are, is proved by all their acts. In the proposed constitution of the state of Deseret they inserted a clause providing for minority representation, although there were but few non-"Mormons" in the Territory then. . . . Notwithstanding this truly American, and Christian, spirit of liberty, trouble arose when unprincipled bigots and ruffians decided to deprive the settlers here of their Constitutional rights, in order to profit by the spoils. . . . But through it all, the people here looked to the government of the American people and the common sense of their nation, for protection against their persecutors and a vindication of the cause of justice. And they were not disappointed. (4 July 1907; see also R. W. Young 1906, 102–3)

Except for claiming that their rights had prevailed on the national stage since 1890, this quote closely resembles LDS rhetoric of the 1880s. Like earlier Mormons, the *Deseret Evening News* could make this claim only by erasing the expulsion of Native American peoples (on trampling of religious liberties, see Deloria 1999).

These worries about rights were increasingly throwbacks to the 1880s. Rhetorical concern for women's rights dwindled after statehood. Smoot kept his seat in the Senate and promptly created a powerful Republican Party political machine containing both Mormons and non-Mormons. The American Party, which controlled Salt Lake City government from 1905 to 1911 but was never a force statewide, fell victim to the country's two-party system, even as church leaders feared that it would resurrect itself (Alexander 1995b, 455–56).[9] Nevertheless, the flare-up of rights-oriented rhetoric reminded both sides of the religiously drawn competition they wished to avoid. More often, the rhetoric was much less caustic, with both sides seeking peaceful coexistence. Appeals to rights, understandably, came less frequently. Perhaps just as important, such petitions gradually lost concern for oppression.[10] Instead, the appeals grew vaguer. When not marked by ambiguity, they increasingly came from a position of strength: the strong claimed the right to maintain their strength. Rights and liberty were seen less as mechanisms to protect the weak; instead, they euphemistically stood for power to preserve and extend American cultural practices globally. Liberty resulted from extending American power. Regional inhabitants suggested that Americans had sufficient rights and liberty. Those appealing to rights were now more concerned with being properly thankful for the American (white and increasingly middle-class) way of life.

Some no longer interpreted the region's past as a struggle for rights. At a speech celebrating Pioneer Day, Salt Lake City's Mayor John Clark said, "[W]hile we enjoy the blessings of advanced civilization . . . let us never forget those noble pioneers who opened up these valleys for us and our posterity, and made it possible for us to enjoy this rich heritage" (quoted in *Salt Lake Tribune,* 26 July 1898). Regional inhabitants were to celebrate and imperialistically extend blessings conferred by American rights. The struggle was no longer to gain or retain such rights. A Fourth of July speaker during the Spanish-American War put it this way: "We now want freedom not only for ourselves but for all, even for Spain herself, and the day will come when the Fourth of July will be celebrated in Madrid as well as in Washington" (quoted in *Salt Lake Tribune,* 5 July 1898).

Defending religious liberties and rights to speak as they wished died slower among Mormon leaders than others. In 1899, George Q. Cannon argued, "We want to see . . . that every man shall enjoy the rights guaranteed by that grand instrument of liberty which God inspired the framers to make. But we differ from many people in regard to our views concerning the manner in which the government should be administered. And we think, as free men . . . we have a right to express our feelings upon this point with the utmost freedom; and that we are not traitors when we do so, but are the friends of the government . . ." (1899, 49; see also Cowley 1900; and John Henry Smith in U.S. Congress 1906, 2:311). George Teasdale, another church leader, said, "Did you ever know this [LDS] people so unpatriotic as to be petitioning the government against any handfull of people?[11] No patriot was ever guilty of anything of the kind. A patriot is a man who sustains the Constitution of the United States and believes in religious liberty. . . . We know how to appreciate liberty and freedom, and we never interfere with other people's doctrines or belief" (1900, 20; see also Young Men's Mutual Improvement Association 1900, 121).

Still, more church leaders began to believe that Americans possessed enough rights and that oppression constituted no significant national problem. Although the Saints had been persecuted historically, church president Joseph F. Smith claimed, the nation had no part in it; rather, assorted unprincipled people denied the Saints their rights (1903a, 73). Another leader also located persecution and the need to struggle for rights in the past: "[B]less our nation—the nation that has given an asylum to this work and the people of God. . . . If the people of the nation have offended in the past, they will make satisfaction; and the Lord is using and directing them . . ." (F. Lyman 1899, 40). John Henry Smith celebrated his American citizenship and claimed to feel no shame in it. All persons have constitutional liberties, he declared: "So long as he interferes not with the rights and liberties of other men, his liberties should be guarded, his rights should be preserved . . ." (1905, 14). Joseph F. Smith said he was convinced that in no other nation could the church have been established with so little opposition; the sentiment for religious toleration and the freedom in the country could not be matched elsewhere. The church president called the United States an asylum for the oppressed (1905, 6).

Church leaders rhetoric on rights grew more one-sided over time. Instead of also representing something to struggle for, sufficient rights were said to exist almost automatically in the United States. The country had progressed, and the time for struggling had passed; Mormons should feel blessed for the freedoms they now enjoyed. John Henry Smith expressed gratefulness that the country guaranteed liberty in religion and conscience. This liberty motivated Mormon immigrants to make the nation their own. The United States was, in his words, "the Zion of God, where the liberties of the human race were assured, where men could bow in reverence and respect to the Supreme Being, and where no man need ask whether they prayed to Buddha, or to Christ Jesus, or to the Unknown God, or to a stick or stone" (1906, 24). The Lord had ordained things, Francis M. Lyman believed, so that in Utah and the surrounding states "[t]his government will contribute very materially to the protection of the kingdom of God. It has done this in the past, and will do so in the future. How grateful we ought to be . . ." (1907, 16; see also G. Richards 1908, 43).[12]

Mormons increasingly contrasted America's blessings with supposed oppressions elsewhere. The Saints had earlier compared countries, concluding the United States was the freest. The difference between 1880s statements and those from the early twentieth century is the latter's unreserved enthusiasm for the country's freedom. In 1880, John Taylor said, "That these things—the rights of men, have not been thoroughly maintained, we are a living example today, and yet notwithstanding this and notwithstanding the scenes that we have passed through, the difficulties we have had to contend with, the persecutions we have been obliged to endure and the rights that have been wrested from us, yet I very much question to-day whether there is any nation in existence in the world where we could find more protection than we can in this Nation, poor as it is" (quoted in *Salt Lake Tribune*, 25 July 1880). For Taylor, there was at least the form and promise of guaranteed liberty in the United States (1880, 102). By the twentieth century, such reserve no longer marked LDS comparisons, as is evident in Joseph F. Smith's pronouncement: "I think it is, a necessity for the Latter-day Saints to take every advantage they possibly can to secure homes

for themselves in Utah, in Idaho, in Wyoming and Colorado, in the ad-
joining states here, and in our own country—our blessed America—under
our grand and glorious government, where life, property and liberties of
men may be protected and not jeopardized by mob-violence, by revolutions,
or by any . . . disruption that so often occurs in some of our neighboring
countries" (1910, 4; see also J. H. Smith 1910b, 11; and C. Hart 1913, 41).
The proper LDS cultural stance toward American rights shifted from critique to appreciation.

In 1912, a disagreement arose among church leaders. According to
Thomas Alexander, it stemmed most directly from the question of whether
church president Joseph F. Smith was unduly trying to influence church
members to vote Republican (1986, 39–41). B. H. Roberts, a member of
the Quorum of the Seventy and a Democrat, had run afoul of most church
leaders in the mid-1890s over a political controversy involving Moses
Thatcher (see below). Since then, according to Alexander, Roberts had tried
to map out a proper space for church leaders to be involved in politics. In
an October 1912 general conference address, he suggested that "in essen-
tials let there be unity; in non-essentials, liberty; and in all things charity"
(1912, 30). He argued that the church ought to be unified in religious matters, but tolerance for varying viewpoints should reign in social and political matters. The example he used to bolster his point is particularly interesting: "[I]f governments become destructive of liberties and rights of the
people, it is the right of the people to alter or even abolish them, and institute new forms that shall, in their judgment tend better to preserve their
rights and their liberties" (33; see also Young Men's Mutual Improvement
Association n.d.a, 121–22). He said he followed Brigham Young in believing that though the Constitution was inspired, it was also not perfect and
that improvements should be welcomed: "[L]et us not think because we believe in the great truth that the Constitution of our country was the product of divine inspiration, that new conditions and constantly changing status would not warrant, from time to time, changes in the fundamental law
of the land" (33).

Perhaps Roberts was also responding to Smith's message in the April conference to the effect that no Saint ought to tolerate any hint that the Constitution might be destroyed or trampled or the notion that the people's sentiment ought to be regarded more highly than the Constitution. Tolerating
these, Smith argued, is the spirit of "anarchism" and "mobocracy" that had
begun to spread throughout the country (1912, 10–11). Roberts's arguments provoked numerous responses from church leaders, though it was
not clear at the time whether they supported or rebuked Roberts's general

point, Alexander suggests. What is interesting is the way the responses addressed Roberts's particular example that the Constitution might need occasional modification. On this particular issue, most church leaders found Roberts's formulation wrong-headed.

Charles Penrose (a Democrat) argued that the Constitution is an essential on which church members ought to be unified: "Now then let us be careful that we do not drift away from that Constitution to be led off into bygone and forbidden paths and bring chaos and finally anarchy and destruction upon this glorious nation" (1912, 68). James E. Talmage spoke of a false progressivism, one that belittled, instead of built on, the past. He said church members needed to beware of imitations of liberty. Although he used examples having little to do with potential constitutional changes (people who do not listen to advice infringe on the rights of those who do, smokers infringe on the rights of nonsmokers), he clearly believed false notions of advancement and progressivism undermined liberty's foundations. Contemporary claims of rights were more likely to infringe on, rather than extend, existing American liberty (1912, 126–27).

In subsequent years (aided by the First World War), expressions of doubt about calls for rights to be extended further within the United States became increasingly dominant among Mormon leaders (Whitney 1916a, 68; J. F. Smith 1918a, 5; J. F. Smith 1918b, 169). Existing rights and true liberty could be protected only by skepticism of new and different claims for rights, by vigilance against anarchy. In particular, only individualist claims (and communally nationalist, as I argue below) should be seriously considered. Regional culture shunted aside the communal rights of those who did not easily fit into dominant narratives of American progress—such as the working class, Native Americans, and immigrants. Rights to be politically or culturally different were confined to a narrow range of politics and culture. Rights and liberty came to mean the freedom of those already well established in society to prosper (through individual property rights, the freedom of capital and labor, the freedom of whites to disregard the needs and rights of other groups, the freedom for political parties to orchestrate political debate, and so forth).[13] Those who were different were either dangerous or unimportant (see the priority of "American" rights over Indian rights reported in the *Salt Lake Tribune* on 12 March 1897).

When Mormons and non-Mormons in the region viewed themselves as subjugated minorities, much regional discourse emphasized the rights of the oppressed. Once regional inhabitants, both Mormon and non-Mormon, perceived themselves as mainstream, they deemphasized minority rights. Instead, they concentrated on maintaining the rights already enjoyed. This shift, though unfortunate, should not be surprising. Increasingly, regional inhabitants spoke of the responsibilities of national loyalty instead of claiming, as an expression of national loyalty, that rights should be extended and expanded in America.

Citizens' Responsibilities

Regional discourse on the responsibilities inherent in national loyalty also shows a narrowed regional accommodation of cultural and political difference by 1920. Not only did this discourse's frequency increase between 1880 and 1920, but the tone shifted from socially analytical to socially prescriptive. Nineteenth-century discussions between Mormons and non-Mormons did not ignore responsibility, to be sure. Both groups thought that the other failed to live up to citizenship responsibilities and needed to be shown the way. Mormons, branded with the un-American label, felt it important to argue that they showed loyalty through distinctive Mormon practices. Non-Mormons, too, asserted that their ideals exhibited true patriotism.

Nineteenth-century Mormons thought that fighting for political and religious rights inhered in citizens' duties. Church president John Taylor made it clear that since the Saints had to fight to maintain these rights, they were responsible for ensuring that the rights extended to others. But, he intimated, the Saints' responsibility lay more in making Mormonism succeed than in making America succeed (*Salt Lake Tribune*, 25 July 1880). Susan Stryker (1992) argues that early Mormonism constituted a cultural and political formation distinctive from the American cultural and political formation. Though born on American soil as a reaction to the social dislocations of capitalist expansion of the American North, Mormon culture conceived of an ontology fundamentally separate from American culture. It came to not depend either positively or negatively on American culture. That is, it was conceived neither as a direct fulfillment of American ideals nor as a direct reaction against those ideals. Its frames of reference were elsewhere, she claims. Making the Mormon Zion flourish was a project neither directly opposed to nor directly dependent on the perpetuation and expansion of the American state (though clearly American fortunes had ramifications for Mormons). Mormonism, like Americanism, was a comprehensive cultural system, claiming authority in most aspects of life. Mormon loyalty could conflict with American loyalty, as non-Mormons consistently pointed out, but the two types of loyalty were not a priori in diametrical opposition, contrary to what non-Mormons were wont to claim.

On the contrary, Taylor suggested that for American principles to be upheld, Mormon ones had to be preserved. The nation would take care of itself, but Mormons' responsibility to America lay in creating a Zion that would become a model for all people. "Have the [Saints] done a good work?" he asked rhetorically at a Pioneer Day celebration. "They have, and let us continue to . . . improve and go on until we shall be as far ahead of this and other nations in regard to science and intelligence of every kind as we are today in regard to religious matters" (quoted in *Salt Lake Tribune*, 25 July 1880). At the same celebration, Wilford Woodruff spoke of the loyalty of the Mormon Battalion in honoring the request of "our government" to supply troops for the war on Mexico.[14] The country now had no justification for destroying the church. Yet while this element of national loyalty ran through the speech, the theme of loyalty to Zion came through more strongly. Mormons' patriotic responsibilities to the nation-state were to be performed under the direction of the church and in ways that prioritized creating Zion. Similarly, the *Home Writer* conceptualized the citizen's duty as voting for People's Party candidates (the church ticket) who would support LDS rights and liberty (14 July 1882, 3–4; and 2 January 1883, 1). While the Saints felt they were not working against the nation, they felt citizen influence was to come through Zion rather than individuals (J. Taylor 1880, 102).

For their part, early regional non-Mormons emphasized the responsibility of obeying and honoring the country. "[I]f around the alters of our country we do not draw with grateful hearts to bless its coming, to try to comprehend its significance, its blessings and glory, then we are not worthy to be Americans, and not fit to be free men," the *Salt Lake Tribune* declared (4 July 1880). In 1889, non-Mormon Fourth of July speakers spoke of responsibility as obedience to the country's laws and development of the country's resources. In a speech to a group of laborers, Arthur L. Thomas, the territorial governor, spoke on a common capitalist theme: "The workingmen are interested more than any other class in upholding the law. Wealth and power could care for itself, but the working classes must always depend upon the justice and generosity of their government. Every workingman should signalize his devotion to the laws and institutions of his country at every opportunity" (*Salt Lake Tribune*, 5 July 1889). Another speech prioritized development responsibilities: "[The country's] sturdy pioneers, with rifle and axe, in the very heart of the continent, blazed the way for an advancing civilization, and a liberty loving people covered the trackless waste with evidences of their thrift and prosperity" (*Salt Lake Tribune*, 5 July 1889).

With Mormons' increasing national identity after 1890, the two groups' rhetoric on responsibility quickly became remarkably similar. Mormons transferred part of their collective responsibility from the church's regionalized Zion to the nation. Both Mormons and non-Mormons prioritized public virtue. They conceived of the nation as a unit; public virtue meant that citizens had to look after the strength of the whole if individuals were to prosper. A YMMIA manual suggested that "[p]ublic virtue is evidently on the increase. A time there was when contagious diseases were smuggled, but today every citizen is an active detective against the hiding of pestilence. . . . More and more the line between the public welfare and individual interest is being obliterated and the individual is understanding more clearly that on the protection and progress of the whole depends his security and advancement" (n.d.g, 67). The manual made clear that strengthening the whole meant upholding status-quo institutions more than accommodating difference within the whole or seeking positive institutional change: "The man who thinks of the United States as my country, will no more deride its institutions than he would trample the flag in the mud, or dynamite the capitol at Washington. It is not *the* government, with him—it is *my* government, I in it and it in me. I for it, and it for me. It and I are one" (69–70).

Non-Mormons also framed the responsibility for being publicly virtuous in terms that closed off space for responsible dissent. The *Salt Lake Tribune* responded to a *Deseret Evening News* complaint about acquitting an accused murderer in Virginia by arguing that the church ought first to "cast the beam out of Utah's eye before we quarrel with the mote in Virginia's eye. . . . [L]et [Mormons] take thought unto the Utah law, and come to the support of the law-abiding people here and join with them in stating that they will foreswear all law-breaking from henceforth, and will join with the well-disposed, law-respecting people here and see that the laws are enforced in their fullness, first of all in Utah" (4 July 1907). The *Tribune* was complaining here about the lack of regional enthusiasm for prosecuting polygamous relationships. Responsible citizenship increasingly meant denying that nonconformist practices could be based on legitimate reasons.[15]

Citizens' responsibilities to support the nation's wars also occupied significant regional attention, particularly among LDS leaders. Love for the nation caused Zion's youth, on counsel from the prophet, to stand against Spain in the Spanish-American War and to cling to the American flag when driven from Nauvoo into Mexican territory, Mormons suggested (Rich 1908b, 102–3; Young Men's Mutual Improvement Association n.d.l, 11–16). Ronald Walker (1992) argues that while LDS leaders felt that war was a general evil, they refused to evaluate particular wars in moral terms, a policy D. Michael Quinn (1984) contends they came to support (despite some disagreement among leaders) only during the Spanish-American War. Mormon leaders wished wars would never be necessary, Walker suggests; but once the country engaged in war, Mormon leaders counseled, a good citizen conformed to the demands of the state. Walker and Quinn both find that, with previous impediments to unqualified nationalism removed by the late 1890s, many Mormons were filled with patriotic and imperialistic fervor during the Spanish-American War. While many Saints were also reluctant to become involved in World War I, once the United States entered, Mormons leaders insisted that citizens should support the war effort (Austin 1917b; Young Men's Mutual Improvement Association n.d.l, 11–16). Despite church leaders' enthusiastic support, Kerry William Bate (1995) reports many residents in a mostly Mormon rural Utah town were ambivalent about the war. They questioned the war's premises much more than church leadership appears to have. (Some individual church leaders also had private doubts, though most of their public action conformed to wartime demands [Lund n.d.; Smoot 1997]).

Mormon leaders also concerned themselves with citizen responsibility for raising a moral younger generation. By doing so, the leaders claimed, citizens demonstrated faithfulness to their forebears who had struggled for blessings. John Henry Smith asked the Saints if they were better citizens than their fathers and mothers and if they had improved on what their parents had given them (1906, 23). Charles Hart asserted that the Saints owed it to the nation to produce "worthy citizens, men who have embodied in their lives those principles that have been taught during this conference" (1909, 116; see also McKay 1912, 56; and J. F. Smith 1917, 6). Part of producing such citizens meant bearing children; Charles A. Callis hoped that Americans would join him in "denouncing the awful crime of race suicide" (1917, 134).[16] LDS ideals of producing model American citizens thus merged with those of more secular organizations.

LDS and non-LDS rhetorics of responsibility also converged on the economic requirements of citizenship. Good citizens had a responsibility to care for themselves individually, as families, and to help develop communities and the region.[17] When Hyrum M. Smith, an LDS apostle and the son of church president Joseph F. Smith, was asked in the Smoot hearings to respond to a claim he made that temporal and spiritual matters could not be separated, he said that he did not mean the church could dictate in voting but instead meant the church promoted the ideals of citizenship: "That is, the looking after themselves, their families, their condition in the church, taking care of their premises. . . . I mean being frugal, industrious, . . . build up their country, take care of their flocks and herds, properly fence their fields . . . and such things as that. That is what I mean by temporal advice" (U.S. Congress 1906, 1:508). Good citizens were responsible for promoting economic development through existing norms and institutions. Utah's Attorney General M. A. Breeden paid tribute to the Mormon pioneers in terms that pointed to an ethic of citizens' economic responsibilities, one that could fully materialize only with the cessation of hostilities between Mormons and non-Mormons:

> To go before, open the way, unfold, tunnel the mountains, bridge the streams, till the soil, subdue the savage, build the home, erect the schoolhouse, build the altar, and raise the cross of Christian hope. This is but a brief index to what a pioneer is. . . . Now, my friends, if we could eliminate all the bickerings and misunderstandings from our borders and be firmly united in purpose, no land could compete with us in our race for the ascendancy in Christian development, business enterprise and social peace and happiness! We have an honest, rugged, liberty loving people in this mountain country, the brightest, bravest, and the best. (Quoted in *Deseret Evening News*, 24 July 1907)

An increased desire to systematize requirements of patriotism and good citizenship accompanied this convergence of identification. One of the YMMIA's goals "is to help in the preparation of young people for the duties of life. The aim is to fit them for good citizenship in the country and in the Church, and to make them thoroughly useful to the age in which they live" (Young Men's Mutual Improvement Association n.d.e, 3). Public schools held similar goals. The objectives of a section on civics were "to acquaint pupils with the different modes of government, and particularly our own government; to inculcate patriotism and love for our country; and to prepare with good citizenship" (Utah State Text Book Committee [1897], 77; see also State Department of Public Instruction 1918b, 69). LDS Church leaders had the same sentiments. One argued that respect for the law could not be enforced simply by the power of the law; people must be taught to internalize it; more systematic training in citizenship was needed (S. L. Richards 1919, 102).

In general, church leaders increasingly insisted that church members should be (and were) loyal to the nation. Church members were to be wary of the forces of anarchy (signified most often by the Mexican Revolution, labor movements—especially those portrayed as advocating violence—and the Russian Revolution). George Albert Smith argued that the United States was a free country only as long as people obeyed the laws (1911, 44), adding (with a discursive form matching that of long-standing appeals for loyalty to the church and its leaders):

> I do hope and pray that the sons and daughters of God, born and reared under the folds of Old Glory, or who have made this their home, may stand true and faithful to the institutions of our country, and may ever raise their voices in defense of the law of the land, for it is the law of God to us in so much as it is for the uplifting of the children of men. Let us not associate ourselves with bands of men, or associations of individuals, who may be finding fault and criticising, striv-

ing to tear down, vilifying men who are called to preside over us, destroying, as far as their influence may be, the free institutions that our Father has blessed us with. . . . Let it be known throughout the land in which we live that in the valleys of these mountains there stands a body of men and women true to the institutions of our country, true to the privileges that God has blessed us with. (45)

Thus the regional discourse of responsibility increased generally and among Mormons grew closer in form to the rhetoric of nineteenth-century non-Mormons. The responsibility of loyal citizenship meant obedience to laws and cultural norms, axiomatic expressions of patriotism, and involvement in capitalist development. It did not mean concern for those with too few rights. No longer did a citizen's or a group's responsibilities include analysis of society and efforts to follow that analysis. For most people, the analysis had already been completed. Instead, the country needed citizens putting national norms into practice. Just as responsibilities of national loyalty narrowed, so did demand for political and cultural conformity.

Super-Americanization

A Liberalizing Project

The turn-of-the-century Americanization of Mormons was very much a project of liberalization. Non-Mormons, both inside and outside the region, worried that Mormons were not sufficiently free individuals. Their culture of obedience to the church made them something other than free Americans. American liberals have believed that individuals need protection from the tyranny of the large social body (Kelly 1984, 20–21).[18] Non-Mormons especially wanted Mormons to become liberals vis-à-vis their church. The church body must not infringe on Mormons' individual political freedoms, non-Mormons argued. This project of liberalism did not entirely cohere. Non-Mormons wanted Mormons to be consummate liberal individualists in terms of the church's influence on their politics, but in reality one "social tyranny" replaced another as the ideal. Mormons were expected not so much to shed unreflective political habits as to transfer them from serving the church to serving the American nation and its political system. Demanding such conformance from Mormons affected non-Mormons as well; they created with Mormons an unusually strong regional ethic of nationalist conformance. The Mormon culture region Americanized not simply by establishing American institutions but also by insisting that regional inhabitants strongly identify with nationalist ideology.

But perhaps those insisting on conformance to the nation were not so incoherent in their liberalism. Liberalism, in its strongest ideological form, claims radical separation between self and others. It minimizes, if not deny-ing altogether, the situatedness of individuals within communities (or dis-courses, depending on one's theoretical preference) and tends to separate spheres of life from one another (Sandel 1984). As such, liberalism's polit-ical forms and intellectual philosophy have been critiqued from a wide range of viewpoints—from the communitarian politics of Michael J. Sandel (1984) to the poststructural feminism of Donna Haraway (1988), for ex-ample. Liberalism, when dependent on this strong notion of individual sov-ereignty, leads to political individuals fragmented from their social context. Each sphere of life loses connection with others. In the case under study, changed regional norms enforced radical separation of religion from poli-tics; the religious individual was presumed to have little relation to the po-litical individual.

An equally serious problem stems from liberalism's deviance from real-ity. Liberalism can never produce the radically independent individual it posits. Liberalism's ideology obscures this fact as well as the social alle-giances that help constitute individuals. Liberals (except perhaps a few lib-eral theorists) do not account for how the nationalist community constructs individuals. In this regional case, Mormons and non-Mormons both saw the region's "Americanization" as a victory for the independent individual. Neither group saw very well that Americanization implied transfer of Mor-mons' political obedience from one institution to another: from the church to the nation and its political system. Regional citizens came not only to *participate* in nation-state politics, as most accounts of LDS Americaniza-tion suggest (for example, Handy 1991, 55–56), but also to expect unwa-vering *conformance* to national ideologies.

Cultural and Political Conformance

The *Salt Lake Tribune*'s report of the Saints' Twenty-fourth of July cele-bration in 1880 (the *Tribune* used the term *uprising*) is a good starting point for showing how cultural and political conformance to American ideals be-came a regional norm (25 July 1880). The report came amid bitter compe-tition between Mormons and non-Mormons for control over Utah politics. Non-Mormons, at least, thought a rivalry had developed between Fourth of July and Twenty-fourth of July celebrations (see also *July Twenty-Fourth* [1888]). The article rhetorically separated the Mormon regional Zion from the United States; the real region, inhabited by real Americans, was Utah:

> The [Mormon] people understood . . . that in some inexplicable manner the so-called region was on trial and they rallied from all quarters and came down on Zion like a swarm of locusts. Old men crippled with rheumatism, young yip-yaps

under banners whose words they could not read, thanks to the policy of the priests to keep the Territory steeped in ignorance, . . . people from all climes and of all colors. . . . It was a *potpourri,* a conglomeration of nationalities, with the American in the great minority, a mass of humanity who thought not of their adopted country, have not a spark of love for Utah, but whose sole and controlling idea was Mormonism. . . . No where so much as in Utah can so many different people be seen.

Mormonism was more than simply a conglomeration of nationalities. To the *Tribune,* the emblematic figure in the parade was a wagon carrying what was supposed to be a happy polygamous family: "There was no happiness visible. One of the wives had a child at her breast and looked tired as did all. . . . All the occupants seemed to be ashamed." It was not just polygamy that dispirited the Mormons; it was the whole system of Mormonism. Mormons did not possess American optimism for life. Nevertheless, the *Tribune* noted, "[d]uring the afternoon the great majority sought refuge from the heat precisely as on the Fourth, by hastening to the different pleasure resorts, etc. The saloons were crowded, and whoever says the Saints are a temperate people is a perfect stranger to the truth."

This article captures many of the significant charges regional non-Mormons made about LDS nonconformance to American cultural norms: Mormonism encompassed too many foreigners and was too liberal toward the different races; Mormonism did not sufficiently require American economic individuality and loyalty from immigrants; polygamy evidenced Mormon cultural degradation; and, in any event, Mormons had their share of vices, contradicting the LDS claim of virtue. In subsequent decades, non-Mormons pressured the Saints into greater conformance with national norms; Mormons themselves wanted to demonstrate that they could be as American as other Americans. These norms of individualist economics, nationalist patriotism, and cultural progress and purity were, of course, regional non-Mormons' idealizations of American life (which had somewhat milder and later—1890s—counterparts in America generally [O'Leary 1999]). However, the norms assumed a kind of ideological reality through non-Mormons', and then Mormons', beliefs that the norms described American life.

In fact, the nineteenth-century non-Mormon suspicion that LDS immigrants were not being Americanized was exaggerated. William Mulder (1957) and Richard Jensen (1987) argue that although the church tried to make the transition to American life easier by encouraging ethnic self-support, the Mormon policy always was Americanization. The church expected converts to learn English and participate in local life. Nevertheless, the perception remained that Mormonism signified unacceptable cultural diversity (U.S. Congress 1906, 2:905, 3:158; Vermilye 1912). Messages continued to come from non-Mormons, both regionally and nationally, that America needed to control its diversity. For example, in arguing for the Senate's right to exclude anyone from its membership, a lawyer representing Reed Smoot's opponents said, "[W]e have entered upon a policy of expansion beyond the seas. . . . [T]he time will come . . . when those islands and their people . . . must be admitted into the Union as a State. . . . What kind of persons they will send here nobody can now predict. Will the Senate put shackles upon itself?" (U.S. Congress 1906, 4:430).

Instead of being satisfied with earlier efforts, church members after 1890 tried to prove racial and ethnic conformance. Mormons, or at least American Mormons, had always identified with white Americans. They felt they were part of the progress of civilization that America represented. But their persecution made them occasionally glimpse similarities between their own situation and that of others, as is reflected in this statement made at a meeting of Mormon women: "We are in as bad a fix as the Chinese, perhaps even a little worse, for when they were driven and mobbed, the President (under the sting of the Chinese Emperor's threats) sends a message to Congress asking for fair play for the Chinamen. But has he, with all that we have suffered, ever sent to Congress demanding justice for the 'Mormons?' No" (*"Mormon" Women's Protest* [1886], 15). Such recognition of similar situations did not foster solidarity with other oppressed groups. Mormons soon strongly distinguished between the civilization they thought they inhabited and the supposed backwardness of others. These others (Native Americans, Mexicans, Chinese) could escape from backwardness only by joining American civilization, of which Mormonism was an agent.[19]

Mormons emphasized their lineage links to founders of the American nation and to the easily assimilated and "civilized" British and Scandinavian races (Gates 1911; Robinson 1912, 76–77; A. Green 1999; Mauss 1999). Immigration to Utah as a Mormon meant that one became a thoroughgoing American and did not retain past loyalties and customs. One did not become a "hyphenated American" (A. Ivins 1911, 119; Nibley 1916, 132–33).[20] Mormons felt they were engaged in a race-building project, the culmination of American civilization (Ballard 1913a, 19–20; Hinckley 1916, 82–83). In the Smoot hearings, Joseph F. Smith showed that he understood Americanizers' expectations. When it was noted that he referred to the Saints as "my people," Smith replied, "I presume that I should not speak of them in that way, for all the American people are my people" (U.S. Congress 1906, 1:317). Mormons thus strove in the early decades of the twentieth century to be loyal to the nation through ethnic and cultural conformance. They

located themselves on the side of racial privilege. While the climate for ethnic and racial minorities was not as unfriendly or violent as in some western states, particularly California, many minorities found Mormons maintained as much cultural separation from them as non-Mormons did.[21] By
most retrospective measures, twentieth-century Mormons possessed all the
conceits of white American identity.

Mormons and non-Mormons also placed a premium on other aspects of
LDS conformance to American cultural norms. The Smoot hearings were one
forum among others that revived the notion of Mormons as un-American
and depraved for tolerating polygamy (as well as for covering it up and protecting lawbreakers) and for differentiating between LDS and non-LDS in
business, social organizations, and formal politics. Mormons were portrayed
as almost irredeemably un-American, with a loyalty to church principles that
superseded their American patriotism. Mormon authority was said to cover
all parts of life; the political and religious were not sufficiently separate.[22]
Non-Mormons essentially charged Mormons with masquerading as white
Americans. Non-Mormons claimed that the Saints' culture of obedience to
the church made them into something else (see also Givens 1997, 121–52;
and London 1919). Mormons—as well as increasing numbers of non-Mormons in the twentieth century—fought these charges and struggled to ensure
that little separated Mormons from non-Mormons other than spiritual beliefs.

One strategy was to concede the point that religion and politics were separate projects and to insist that Mormon loyalty to the church did not (and
would not, almost by definition) interfere with national loyalty. Here the
church acceded to the general understanding among American Protestant
leaders that the relatively new notion of separation between church and state
meant church leaders and missionaries were not to speak on politically partisan issues, at least not very often (Handy 1989, 293–94). Churches and
government were to recognize a distinction between religious and political
spheres. Nevertheless, if friendly cooperation worked to the mutual benefit
of both, the line separating the institutions could blur a bit. Scholars recognize that nondenominational Protestantism was assumed to be the basis
of American life, both in the project of Americanizing Mormons and elsewhere (Handy 1991, 19–25; Landsman 1998; Gordon 2002). Americans
were not quite ready to let Mormons join in this cozy agreement between
Protestantism and the state. A trust-busting Congress viewed Mormonism
as a monopoly that needed to be reined in (Flake 2000, 190–222; Gordon
2002, 183–87). Americans thus tried to ensure that a stronger notion of
separate spheres kept Mormonism out of politics.

Such sentiments marked the Smoot hearings where exchanges between Smoot's opponents and Joseph F. Smith resembled conversations between a schoolteacher and a pupil who is able, but reluctant, to give the desired answer. When asked what members should do if the law of the land and the law of the church differed, Smith went halfway and said that members were free to do as they wished. To some, the church took precedence, while others obeyed the nation. After more prodding by senators, however, Smith replied, "I think under the discipline that we have had for the last twenty years our people would obey the law of the land" (U.S. Congress 1906, 1:312–14, quote on 314). When B. H. Roberts was asked a similar question, he gave a similar answer: it would depend on the circumstance. Roberts said he could imagine situations where the nation's claim was more compelling and other situations where church's had priority (1:734). Smoot himself went even further. Unless he received a direct revelation from God—which he claimed he never had[23]—the law of the land would come first. He said he did not know of any church principle superseding the laws of the land; if anything, national laws were more binding, since the church enjoined obedience to the laws of the land (3:248–52).[24] In Smith's and Roberts's cases, even though they resisted giving the full answer desired, they both knew what it was, at least partially conceding that religion and politics could be separated.

The Smoot hearings separated religion and politics in other ways as well.[25] The primary lawyer against Smoot's seating asked a regional non-Mormon witness if ordinary lawbreaking differed from breaking the law because of a deeply seated religious belief. While the witness saw no difference, the lawyer (representing the fears of some regional non-Mormons) thought that breaking the law due to religious belief was a much greater menace to the government (2:834). He implied that, at least in the case of Mormonism, religion ought to go to more than ordinary trouble to keep from interfering with political matters. The fact that Mormons believed in revelation, coupled with the fact that they had historically (and in some cases still) said temporal and spiritual matters could not be separated, meant that a different, somewhat more rigid standard had to be applied to Mormons (3:470–78). "The acts of Senator Smoot [never specified other than membership in the church and its hierarchy; Smoot's opponents could find nothing specifically objectionable that he did] and his associates deny the sovereign; they repudiate the lawful government. . . . [T]hey are subversive of government. They do not merely breed anarchy, they are anarchy," he declared (3:478). Until the Mormon church demonstrated over a period of decades that it would act politically like a Protestant church, many non-

Mormons refused to treat it as anything but a threat to the government, one that required an extra thick wall of separation between church and state. Although Smoot eventually gained his seat, although many non-Mormons argued that such an interpretation was extreme, and although those fighting against the church could be branded as a small minority with primarily theological quarrels (1:601–7, 3:687, 3:720–21; see also Shipps 1987, 352–53), a majority of committee members incorporated this position in their report (4:467–97).[26]

Mormons knew they faced powerful opponents enforcing a separation of religion and politics. They had to reproduce the impression that religion and politics were essentially separate (and separable) projects. They could not afford to argue anymore that the church's claims might challenge the nation's interests in any serious way. The church would be allowed temporal authority to the extent that it looked after its own institutional economics and produced nationally useful and loyal citizens, but little further (U.S. Congress 1906, 1:75, 1:506–7, 3:133). In accepting the notion that religion and politics did not overlap, the Saints gradually downplayed a fundamental nineteenth-century tenet. Yet as Thomas Alexander (1986) and Susan Stryker (1992) argue, becoming a church in the accepted sense (renouncing the possibility of competing with the nation for loyalty) allowed the Mormon church to survive and even retain many distinctive doctrines.[27]

While the Smoot hearings focused on disciplining the church as an institution by asking whether it kept its authority out of politics, liberal expectations went beyond the church itself to individual members of the church. Mormons joined what Robert Booth Fowler calls a nation of liberal Protestant individuals (1994, 212). The strength of LDS Church–state separation implied an unusually strong regional norm of conformance with nationalist ideologies, however. Mormons learned that, unlike Protestants, they could not even indirectly mediate their American identity through their religion. The hearings reminded Mormons they were being held to a stricter standard than other Americans were. Smoot's opponents claimed Mormons took a temple oath binding them to fight against the nation (Smoot's opponents never satisfactorily established either what this oath meant or if there even was an oath setting Mormons against the nation in even an indeterminate sense). Instead of freely deciding whether the nation deserved their loyalty, as most other citizens were free to do, Mormons needed to claim they had taken no such oath and that they had nothing but loyalty to the nation (U.S. Congress 1906, 1:436–37).

The hearings also showcased liberal expectations through discussion of the Moses Thatcher controversy. Thatcher had been a member of the church's

Quorum of the Twelve Apostles when he ran for Congress in 1894 as a Democrat. Other church leaders complained then that he acted wrongly and should have consulted church leaders before running. They claimed that the church had a rule requiring high church officers to seek church permission before running for public office.[28] Thatcher held that he should not have to discuss his political practices with church leaders; eventually he was expelled from the quorum. Later, during the Smoot hearings, church leaders claimed a series of events beyond the candidacy question showed that Thatcher no longer cooperated with other church leaders and provoked the expulsion (on these other events, see Lund n.d., 12:77–96). Regarding the candidacy, church leaders argued the fundamental issue was not Thatcher's independence but whether the church could determine if its leadership would devote enough time to ecclesiastical duties.

Thomas Alexander maintains that the church leaders' motives were less innocent than their arguments suggest (1986, 8–11; and 1992, 252–54).[29] Republican church leaders in the 1890s were, in fact, allowed to exercise greater political influence than Democrat church leaders. But, Alexander argues, such political partisanship may have been as much (or more) a case of Mormon leaders' trying to deal the best they could with a no-win situation as their harboring continued desires to control Utah politics. Because Mormons blamed the Republican Party for the 1880s national fight against the church, most church members leaned Democratic when the church ended its own political party in the 1890s. The motivation of church leaders, Alexander claims, was to ensure that a majority of church members did not join the Democratic Party. Without any political maneuvering, a majority of Mormons would have been Democrats. Church leaders figured that if most Mormons were Democrats, the church would face the charge of control over Utah politics all over again. Better, they reasoned, to give behind-the-scenes support to the Republican Party in hopes Mormons would divide more or less evenly among the two parties than to face renewed charges that Mormons rejected the American two-party system (Alexander 1991, 310–20). Whatever church leaders' motivations, some regional non-Mormons regarded the rule regulating church leaders' political activity as evidence the church would not willingly give members political independence (E. Lyman 1986). Smoot's opponents' lawyers used the Thatcher incident to argue that church leaders should not join the Senate.[30]

Smoot's opponents pursued this argument further through the B. H. Roberts case. Roberts shared Thatcher's situation in many ways. A church leader who ran for Congress in 1894 and 1896 as a Democrat and who at first disagreed with the rule, he shared Thatcher's concern that church leaders had unfairly promoted Republican Party interests (Alexander 1986, 9–11). However, church leaders eventually persuaded him that they were not trying to infringe on his independence or seeking to retain control of Utah politics but instead were merely attempting to ensure that the church's affairs were not neglected (U.S. Congress 1906, 1:723).[31] Nevertheless, even this understanding of the church's rule did not suit many senators in the hearings. Any such conception, Senator Joseph W. Bailey from Texas said, was "irreconcilable with the duties of good citizenship. It seems to me a man must always leave himself free to serve his country . . . and he must do that without agreeing that he will first obtain the permission of any religious, industrial, or business association" (1:726). The hearings taught Mormons that nothing takes priority over the nation and that their church membership and obligations should have nothing to do with their political activity.

What bothered some non-Mormons most was the possibility that, regardless of whether the church reduced its political activity, many members were individually unwilling to take the church out of their politics. In spite of Mormon attestations to the contrary, Smoot's opponents did not believe most church members had truly separated church and politics. Orlando Powers, perhaps Smoot's opponents' most credible witness, expressed the view well: "It is the un-American domination by the hierarchy of the people of that faith, the constant teaching that they must obey counsel, the belief that the head of the church is inspired and speaks the word of God when he is inspired and the interference in our political affairs . . ." (1:885). Powers followed Smoot's opponents' lawyer in believing that Mormons would not "ever achieve individual independence as long as this doctrine . . . is the doctrine and policy of the church" (1:921). While Powers expressed respect for Mormons in many areas, on this lack of political independence he said, "I would condemn the people; . . . it is such an un-American doctrine, so contrary to the spirit of our institutions, that the Mormon people ought not to permit it to prevail" (1:923).

Smoot's lawyers took the strategy of trying to prove that, contrary to Powers's claims, Mormons acted as independently and individualistically as anyone else. They brought Mormons and non-Mormons to the stand to testify that Mormons did not expect political counsel from church leaders or necessarily follow it in the rare cases it was given. W. J. N. Whitecotton, a non-Mormon lawyer from Provo, Smoot's hometown, said the Mormon people "very strongly resent interference from anybody. I never met a man who admitted that he had been approached by any church authority to be influenced in his vote, but I know that the people pride themselves in independent suffrage and I do not believe any considerable number in Utah will accept any dictation from anybody" (2:672). Whitecotton, as well as other witnesses, testified that Smoot's previous activity in the Republican Party, not his church leadership, made him the inevitable candidate for the Senate; that many Mormons opposed Smoot's nomination; that he never heard Smoot was the church's candidate until the hearings; and that most Utahns endorsed the church rule about church leaders' receiving permission before running for political office, construing it as a leave of absence, not an endorsement (2:681–83).[32]

This argument about church members' individual political independence often relied on discourses of manhood. As feminist political theorists argue, the concept of the liberal individual is rarely as universally encompassing as it seems. When most people have referred to the liberal individual, they mean a man, not a woman. They take the separation between public and private spheres and women's relegation (with implied power differentials) to the private sphere as givens (Pateman 1989; Pateman and Shanley 1991). Both sides' arguments over individual Mormons' political independence betray this assumption.[33] True American citizenship came to be equated with the gendered notion of manhood. When Joseph F. Smith denied that the consultation policy for church leaders on political candidacy eliminated political independence, he used the language of independent manhood. Church leaders regularly consult one another on many issues, he said, adding, "They have not felt that they were sacrificing their manhood in doing so, nor that they were submitting to improper dictation, . . . nor that to any improper degree were their rights and duties as American citizens being abridged or interfered with" (U.S. Congress 1906, 1:170). Similarly, William Hyde Stalker gave a speech against Mormon power by arguing that his father, an excommunicated Mormon, "committed the unpardonable sin of asserting his manhood, trading where he pleased and exercising his right as a citizen" (quoted in 2:638). Manhood and independence, to church opponents, depended on not blindly following the wishes of church leaders. Henry W. Lawrence, a former Mormon, testified that he left the church when "I simply asserted my independence and manhood . . . I simply got to a point where I commenced to doubt the system and commenced to think for myself. That made me act a little independent" (4:104).

This normative, gendered liberal individualization of Mormons only went so far as to separate individuals from their religious moorings. Non-Mormons did not actually expect Mormons to become radical individualists; they only used such rhetoric to enforce a certain church-state relationship. Despite—or maybe because of—the liberal emphasis on individual decision making and manhood, what replaced Mormon political unity was not so much independence (if independence derives from making sense of connections between communities and discourses to which an agent is subject) as a new kind of conformance—political party conformance. Liberalism's account of the separation between public and private is inadequate. As a result, liberalism tends to see neither its own gender specificity nor its need to be supplemented by more communal ideologies (in practice, usually nationalistic). When political ideologies took the place of religious ideologies for Mormons, few people noticed that the ideal of the liberal individual was compromised by insistence on nationalist conformance. Both regional and nonregional non-Mormons expected church members to find a place within the American two-party system and to be as loyal and unthinking in political party allegiance as it was supposed they had been to the church. Non-Mormons wanted not so much independence in Mormons as fragmentation and separation of loyalties. Mormons were expected to transfer political rootedness and allegiance from the church not to the sovereign liberal individual or even any regional community but to either of the two major national political parties and the two-party system.[34]

The Smoot hearings made it clear that voting the political party line and not wavering from election to election evidenced Mormon "independence." The minority report, recommending Smoot's seating in the Senate, noted that it was understandable that not all forms of church mandates had completely ceased but that Mormons had rapidly improved their political habits. It reported that Mormons stayed closer to voting the party line (either Republican or Democratic) and not switching parties from election to election than did non-Mormons (4:523–24). The hearings almost literally constituted a site at which—to adapt a phrase from Paul Kleppner through Swierenga (1989, 161)—political parties were anointed as "political churches" with conformance to their ideologies amounting to "political confessionalism."

Since Smoot's opponents asserted that Mormons were not necessarily Republicans or Democrats but that they were Mormons first and party members only secondarily, Smoot's lawyers presented witness after witness, both regional Mormons and non-Mormons, who claimed that the vast majority of Mormons were no longer politically influenced by the church. Instead, Mormons had become loyal Democrats or Republicans. Many witnesses argued that Mormons conformed to a party line as much as or more than non-Mormons did. For example, Mrs. W. H. Jones, a Salt Lake City Methodist active in the Republican Party, said she had been active in the Liberal Party when it existed. "I . . . thought a Mormon ought not to live." But now, she claimed, the Mormon Republicans she knew stayed as faithful to the party as the Gentile Republicans, perhaps even more so (U.S. Congress 1906, 3:175, 3:177).[35]

The true measure of Mormons' acceptability lay not in political independence per se, since non-Mormons expected them to replace one type of conformity with another. Rather, it came in independence of spheres (religious from political) and greater conformance within the accepted political sphere. The Americanization of Mormons and Utah, in this respect, was a project of fragmentation. Private religious viewpoints were supposed to be separable from and not affect public political opinions.[36] Non-Mormons did not simply want the church to stop dictating political stances to its members and expecting compliance. They also did not want the Saints, even as individuals, to bring their religious experiences to bear on analysis of social conditions. Nothing about the Saints' experiences as Mormons (unless it conformed to Protestant/capitalist views) was to affect the world of politics. They wanted fragmented individuals whose lives reflected a radical separation between religion and politics and who could be counted on to conform to the country's norms of political party allegiance. They established greater separation between Mormonism and the state than between mainstream Protestantism and the state (Handy 1991, 30–36).[37] The Mormon culture region became a place of unusually strong norms on separation of church and state and on political party loyalty.

Mormons' conformance to national norms also took the form of defining their own experiences as contributions to American norms and American progress (see also Foote 1997, 246–62). Mormon cultural and social uniqueness came to be figured as a part of, rather than distinctive from, American life. The Saints often found parallels between themselves and American colonists. Although such references had always been designed to place the Saints within the American tradition (see the report of the Twenty-fourth of July parade in *Deseret Evening News*, 26 July 1880), these allusions shifted over time from emphasizing the right to protest against oppression to focusing on American conformance. When H. C. Brown spoke of rights denied virtuous Mormon women by antipolygamy legislation and withdrawal of suffrage, she said, "We are here, not as Latter-day Saints, but as American citizens—members of that great commonwealth which our noble grandsires fought and bled to establish . . ." (*"Mormon" Women's Protest* [1886], 12). The *Home Writer* argued in 1882 that the Puritans, once persecuted, had become persecutors "and now cry aloud for the destruction and Extirpation of a body of people who have done as much to build up America in the West as they themselves have to build up America in the East" (24 February 1882, 4–5). Although this passage foreshadows the stronger later identification of the Mormon region with the American West, it does not quite identify Mormons with other westerners. Rather, it implies that just as

eastern American society arose out of Puritan culture, western society originated in Mormonism.

Later references seek less to justify LDS difference than to locate LDS similarity to the rest of the nation by comparing Mormons with the nation's
founders (see, for example, Gates 1911, 21–22). When asked whether LDS
leaders once controlled members' votes, even the former Mormon John P.
Meakin suggested that Mormons had simply participated in the American experience "like the Pilgrim fathers in early times" (U.S. Congress 1906, 2:801).
Mormons intended not so much to assert difference, this answer implied; instead past circumstances required creating a society that was distinct from the
rest of the country but still modeled itself on the revered national founders'
experiences. Now that Mormons had weathered the early storms, they could
wholeheartedly conform to the contemporary American experience.

Mormon interpretations of American and Utah history began to parallel
secular views. Earlier Mormon accounts of U.S. history and politics centered
on the Constitution (Editorial in *Deseret Evening News,* 3 July 1890; Young
Men's Mutual Improvement Association 1891, 1895). Increasingly, American progress joined the stories (*Wasatch Wave,* 30 July 1905). Both Mormons and non-Mormons framed Utah history, especially Mormon history,
as another part of the development and progress of the American nation.[38]

Most important, both Mormons and non-Mormons drew Mormons into
national conformance and unity by interpreting Mormon regional history as
part of the larger story of the American West. A *Salt Lake Tribune* editorial
signaled the beginnings of a shift from conceptualizing Mormon history as
an anti-American (or at least nationally neutral) project to viewing it as a
piece of the larger American saga: "We think the Mormon people should celebrate Pioneer day [24 July] with more enthusiasm. . . . The coming hither of
that little band was a great event. . . . It is on such step that history mounts
its stairs, and such an event should be honored" (25 July 1889). Later the
theme was further developed. In an 1898 celebration, non-Mormons praised
the work of the Saints. C. C. Goodwin, publisher of the *Salt Lake Tribune,*
said the Mormon "pioneers came here to found and build up a new civilization" (*Salt Lake Tribune,* 26 July 1898). Whether he thought so then, such
sentiments increasingly meant that Mormons came not to escape American
civilization but to establish American civilization in an uncivilized and barren land (see the prayer by the Reverend Iliff opening the celebration in the
Salt Lake Tribune, 26 July 1898). Even in 1907, with renewed mistrust between Mormons and non-Mormons, the *Tribune* stated:

> We . . . join heartily in the spirit with the appropriate celebration of the day [24
> July], and trust that as the years go by the observances of the day will broaden,

and will lose their rigid sectarian character, taking on more the shape that such observances do in other States, as a civic remembrance of the pioneers who first brought such civilization as they had to the wilds and unbroken wastes of America. . . . We observe signs of the broadening of spirit and observance here from time to time and rejoice in them. (24 July 1907)

Mormons were of similar minds; they, too, increasingly framed Mormon history in terms of national progress and development. Early on, this interpretation was not very coherent, but there were signs it would develop. In 1890, the *Deseret Evening News* wrote, "Some sneers have been indulged in by persons who are ever ready to misinterpret the motives and acts of the majority of our people over the fact that the Twenty-fourth of July holds so dear a place in their hearts. But have we not all good reason to commemorate the day when the pilgrim band who led the way to these valleys came out of the canyon after their weary journey, planted the flag of our country upon this then Mexican soil and marked the spot for this fine and prosperous city?" (23 July 1890). Later Mormon expressions converged with non-Mormon interpretations, as is reflected in a 23 July 1898 article in the *Deseret Evening News*: "The entrance of the Pioneers in Salt Lake Valley . . . will always be gratefully and reverently remembered in this region as one of the great events in the history of our country during this century. It was but a small band . . . but it was the advance guard of the hosts that under Providence were destined to conquer an immense region for civilization and for the heaven-born principles of which the American Constitution is the most perfect expression in existence" (see also the editorials and special section commemorating LDS pioneers in *Deseret Evening News*, 24 July 1907).

By the 1910s, little separated the way Mormons and non-Mormons viewed the pioneers and regional history (see, for example, *Deseret News*, 24 July 1916 and 24 July 1920; and *Salt Lake Tribune*, 24 July 1920). LDS/regional history no longer justified complaints against the nation. Instead it gave Mormons and non-Mormons reason to jointly affirm allegiance to the American nation's progress.[39] The increasing emphasis in both Independence Day and Pioneer Day celebrations on recreational pursuits rather than on more strictly patriotic activities also could occur only with growing agreement on this Americanized interpretation of regional history.[40] As the *Tribune* argued in an article noting how Independence Day was given over to amusements:

There was no organized celebration of the day, no parade and no oratory. With the absence of the flamboyant spread-eagleism which has characterized the day on past occasions—sometimes with so little, real intrinsic value—but the people themselves were fully imbued with the spirit of the day; they did not require any orator to tell them of their country's greatness and its achievements—its past, present, and future; they know these things and realize them with the real American conditions which surround them and begin to prevail generally in Utah. (5 July 1907)

This desire for regional agreement and unity also manifested itself in the Smoot hearings. Some of Smoot's opponents claimed that Mormons were still too clannish, but Smoot's lawyers produced witness after witness who disputed the claim. Mormons and non-Mormons wished to be (and in most respects were) united in the region, they argued. Other than religious belief, nothing essential separated Mormons from non-Mormons, or would within a few years (see, for example, U.S. Congress 1906, 3:344–49). According to Mary G. Coulter, a non-Mormon member of the state legislature that elected Smoot a senator, "The West is a rapid-moving, fast-growing country and we are bound to overcome [polygamy and church political dictation] in time. . . . But those of us who have witnessed the old-time antagonisms and who are living and working for the new growth and progress, do not believe in inquisitorial methods." Most people think that colonization, education, and development "will, in time, eradicate all of the old and objectionable conditions" (3:170). Non-Mormons used the term *young Utah* to refer to the younger generation of Mormons eager to put the past behind them, cooperate with non-Mormons, and embrace American culture (3:759; Ericksen [1922] 1975, 77). Even some of Smoot's opponents admitted that Mormons and non-Mormons had become more similar, although they added that dominance by the church itself prevented some members from moving in this direction as fast as they wished (1:883, 1:929).

Increasing numbers of non-Mormons expressed a regional consciousness. The problems of the past could not be solved by legislation from outside the region, they argued; instead, it took people with sensitivity to the strength of Mormon belief and appreciation for the Mormon people to bury nineteenth-century tensions. Such sentiments manifested themselves in regard to men married plurally before the Manifesto who continued to live with more than one wife. Joseph F. Smith explained how he continued living plurally without prosecution: "[T]here is a sentiment prevailing, an all-pervading sentiment, in Utah, among Mormons and Jews and Gentiles, not to interfere with men's families who entered that plural status before the manifesto was issued and before statehood . . ." (U.S. Congress 1906, 1:153).[41] Although many witnesses regretted that these cases were not prosecuted, wished that polygamy could die faster, and doubted the church's sincerity about ending polygamy, few disputed this general regional understanding. Most non-Mormons had come to realize what Mormons had faced previously as well as the strength of their religious convictions and were disinclined to stir up old antagonisms within communities and Utah. Orlando Powers captured the view of many non-Mormon witnesses (though there were disagreements over his assessment of the speed of change):

> First of all, of course, we want peace in Utah. We would like to be like the rest of the country. We want to make of it a State like the States of the rest of the Union. We want the Mormon people to be like the rest of the American people; but we realize that there is a condition there which the people of the East do not— and I presume, can not—understand.
>
> . . .
>
> The bitterness that was so intense between Mormons and gentiles that it is hard to describe it, has in a great measure passed away, although it exists, unfortunately, to some extent yet.
>
> . . .
>
> I have great faith in the people, not only of the country at large, but of Utah. I can not believe otherwise than that in this free Government, after a time—that is the trouble; I fear I will not live to see it—the Mormon Church will take its place, where it ought to take it, like the rest of the churches, in the country. (1:884, 1:897, 1:898)

The very act of asserting a "there," where inhabitants held normative practices outsiders were unlikely to understand, was a place-creating act (Curry 1999, 99). Regional inhabitants thought Mormons and non-Mormons should not be culturally separate in the region. No longer was it taboo for non-Mormons to praise Mormons' virtues and feel pride in the region's development (U.S. Congress 1906, 2:495, 2:742, 2:794, 3:396, 3:758).[42] James E. Talmage, an LDS leader, argued that God separated Mormons from the world only to allow them to be trained; God never intended them to stay isolated (1919, 96). Questioning the meaning of national loyalty, like separatism and other elements of Mormon radicalism, became historical contingencies that made sense at the time but had little relation to twentieth-century regional society. Likewise, national organizations hoping to have a regional presence, such as the Red Cross during wartime efforts, learned to live with the Mormons. Such organizations served their own interests by putting aside preconceptions about Mormons and working through the church's organizational structure (Alexander 1986, 47–48). Mormons and non-Mormons thus found a basis for cooperation by moving beyond past antagonisms over national loyalty, just as they had with conflict over capitalist development (Poll 1987, 327–29). It seems that Mormons had forgotten, suppressed, or regarded as merely an artifact of the age their sentiments of 1880 that were reflected in this *Deseret Evening News* declaration: "We say that if the price of Statehood is an unholy alliance with the debasing and corrupt thing in this degenerate age called civilization, God Almighty grant that she may remain in her present condition of territorial spinsterhood!" (6 July 1880). Mormons never fully explained how "civilization" changed enough for Mormonism to warmly embrace it in the twentieth century.[43]

Nathan O. Hatch argues that a key feature of new nineteenth-century American religious movements was their democratizing tendency. In spite of the irony of their own nondemocratic structures, these movements denied the strong distinction between laity and clergy, empowered ordinary people, and promoted aspirations to overthrow coercive social structures (1989, 96–97; see also Leone 1979). Even in the late 1800s, such democratizing tendencies no doubt appealed to many new and established Latter-day Saints alike. Most non-Mormons and some Mormons, however, felt the church increasingly reinforced its own undemocratic structures and gave less power to society's dispossessed. Rather than rethink communitarian democracy, they opted for American liberal nationalist individualism. They thought the region needed stronger conformance with national norms, not any fresh evaluation of those norms.

Jumping on the Bandwagon

The regional effect of changes in the discourse of rights, the rhetoric of responsibility, and the importance of cultural and political conformity was that regional inhabitants jumped on the national bandwagon. The Mormon church, in particular, sought ways to address its decreasing power in members' lives. While members moved away from religious unity in politics, conformance to the American system—not strong political individualism—became the norm. In this context, the LDS Church reinterpreted its relationship with the nation in a way that gave it additional purchase in members' lives. By identifying more strongly and consistently with the nation (as Protestant churches already did), the church regained a political influence to which other Americans could not easily object. Religion and liberal politics, while competitive in many ways, can also be complementary (Kelly 1984, 24–25; Fowler 1994, 202–8). Religion contains powers of legitimation and conviction that are very useful to politics. When these powers act in the service of the state, as Mormonism's came to in the early twentieth century, the state has much less reason to object to religion's political influence.

Within the transformed region, questioning the meaning of national loyalty became a nonviable option for both Mormons and non-Mormons. A few groups, like the socialists, tried to debate the issue by proposing a socialist internationalism, but dominant regional conversations increasingly marginalized their viewpoints. By failing to enter into productive conversation with Mormons, socialists limited their impact on those Saints who may have inclined toward internationalism. For those who chose to remain within the mainstream of regional life, either as Mormons or non-Mormons, few options appeared beside jumping on the national bandwagon and giving unquestioned loyalty to the nation-state. For Mormons, these options narrowed partly because of changing doctrinal emphases. Mormons' focus shifted somewhat from the regional to the national scale. The LDS notion of Zion expanded to encompass the nation.[44]

The nation as a key political actor, with a significant destiny, became more important in Mormon thought. Before 1890, but decreasingly thereafter, Mormons spoke of the United States as the context in which the church and Zion would develop and work out their destiny. The important thing about the nation was that it provided religious freedom and liberty; whether the nation expanded or flourished was relatively unimportant as long as it allowed the regional Zion to grow and progress. Early Mormons held that America's free institutions provided support for the ultimately greater kingdom of God (Hatch 1989, 102–3), not the other way around. The nation was the context; the church, with its regionalized Zion, was the actor. In 1880, the church's president, John Taylor, argued that church members should sustain the national government where possible and call for reform in the nation. But the reason was less that the nation needed to perform any special labor than that the Elders of Israel (the LDS priesthood) would eventually raise a standard of freedom to the world, and they needed a suitable environment in which to prepare for that moment (J. Taylor 1880, 102; for remnants of this view, see also F. Lyman 1899, 40; and J. H. Smith 1906, 23–24).

After it became clear that the United States was not about to crumble because it persecuted the Saints, a greater sense of American national destiny emerged among the Saints. The Manifesto, the end of the LDS People's Party, and the postponing of millennial expectations signaled that the LDS leadership saw the need for closer contact between the church and the world (Alexander 1991, 262–305). Almost a year before the Manifesto, church leaders began planning for a new relationship with the nation (Alexander 1991, 257–59). Earlier statements claimed that the fortunes of all nations, including the United States, were separate from Zion's destiny and subject to God's discretion (Alexander 1991, 237–39); now the idea gained strength that the United States would play an important role in helping the Saints and Zion accomplish their destiny. To Joseph F. Smith, God created the nation so that the kingdom of God could be established. Yet the nation was not simply a context of liberty. It also promoted freedom through its power

and might: "If the Lord had not prepared the way by laying the foundations of this glorious nation, it would have been impossible . . . to have laid
the foundations for the coming of His great kingdom. . . . His hand has been
over this nation, and it is His purpose and design to enlarge it, make it glorious above all others, and to give it dominion and power over the earth,
to the end that those who are kept in bondage may be brought to the enjoyment of the fullest freedom and liberty of conscience possible for intelligent men to exercise in the earth" (1903a, 73; see also F. Lyman 1907). A
regional Zion was no longer the only important actor in the LDS eschatological drama. America's increasing strength and power was desirable in its
own right.

Church leaders began reminding Saints that Joseph Smith had once called
all of North and South America the land of Zion (G. Cannon 1898a, 83–85;
Roberts 1908, 106–7). God's work lay as much in the national Zion as in
the regional Zion. "Many people," George Q. Cannon noted, "imagine that
when we talk about the triumph of the Church of God we mean to confine
that triumph to those who belong to our Church. Not so; this is for the
whole world. It is for all America, as well as for Utah. God has made most
glorious promises to this nation, the Lord has destined to make it the head
of all the nations of the earth . . ." (1899, 48). Increasingly, God would establish his ways as much through the might and influence of the United
States as through LDS missionary efforts. No real difference existed between the nation's interests and those of the church and kingdom. Instead
of supplanting the nation, as was earlier expected, the church would perfect it (J. F. Smith 1907). The nation and the church were related, "not [as]
a union of church and state, but the relationship of a common purpose, and
that purpose God's—he who was the founder of this Church and also the
founder of this nation," Orson Whitney declared (1909, 72). God was just
as willing to fight the nation's battles as to protect the Saints (Robinson
1908, 75–77). Church leaders interpreted the biblical prophecy that the law
would go forth from Zion and the word of the Lord from Jerusalem to
mean that God would establish American principles of government
throughout the world as the gospel spread from Salt Lake City (Robinson
[1907, 93–95] and Roberts [1908, 108–11] are two of many such interpretations). Some essentially equated the LDS gospel and American liberty
(Whitney 1909, 72–74; on attempts elsewhere to link religious identity and
national identity, see Gallaher 1997; and Raivo 1997).

Similarly, the Saints' own mission was as much to make Americans as to
make Mormons. Samuel W. Richards, a former president of the British mis-

sion, recounted that when the British government asked him why so many converts were emigrating, "I told them that I was sending people to a country where they could own a farm and be as independent in their living as the lords and peers were there" (1905, 88; see also F. Lyman 1909a, 120–21). When the church was put on the defensive by the American Party's accusations and the Smoot hearings, church leaders felt compelled to proclaim the Saints' national loyalty. The church thus not only taught Mormonism but also spread the gospel of the United States. As Ben E. Rich succinctly put it, "We keep an army of . . . men out in all parts of the civilized earth teaching, what? That God made the government of the United States! That is part of their missionary work, distributing the proof, given to us by revelation from on high, of the fact that this government is a part of the work of God, the only government upon the face of the earth that He has set up . . ." (1908a, 41). Rich argued that no other people could possibly be as devoted to the government of the United States as the Saints were, because they knew how and why it was established: "We believe, as part of our religion . . . that the organization of the government of the United States was accomplished by the power of God. . . . No man is baptized into the 'Mormon' church, whether it be in the United States, England, Germany, or any other country, who does not accept as a part of that faith these truths . . ." (1908b, 102).

Just as in their relations with Native Americans, Mormons sought legitimacy for nationally colonialist attitudes, aspirations, and privileges. By the second decade of the twentieth century, the United States, according to most church leaders, had a clear mission to perform beyond providing protection for Zion and Mormonism. The church's president, Joseph F. Smith, spoke of the Mormons' loyalty to the nation during the Spanish-American War and said that Mormons wanted to see "the benignity, the honor, the glory and the good name and the mighty influence for peace of this nation extended abroad, not only over Hawaii and the Philippines, but over the islands of the sea east and west of us. We want to see the power, the influence for good, for elevating mankind, and for the establishment of righteous principles spread out over these poor helpless peoples of the world, establishing peace, good will and intelligence among them, that they may grow to be equal, if possible, to the enlightened nations of the world" (1912, 7).[45] During and after World War I, speaker after speaker spoke in general conferences on how the United States was destined to establish principles of liberty, righteousness, and justice throughout the world. Church leaders disagreed among themselves over the righteousness of the war and whether the League of Nations was the instrument to spread God's principles to all the earth, but few disputed that

God's principles were those of the United States and that God aimed to establish them on earth through U.S. power and virtue.

Thus, while church leaders spoke of a regional Zion's fortune less often, Zion's destiny did not disappear. Instead, it was displaced from the regional to the national scale. "[T]his Nation is sending the law of liberty from Zion unto the uttermost parts of the earth, and its mission will not have been completed until democracy is made safe for the world," Walter P. Monson declared (1918, 56). Whether supporting League of Nations nationalist internationalism or Republican Party isolationism, church leaders sat comfortably on the American bandwagon and asked church members to join them. The church had found a way to influence its members' politics so that non-Mormons (both regionally and nationally) could not object. While Mormons gave their own additional meaning to views about national destiny, they did so in a way that caused no conflict with non-Mormon nationalist visions. Regional inhabitants were now on a nationalist bandwagon.

Conclusion

The process of Americanization entailed recognizing that the Mormon region and the nation were two different, but overlapping places, each with a fundamentally different set of expectations, and setting nation over region so that expectations no longer differed so radically (on hierarchical relations between places, see Curry 1999, 101–3). Non-Mormons used two primary strategies in their efforts to Americanize Mormons and Utah (some non-Mormons inclined more toward one, while others leaned toward the other). At times, both regional and extraregional non-Mormons highlighted the possibility that Mormons would revert to their nineteenth-century practices. The Smoot hearings and the American Party manifested this strategy. At these moments, additional legislation against Mormons loomed large. Non-Mormons focused on polygamy that had not died out and had not been removed from the hearts and minds of some Mormons. Similarly, they found some church leaders who continued to be involved in politics and who used ecclesiastical influence to support their politics. Non-Mormons worried that the Saints' religious allegiance could still bring Mormons into opposition with the nation. To use Orlando Powers's terminology, non-Mormons worried that the LDS Church had not yet become a church like any other church and that the Saints had not quite become Americans like any other Americans. These non-Mormons (most often found among frustrated Democrats, strong Protestants, and former Mormons) insisted on the Saints' conformance with national norms and reminded them that legislation could be reinstated. They did not let the Saints forget that many Americans still regarded the church's very existence as unfortunate and that the nation had the power to weaken or even destroy the institution.

While this strategy almost certainly brought Mormons into closer conformance with national norms, it failed to make the church into simply another church. Americanization did not imply complete Protestantization. For one thing, Protestant national hegemony declined somewhat in the early twentieth century. In addition, as Thomas Alexander (1986) and Susan Stryker (1992) argue most persuasively, the church internalized many "objectionable" practices and "un-American" habits. That is, they no longer tried to enforce these norms on all aspects of members' lives, yet they retained some of the norms in a manner America found proper for churches (management of church property, capitalist charity toward the poor as a nonenforced ideal for members, and the like). The church found "religious" ways to impress upon members that they constituted a separate people (O'Dea 1957; Shipps 1985; Alexander 1986; Davies 1989). While regional battles between Mormons and non-Mormons continued after the demise of the American Party, none approached nineteenth-century intensity.

The second major strategy, the one that accommodated a continuing Mormon sense of religious separateness and eventually became dominant, was to sanitize, suppress, or ignore the social implications of past struggles between the Mormons and non-Mormons. Mormons and many regional non-Mormons pursued this strategy with equal vigor. Both felt the best way to achieve peace and prosperity was by finding commonality and ignoring difference. In contrast to socialists and labor unions, non-Mormons interested in capitalist development found few reasons not to cooperate with Mormons. These non-Mormons realized they could deemphasize past LDS social radicalism. They instead focused on socially conservative aspects of LDS history; LDS history became yet another brick in building the nation. The early Mormon struggle, though a bit unusual for historical reasons, amounted to little more than another episode in the American West's development. The majority of Mormons were also interested in regional peace. They knew that their church's survival depended on better relations with the nation; they were also eager to find regional commonalities and move into mainstream American society. They, too, assigned the socially radical Mormon past to historical contingency—to persecution and the requirements of building a frontier society. In the twentieth century, with statehood achieved, they interpreted Utah history as the story of a loyal people separating for a brief historical moment from the rest of American society until America appreciated their loyalty.

The memory of regional history thus shaped regional norms through both presence and absence. With both strategies, the regional capacity to critique the nation in any significant social sense—or the church for that matter—diminished. While people might call for increased individual moral virtue in the nation, the sense all but disappeared that the nation could be party to—and therefore ought to pay attention to—the oppression of particular people. Subjugation of Mormons was relegated to the historical past. Non-Mormons' sense that they were not extended American rights also weakened. Socialism made claims against the nation for a time, but it quickly lost regional influence. Labor unions, though strong among some regional inhabitants, particularly non-Mormons, tended to be too jingoistic to make powerful claims against the nation. Gender oppressions faded into the background with the achievement of suffrage, and racial oppressions were still too hegemonic to assign culpability to the nation. The LDS Church, by merging its destiny with America's destiny and starting to behave like other churches, insulated itself from some critiques of power relations between leaders and members. Most Mormons were happy to jump on the nation's bandwagon, from which some began the journey to a later superpatriotism. Most non-Mormons were willing to center themselves firmly on this bandwagon as well. By 1920, the Mormon culture region's dominant moral order suggested that to question the nation's power and norms was to unleash the forces of anarchy, religious struggle, and unwelcome authoritarianism. Could there have been any other way to bring about a peaceful regional home, given the enmity of previous battles between Mormons and non-Mormons?

CHAPTER FIVE

A New Type of Home

The Mormon region was transformed between 1880 and 1920 largely because of struggles between Mormons and non-Mormons. Mormon otherness in America rested on a host of characteristics. Aside from being theologically different from mainstream Protestantism, important though this was, Mormonism of the nineteenth century constituted a sociocultural system distinct from that of the American system. Nowhere were these sociocultural differences more important than in the daily interactions between Mormons and non-Mormons in the region. Divergence on gender, economics, and national loyalty resulted in high tensions. Nineteenth-century Mormonism institutionalized these differences through polygamy, the United Order, cooperatives, boycotts of Gentiles, a single political party, and the skeletal form of an independent kingdom of God. Non-Mormons found the institutions and accompanying sociocultural practices alien. LDS success in establishing these norms, enjoining church members' adherence, and gaining converts led non-Mormons—inside and outside the region—to regard Mormonism as a national threat.

Non-Mormons moved to the LDS stronghold in increasing numbers during the last half of the nineteenth century. There they joined members who had stopped believing in the church or its leaders to oppose the church. These regional inhabitants feared exposure to polygamy would jeopardize their moral purity. They found economic opportunity limited by Mormon communitarianism. And they felt like noncitizens in their own country because of Mormon political aspirations and control of politics. The combination of being predisposed to an American frontier mentality and finding themselves surrounded by LDS polygamy, communitarianism, and questionable loyalty led them to insist on particularly narrow conceptions of American ideals. These regional opponents of Mormonism united with many extrare-

172 TRANSFORMATION OF THE MORMON CULTURE REGION

gional non-Mormons, who feared the national consequences of Mormon polygamy and political power, in the struggle against Mormonism.

A struggle between Mormons and non-Mormons over meanings of gender, economy, nation, and Mormonism ensued. A regionally specific set of social and cultural processes (sometimes labeled Americanization) resulted. Non-Mormons held more power in these battles, and the "offensive" Mormon institutions did not survive. The norms associated with these institutions did not immediately die, however. Instead, the norms became subject to regional renegotiation. Although outsiders to the region played some part in the renegotiation, the norms gained regional specificity as inhabitants, Mormon and non-Mormon alike, socialized themselves into these altered norms.[1]

This chapter summarizes the transformation and recenters the concept of region by examining the discourse of the home. Previous chapters separately analyzed the moral orders of gender, economy, and nation, yet the transforming norms strongly affected one another (see also Gordon 2002, 183–220). Although this interdependence is implicit in previous chapters, the connections are more fully explicated in this chapter. In all cases, regional inhabitants engaged in a regionalized "politics of home" (Honig 1994). That is, they desired a place safe from contention and conflict. Distinctions between Mormons and non-Mormons made battles appear inevitable in the nineteenth century; in the regional transformation, both groups sought ways to erase or contain difference and the resultant conflict. Regional inhabitants, to their immense credit, successfully created such a safe place. But, from a retrospective view, the process also had its downside. As Bonnie Honig (1994) argues, the politics of home invariably shuts off potentially productive conversations deriving from difference.

In this regional transformation, the Mormon church lost much formal power, yet it found new and more narrowly "religious" ways to ensure devotion from its adherents. In the meantime, Mormons became cultural American nationalists, not just legally American. Utah gained statehood, and its economy became simultaneously more unified and more integrated into American capitalism. Mormons and non-Mormons found they could live with each other and developed new coalitions of power in politics and business. The characterization of the transformation as "Americanization" is at once accurate and misleading. It captures the fact that the Mormon region began to look and feel much more like the rest of the United States. The label misleads, however, by obscuring the importance of regionally specific changes, the resultant regionalized compromises, and the narrow version of American norms the transformation incorporated. The term inadequately captures the process of finding a place for the Mormon culture region within the American system of regions.

Distinctive regional structures of moral expectation relating to gender, economy, and nation emerged from the transformation. The dynamic between Mormons and non-Mormons in the region meant that these categories were subject to almost constant debate in 1880. In 1920, the disputes remaining between Mormons and non-Mormons reminded regional inhabitants of the much more bitter disputes of the past—a condition to which they dared not return. Thus key elements keeping the region distinctive were a collective memory of past troubles and a collective fear of returning to the battles. This milieu translated into a general unwillingness fundamentally to question dominant structures of power. Proper regional citizenship demanded general agreement on issues of economy, gender, and the nation. Both sides of the Mormon–non-Mormon divide understood that they could not afford to question dominant social categorizations too deeply because doing so might reopen old wounds. That is not to say that questioning power structures became impossible or ceased to occur. The point is that increasingly such resistance was taken less seriously regionally, and resisters found themselves out of favor with, or ignored by, mainstream society.

The Politics of Home

Previous chapters in this book convey a story about home. Mormons came to the Great Basin in search of a home free from persecution and violence. Although they did not escape anti-Mormon sentiment in their new home, Mormons lived without fear of frequent violence. Non-Mormons also came to the region in search of homes. The Mormons were much more successful in establishing the types of homes they desired (in the sense of communities and region) than the many non-Mormons who often felt out of place in a Mormon-dominated region. By the 1880s, with an ever-increasing non-Mormon population and effective regulation of Mormon power and practices finally in place, Mormons began to feel their home was once again under attack. Non-Mormons envisioned finally creating the home they desired. Both Mormons and non-Mormons used *home* as a metaphor for the regional society they wanted to create. By 1920, this regional home was transformed in favor of non-Mormons. Home began to feel more like the rest of the United States.[2] In spite of the changes, the continued reliance on the metaphor of home suggests that Mormons, especially, yearned for a distinctive region. Even with an increasing use of Zion to refer to the United States, Zion still had the connotation of a regional home.

Regional inhabitants also often used *home* in the household sense. Both Mormons and non-Mormons of the 1880s insisted they were trying to protect the home in their battles against each other. Mormon polygamy and patriarchy constituted threats to the American home in the minds of many non-Mormons, while Mormons asserted the virtue of their own homes and claimed American society destroyed homes by rewarding vice. The increasing desire on both sides to codify the ideal home points to interrelationships between the emergent moral orders of gender, economy, and nation. Both sides failed to see that their commitments to the home depended on a rather specific and narrow regional codification of the function of the home in relation to the nation, the economy, and gender.

By 1920, the "proper" home symbolized narrowed moral orders in each of these areas. I examine this discourse of the home primarily through LDS statements, but I think the conclusions apply regionally. After all, non-Mormons pushed for and showed Mormons how these transformed norms operated. While both Mormon and non-Mormon cultures narrowed in a regionally based consensus, Mormons (perhaps partly because of church efforts to retain influence over members) depended more strongly on the politics of home than did regional non-Mormons. In particular, Mormons retained a more acute sense that the region was a home. As part of this politics of home, the region was refigured as a private space, a haven, and a refuge devoid of politics.[3] Like "female" spaces, which also tend to be figured in this way, the region lost its connotation as a space of possible fundamental social change. The politics of home figured the region as a place where some types of basic difference could not be countenanced.

The Ideal Home

Some non-Mormons justified attacks against Mormonism as defenses of American homes (see also Gordon 2002). Mormon homes, especially polygamous homes, they argued, were not happy and did not convey proper values, such as patriotism. A non-Mormon Fourth of July speaker argued that, by contrast, "in the American home, sacredly guarded by law and public opinion against intrusion, the children of the Nation are reared in reverential affection for their country and their country's flag. . . . In the American homes have the youth of the Nation been taught that the highest and holiest duty of man is obedience to the laws of his country, and, that by intelligent and unremitting labor only, may he hope to attain his best estate" (quoted in *Daily Tribune*, 5 July 1889). Similar complaints against Mormonism—especially Mormon polygamy—persisted, often articulated by evangelical Protestants, long after the Manifesto was issued. A fund-raising appeal by the International Council for Patriotic Service ([1912]) noted that its "chief purpose at this time is the defence of this nation and its homes against the evils of Mormonism." It continued:

> Our civilization is founded upon the integrity of the home and the social unit of the monogamous family. The very thought of polygamy, reversion toward a practice current in semi-barbarous stages of man's development, is abhorrent to all true Americans. . . . Do you wish those who profess belief in this practice, who teach and practice its doctrines, to gain political control over you, your community, your state, and your nation? For years now, very subtly, The Mormon Church has slowly, but nevertheless surely, broadened its sphere of activity, extended the practice of Polygamy and quietly secured a hold upon our political machinery which threatens the disintegration of our nation's fundamental institutions. . . . Now won't you help? . . . This evil threatens the home.

Mormons, of course, rejected these charges (relics from the 1880s) and countered that they were the defenders of domestic virtue. Earlier, they had suggested that antipolygamy legislation compelled plural wives to testify against their husband. Such a practice was inconceivable in other civilized countries, argued Ruthinda Moench. Such revealed secrets between husband and wife meant that the "sanctity of the home circle" was being destroyed (*"Mormon" Women's Protest* [1886], 27). By 1920, Mormons still argued that one of Mormonism's contributions was its teachings about the home. This continuity of emphasis on the home may have helped Mormons feel that little had changed in the process of Americanization, but it masked changes in the concept of home itself. Michael Dalton Palmer argues that nineteenth-century Mormons never felt a great need to separate family and home from the rest of society. Home was one institution among many in Mormonism. Little sense existed that home and family were independent units. Zion, Utah, and Kingdom implied security as much as home. By the early twentieth century, the nuclear family was installed as the proper group to reside in the home, and the home with such a family came to be seen as *the* fundamental unit of society (1982, 135–69).

The proper home existed in an increasingly narrowly defined form. By 1920, it appeared as what is today called the traditional nuclear family: father, mother, and children tied together under one roof with patriarchal power distribution. Husband and wife were to be bound together by romantic love. The father went outside the home to work to provide material goods for the family, while the mother stayed at home and reared the children. This is not to say that this ideal did not exist in 1880; it clearly did, even in polygamy—allowing for adaptations (Embry 1987). But some elements of the ideal were not as strong, and many variations existed in practice, with less stigma attached. Polygamous families existed (usually by necessity, [Daynes 2001, 133–36]) where each woman was largely in charge of her own and her children's affairs, with little input from the father. Particularly strong notions of patriarchy characterized many polygamous marriages, with much less emphasis on romantic love (Embry 1987). Many households routinely hired a girl to assist the mother with household chores. Divorce, though never encouraged, was relatively common in 1880, whereas strengthened social controls made it much less so in 1920; divorce carried less dishonor in the earlier years than it later came to (Campbell and Campbell 1992). Neither had it been uncommon, especially among non-Mormons, for men to live alone, since they had migrated to the region for economic opportunity. These variations did not unseat the "traditional" home as the ideal, but they did prevent it from being widely considered as the only home from which responsible citizenship could emanate. By 1920, the traditional home was the primary place for citizens to develop proper values.

Mormons and non-Mormons valued the home and called it the basic unit of society prior to the turn of the century, but by 1920 this label had additional meaning. A particular form of the home was now a model for society. Girls and boys could learn the gender roles and authority that men and women assumed in society by observing family relations in their home. A properly functioning home came to be seen as necessary for a properly functioning economy. Men's ability to provide labor outside the home depended on women's complementary labor in the home. Children learned more than loyalty to the nation from their mother's teachings; the home also provided a model of obedience they could carry over to relations in the nation. In 1880, societal relations were not always to be modeled directly on home relationships, but by 1920, more often than not, they were.

Consider the contrast between earlier norms and later norms in the following three sets of quotes (some of which also appear in earlier chapters). Each quote draws on the discourse of home, but norms appealed to earlier differ from later ones. The first quote from the first set points out the value of polygamy in domestic relations:

[The American idea of government is] founded on the Christian idea of home, where one father and one mother, each the equal of the other . . . rear about the hearth-stone an intelligent and God fearing family. Patriotism springs from love of country, which is born of love for home. . . . Has not every woman the undeniable right to be an honorable wife and mother[?] . . . Hand in hand with celestial [plural] marriage is the elevation of woman. In church she votes equally with men, and politically she has the suffrage raising her from the old common way, monogamic serfdom, to political equality with men. Rights of property are given her. . . . If any woman at an advanced period of her life wishes in a measure to retire from her husband's society with his consent, this is her own individual privilege with which no one has the right to interfere. (Romania B. Pratt, in *"Mormon" Women's Protest* [1886], 28–31)

Defending the home and the family are important here, but home situations beyond the nuclear family seem possible. Pratt's ideal home is not very hierarchical. Wives have latitude in constituting relationships with their husbands. Women should claim equal authority with men.

A second quote from the nineteenth century narrows the scope a bit:

Woman, without having lost anything of her gentleness and grace, no longer accepts that once famous axiom, "man should support woman." She cares not for adoration alone, but wants to carry her intellect and activity into spheres suited to her. She claims that every human being is best judge of his or her own aptitudes, and is willing and anxious to labor to conquer her civil rights. . . . In the family the natural task of the woman is the management of domestic affairs—the training of the children and the comfort of the husband, of whom she should be the inspiration. By the side of the eminent man, yet in the shade, there is always a woman. This career of hidden utility and modest devotion is well suited to her; yet, to exclude woman from active occupations and confine her to the cares of the household is to attempt an impossibility—to close the way to progress. For there are many women who will not marry. Many who are left widows without resources, who could never remain pure, except by engaging in some active employment. . . . (L. Smith 1890, 175–76)

In comparison with Pratt, Lizzie Smith assigns women a more modest, deferent nature. The home is woman's sphere. Nonetheless, she insists that this sphere is not woman's only sphere. Women have many more interests and talents than can be pursued strictly in the home. Women should have the opportunity to work outside the home, for example, if they want to do so. Outside work instead of defiling women can help them remain pure.

By 1920, the following sentiment was more common:

Much is expected of woman in this new life upon which she is so determinedly entering and thoughtful people are asking what will be the result not only on civic life but on women themselves. Will they lose the charm of their sisters in past ages? Will they lose sight of the high ideal that woman as successful wife and mother reaches her highest glory and gives her greatest service to mankind? . . . We hope that women will not forget in their race after new laurels that this new field is not so great nor important as the old, old one of wifehood, motherhood, homemaker. If they fail here all else will be as dross for home is the structure on which the nation rears its superstructure. (" 'Woman's Day' " 1920, 285–86)

By 1920, women were to live their lives even more strongly in the service of men than they had in 1880. This quote is the reverse of Lizzie Smith's quote. Instead of women having important interests in addition to the home, it suggests that home is the only truly important place for women (see also Iverson 1908, 70–71). By implication, separation between men's and women's work has hardened (although for some ambiguity on this issue, see Smoot 1909, 70–72).

The next set of quotes illustrates separation between men's and women's participation in the economic sphere. It also shows the shift from a communitarian ethic to a narrower responsibility for the well-being of one's home. "If it be verily true that [women] have not time [for personal development], (which I believe is the case with the majority of wives and mothers) is it not because we willingly place ourselves on the altar of sacrifice, and bear heavy burdens that ought to be shared by husbands, children, and in some instances by communities" (Editorial 1894b, n.p.). According to this quote, the separation between home and the community was greater than it ought to have been. Community members should help care for one another; all responsibility should not rest with the mother or even the family.

The following passages come from YMMIA manuals, the first from 1913–14, the second from 1912–13. Americans feel deeply that "[w]hen once a young man leaves home, his first responsibility is to provide for himself the natural and legitimate wants of respectability. Should he become a family man, or when he becomes one, as he doubtless will, then other lives have a claim upon his manhood. . . . Although he is bound to supply maintenance to no one outside the family, a man must as a citizen, in part, at least, assume the responsibility for the community dependents, including the poor, the sick, the maimed, the orphaned, and the mentally incapable. Citizenship demands this" (Young Men's Mutual Improvement Association n.d.e, 48–49). Although something of a communitarian ethic remained, it was more an ethic to fit the demands of an individualistic, capitalist society. Community economic responsibility (defined squarely in terms of nationalist identity) consisted of the charity relationship; responsibility was not so much because of a shared community membership. The obligation for finding people to help in the community depended more on individualist than communal expectations. Gender distinctions between men and women had hardened. A man had specific responsibilities to provide for his family, whereas women and children figured more as dependents and home workers whose primary function was assisting the husband. The next quote likewise involves individualist, capitalist norms: "Permanency of possession is a factor in the production of stability of character. The nomadic races are incomparably behind the home-building ones. The most desirable citizen is a home builder and a home owner. The most desirable community is a community of home owners" (Young Men's Mutual Improvement Association n.d.d, 58). Economic prowess of the (male) individual defines the quality of the community. While capitalist ownership was not new in Mormonism, its place became cemented, linked to an ever stronger ascription of virtue.

The following excerpts show a shift in ideals of national loyalty—from a rhetoric of rights and protest to one identifying with national power and might—through the discourse of the home. M. Isabella Horne, speaking at a protest meeting, declared, "If it does no other good, it will be a matter of history to be handed down to our posterity, that their mothers rose up in the dignity of their womanhood to protest against insults and indignities heaped upon them. . . . It has been said by the chief executive of the nation, 'I wish you could be like us.' And what is that? They marry one wife and degrade as many women as they choose. God forbid that we should descend to their level!" (*"Mormon" Women's Protest* [1886], 8–9). Late nineteenth-century LDS women asserted political rights usually exercised by men. These Saints felt compelled to scrutinize national norms and protest those they disliked. Mormons considered themselves part of the nation, but they felt no special need to make their own cultural values correspond to those dominant in the nation.

The next two passages from the *Young Woman's Journal* are from midway through the period and show partial shifts in dominant LDS norms. "Through the renovation of its home life, the whole nation must yet be purified and lifted out of the political and social quagmire into which it has fallen; and where should this regenerating influence first be felt, if not in Zion?" ("Home Builders" 1900, 377). Zion's and the nation's norms still apparently did not exactly equate, but a stronger sense exists that they ought to coincide. Zion would model virtue for the rest of the nation rather than protest the difficulty of achieving virtue because of the rest of the nation (see also A. Ivins 1911, 120). The next quote, also from the middle of the period, identifies the home with the nation:

> The home is the unit of society, that is, it is the cornerstone of society. A collection of these little units, or families, form a village, town, city. A collection of towns form a county; a number of counties a state; a number of states, a country. . . . All governments recognize the fact that divided authority is not authority; therefore one person is placed at the head of each department or government. The same principle holds true in the home; and for that reason God placed husband at the head of the family, and He tells us that we should obey our husbands

in righteousness. As soon as young wives recognize this principle as an ethical law, much of the friction between husband and wife will vanish. ("Ethics for Young Girls" 1900, 94–95; for similar arguments by nineteenth-century antipolygamists, see Gordon 2002, 180)

Latter-day Saints increasingly saw the nation as fundamentally a compilation of homes, just as the church was a collection of families (Palmer 1982, 181). National virtue depended on home virtue, since home and nation differed merely in scale, not in kind. Authority exercised in the nation and the home had the same essence; hierarchical and patriarchal order characterized both.

The final quote, by Charles A. Callis, a Mormon apostle who articulated later LDS norms, extends the sentiments: "[W]hen the home is undermined, when the influence of the home is weakened, then the power, the prestige and the might of this great republic is correspondingly weakened" (1917, 134). National might and stature now held great importance (Mormons had jumped on the national bandwagon) and depended most fundamentally on the strength and the order of homes (see also Smoot 1910, 70). The home was increasingly seen as *the* model of society, the foundation of the nation—the nation was the family writ large (S. L. Richards 1920a, 97). The Saints were the most patriotic citizens in the nation because of their teachings about the home (S. L. Richards 1917, 139–40). Loyalty became conformance to dominant norms. Just as children and wives were taught not to protest too much at home, fundamental protest in the nation became increasingly discouraged. Instead of leadership moderated through equality with women, men were to temper leadership in the home through gallantry. This sense of gallantry (with implied power differences) extended outside the home to men's and women's relationships generally (Young Men's Mutual Improvement Association n.d.d, 56–57).

While the three sets of quotations represent general trends, LDS culture was not monolithic. An important distinction developed in the early twentieth century between those who believed Mormonism was part of national (and sometimes international) moral and material progress and those who saw the church holding out an example to help the nation to reverse its moral decline. A passage from the *Woman's Exponent* (probably written by Emmeline Wells) illustrates the first position:

[W]omen are anxious for better advantages and especially for the betterment of the home. Today the nations of the world stand for better government and for domestic purity and culture beginning in the home—and who can declare that homes are not better and cleaner and purer than they were in olden times? . . . [T]he world is becoming better, because the advanced education of women means the higher civilization of the entire globe. It means better homes and surroundings and with all better lives are higher anticipations, better conditions in the state and nation and progress everywhere. ("Progress of Women in the Last Seventy Years" 1912, 44–45)

A few years later, the *Relief Society Magazine* featured an article on LDS women and homes that articulated the second viewpoint (probably written by Susa Young Gates):

> Today, more than at any other period in the world's history, there is a determined effort to break down the barrier of the home. This is not altogether the fault of the deliberate childlessness of the wife, the club attractions for both husband and wife, nor to the increasing popularity of the cozy flat in the forest of apartments which every great city multiplies. These are all but manifestations of a disintegrating force within the social body. However this may be, our Relief Society sisters are the keepers of the keys of home life and home traditions among this people, and eventually in all the world. . . . ("The Relief Society Woman and Her Home" 1915, 477)

While both attitudes—politically progressive and conservative—had been prominent in Mormonism for some time, the conservative one slowly gained dominance. The spate of support among some for the League of Nations after World War I seems to have been the last major expression that the world was progressing through the leaven of the church and would continue doing so until Christ's second coming. Increasingly dominant thereafter was the view that while Mormons stood for American ideals and supported the government with model citizenship, the forces of modernization (individual mobility and breakup of communities, loss of enforcement of communal strictures of piousness, increasing anonymity of public life, increasing capacity of youth to seek recreation) brought moral disintegration to the nation and world. Mormons by 1920 may not have felt under siege as they did in 1880, because the nation was allowing them to live the (recast) practices of their religion, but a few Saints began to bemoan the loss of public virtue through accommodation to the rapidly modernizing American culture. This sense of loss marked the beginning of an LDS political conservatism that called more on the virtues of an idealized American past than on traditional Mormonism.

A Regional Home

Once the Mormon region joined the U.S. regional system and once LDS leaders connected LDS fortunes to America's destiny, Latter-day Saints figured the region as a haven for American values, morality, and decency. LDS historical narratives supported the view that the region housed a people of particularly strong morality. The "cradle of liberty" was the regional mountains, claimed Stephen L. Richards (1919, 105). Many came to see God's will in the Saints' having to leave their original Zion in Missouri and come to the Rocky Mountains (see, for example, Robinson 1912, 76–80; for an opposing view, see Whitney 1917, 50–51). Mormonism retained a strong regionalized sense of home (Poll 1987). The region was the place where Mormons did not have to apologize for their religion. It was (in spite of—or perhaps because of—the normative changes) where they felt part of mainstream society. Mormons still felt like hosts there since, for example, non-Mormons had to learn the LDS vocabulary to interact effectively. This strong desire for a regionalized home may have persisted in separating Mormons from non-Mormons. Or, at least, non-Mormons created a somewhat different type of home. While non-Mormons found the regional home more amenable in 1920 than in 1880, they still did not attach quite the same sentiments to the region that Mormons did. Theirs was still more exclusively a language of regional boosterism (which Mormons joined, to be sure [Bishop and Holzapfel 1993]) than that of a regionalized home. Even though non-Mormons increasingly extolled regional virtues, the region was home first and foremost to the Mormons. The appellation of Zion could still be invoked, and this sense of regional identification continued to help both regional Mormons and non-Mormons learn their places in society.

Yet the Mormon culture region in 1920 was not the same as it had been in the 1880s. Or, to be more precise, the social and cultural characteristics producing the regionally specific effects had been altered. Some elements remained—for example, Mormon numerical dominance (though at its low point) and some of the cultural distinctiveness of Mormonism; the region was still not easily confused with any other. But much had changed by 1920. The Mormon–non-Mormon dynamic still socialized people within a specific, essentially contiguous space, but it had different characteristics than it had had earlier. For one thing, the dynamic operated much more inside the region.

This internalization of Mormon–non-Mormon conflict seems at odds with a simultaneous greater externalization of Utah's economy. Outside capital became more important to Utah's economy, and the economy became much less organized along Mormon–non-Mormon lines. Little economic content remained in the cultural tensions between the two groups by 1920, aside from residual wariness about communal activity. Even debates about LDS leaders' corporate control stemmed more often from capitalist competition than from religious division. To the extent that regionalized socioeconomic processes existed, the region was the American West more than it was the Mormon culture region. Capitalist economic processes acquired meanings distinctive to the Mormon culture region by 1920 mostly because of the structure of regional culture and memory.

The Smoot hearings and Protestant complaints about Mormonism were the last gasps of conflict between Mormons and non-Mormons at the national level. National concern about Mormons did not immediately end after 1896, but such worries were much weaker by 1920. It became difficult to sustain the argument that Mormonism still constituted a vital threat to the nation. After all, almost all Mormons had repudiated polygamy, and Utah's statehood and Mormons in positions of national influence had not damaged the nation. Non-Mormons inside the region did not suddenly agree with everything the LDS Church did and all aspects of LDS culture. The survival of the Mormon church as a powerful institution ensured that the Mormon–non-Mormon dynamic did not die. Yet regional non-Mormons came to feel that such differences should be regional matters rather than national. They increasingly resented outside influence in dealing with Mormon power and culture, regarding it as meddling.[4]

While the LDS–non-LDS dynamic was earlier a means of expressing contempt for each other's social and cultural systems, it contained a much stronger element of cooperation in 1920. Mormons and non-Mormons realized that differences between the two groups remained and that such differences sometimes led to clannishness. But both sides, by and large, determined not to let these differences come in the way of regional cooperation and peace. The changes that took place between 1880 and 1920 were very productive in many ways. Surely few regional inhabitants wanted to return to the type of regional society that existed in 1880. That there was no longer a large region where radical separation reigned between religious groups, where Mormons exhibited a siege mentality,[5] and where almost all white non-Mormons felt like strangers in their own country was a profoundly positive development (Flake 2000).[6]

Because of the regionalized compromises reached between Mormons and non-Mormons, the Latter-day Saints were able to refigure the region as home. They dreamed, in Bonnie Honig's words, of "a place free of power, conflict, and struggle, a place—an identity, a private realm, a form of life, a group vision, unmarked or unriven by difference and untouched by the power brought to bear upon it by the identities that strive to ground themselves in its place" (1994, 567). While Honig argues that the yearning for home never disappears, she suggests that such a home is a never-realizable dream, even a dangerous one: "The dream of home is dangerous, particularly in postcolonial settings, because it animates and exacerbates the inability of constituted subjects—or nations—to accept their own internal divisions, and it engenders zealotry, the will to bring the dream of unitariness or home into being. It leads the subject to project its internal differences onto external Others and then to rage against them for standing in the way of its dream—both at home and elsewhere" (585). Better, she argues, to resignify home as a place containing at least some differences, dilemmas, and conflicts, and better constantly to negotiate these differences (587).[7]

According to this view, it might have been better for Mormon and non-Mormon efforts at regional peace to stop somewhere short of the regional compromise they reached. Fundamental differences between Mormons and non-Mormons in 1880 produced a radically transformed region by 1920, yet the new regional norms closed off possibilities for further fundamental change. Achieving general peace was vital, but the process may have gone too far in displacing difference. Instead of trying to eliminate the difference between Mormon and American (or shunt it off into a separate religious sphere), perhaps it would have been better to recognize that difference. Instead of fragmenting the identity of LDS Americans so that their Mormonness would not affect their political ideologies, perhaps it would have been better to let Mormons (and non-Mormons for that matter) allow the multiple influences contributing to their individuality to come into greater contact with one another. Instead of allowing Mormons to feel as if they had reestablished a home completely safe from outside meddling, perhaps it would have been better for regional culture to have the Saints continue to understand that America stood ready to critique their practices (and perhaps Mormons would have been more inclined to critique American practices). From these somewhat uncomfortable spaces, Honig implies, derive the space for a serious and even socially radical politics. Perhaps from such uncomfortable spaces, white Mormons and non-Mormons would have been less prone to classify themselves as proper regional citizens and those who differed from them as so fundamentally other.

Regional Achievement and Regional Loss

Something was lost in the transformation of the region: the willingness of many people to seek fundamental changes in American society and dominant institutions. Because Mormons seemed so un-American to most nineteenth-century Americans, non-Mormons insisted strongly on an agenda of Americanization. They justified their agenda partially in terms of protecting Mormon women and purifying the home. But, as Deniz Kandiyoti finds is often the case with recent nationalizations, nationalist reform on behalf of women did not "increase the autonomy of individual women, but [harnessed] them more effectively to national developmental goals" (1994, 386). Mormon women's position was reworked through the Americanization of Utah; they became more effective mothers and wives in support of narrowly defined national development goals. Likewise, Mormon men were "liberated" from the church's authoritarian tendencies, but they were simultaneously compelled to assume more economically individualist and politically nationalist identities. Non-Mormons produced a rather one-sided image of American citizenship, one that valued cultural conformity, economic individuality, order, and normality over rights, welfare, equality, and cultural tolerance. Their desire to Americanize Mormons led regional non-Mormons to assume characteristics they hoped Mormons would embrace. They insisted that there was little fundamentally wrong with American cartographies of gender authority that suffrage had not fixed. They found few viable alternatives to boosteristic capitalist development. And they saw scant value in a national loyalty more critical than an unabashed enthusiasm over national power, might, and "civilization." America generally had experienced somewhat similar shifts during the 1890s (Faragher et al. 2000, 547–608). These broader changes undoubtedly added to the momentum of regional shifts, but they also obscured recognition of regional culture's particular trajectory. Shifts toward regional conservatism were consolidated rather than questioned during the Progressive Era.

Retrospectively, one would have hoped that non-Mormons' encounter with nineteenth-century Mormonism would produce a more fruitful conversation over these fundamental social issues. Apparently it did not. Turn-of-the-century white American culture tended to obliterate or compartmentalize difference more than it allowed difference a place in cultural politics. Non-Mormons insisted that Latter-day Saints could not be adequately gendered American citizens on LDS terms. Regional citizenship came to imply that only nationalist terms would do. Just as with Native Americans, non-Mormons insisted that the Americanization of Mormons meant their way or no way.

Mormon culture, too, lost its willingness to question dominant structures of power. This inclination was always fragmented in Mormonism because of the tendency to obey religious authority, but nineteenth-century Mormons capably questioned the social structure of American society. By 1920, Mormon authority had been altered in such a way that the church could still safely request obedience. This change occurred through a refiguration of the difference between Mormon identity and American identity. By 1920, since the church acted politically like other churches, it was (mostly) no longer vulnerable to accusations that it exceeded its authority. In this much more apolitical religious sphere, it could still claim members' obedience. The church also accepted the nation's view of itself, which further allowed the church safely to call for conformance (to nationalist ideals).

Mormons emerged from this period of Americanization with their church and belief structure still intact, with confidence that they perpetuated their forebears' legacy, and with a continued sense of a regional home. These were no small accomplishments, given the forces that had been arrayed against them. But such accomplishments could only be achieved, it seems, by most Saints' losing awareness that Mormon culture once encompassed a social agenda offering fundamental alternatives to the national status quo. The generation of Mormons raised in the early twentieth century thus understood church history much differently from the way nineteenth-century Mormons regarded it. While this loss was significant for both Mormon and regional culture, the Americanization process must be credited for the regional peace it brought; it solved the problem of debilitating antipathy between Mormons and non-Mormons.

In one important way, the loss was more significant for regional culture than for LDS culture. Mormonism can probably never escape the fact that it fundamentally confronted American norms, since that challenge is rooted in church doctrine and history (Quinn 1987). The region, however, can never call upon such a history. The regional history of Mormon–non-Mormon interaction instead suggests that particularly strong national conformity is the key to avoiding unmanageable conflict.

Mormons and the Contemporary Mormon Culture Region

Much of this afterword does not result from the systematic research underlying the rest of the book; instead, it is more personal and speculative commentary. I consider myself a regional insider in many ways, but personal circumstances have moved me toward the viewpoint of an outsider in recent years. When I first wrote this afterword, I was working in Taiwan. When I told students that I came from Utah, those students who made an association usually said, "Oh, Karl Malone and the Utah Jazz." A small number also asked the questions I usually hear in the United States: "That's where there's lots of Mormons, isn't it? Are you Mormon?" Such episodes reveal the partial and uneven pictures that globalization paints. Few institutions, events, issues, or forces have more power currently to shape regional images globally than the National Basketball Association (NBA) and its superstars. Karl Malone's reputation now does more in much of the world to make the area I come from intelligible than does knowledge about Brigham Young, Susa Young Gates, Franklin Spalding, B. H. Roberts, Reed Smoot, Joe Hill, Gordon B. Hinckley, Orrin Hatch, Mike Leavitt, or anybody else. Part of me bemoans history's apparent irrelevance, yet I also recognize an opportunity to refigure the region. Impetus for transformative politics is often located where we do not expect it to be (M. Brown 1997). I want to explore a possibility for contemporary regional change by first considering images of Mormons/Utah/region in connection with images of the Utah Jazz (see also Shipps 2000, 98–123). In significant ways, such images have converged recently.

Chiung Hwang Chen and I recently analyzed representations of Mormons in the American news media over the past six decades (1999). We argue that this medium has portrayed Mormons in much the same way that it has characterized Asian Americans, that is, as "model minorities." Both groups even currently typify upright (and uptight), successful American citizens. Many news stories noted what a different place Utah is compared with the rest of the United States. A general manager in a large international firm contended that "the cultural norm [of Utah] is to work together and make a profit" (quoted in Donnelly 1991, 22). Utah exemplifies Ronald Reagan's vision of America, the *New York Times Magazine* reported: "a nation of pious, striving, self-reliant and politically conservative 'traditional' families where men work hard at their jobs and women work hard in the home raising their children" (R. Lindsey 1986, 24). In this discourse, Utahns, because of the Mormon influence, are patriotic and businesslike; workers do not complain about bosses and would rather succeed as a group than achieve personal glory. Utah has represented nineteenth-century America, embodying the wholesome values modern society is supposedly losing (Carmer 1962, 65; H. F. 1987, 42). The differences that mark Mormons and Utah (often conflated) are not all positive, however. Mormon conformity, lack of creativity, and intolerance also makes Utah an unusual place (on contemporary images of Mormons, see also Givens 1997, 153–67).

As an addicted Utah Jazz fan, I regularly read national commentary about the team. For years after the Jazz first moved to Utah, sports writers frequently remarked that the term *Utah Jazz* was an oxymoron. Jazz represents everything that Utah—with its Mormon influence—does not represent, and vice versa. Such commentaries dominated when the Jazz was a losing team. Writers changed their line after a long run of club success. Now the team epitomizes hard work, toughness, and success. It is a model NBA franchise—a throwback to another era amid widespread accusations of NBA players' laziness and glory-seeking. Story after story asserts essentially that "they do things differently in Utah"—they work for their success, they don't seek the limelight, they keep coming back year after year. For example, the sports writer Frank Hughes (2001) reported, "In Salt Lake . . . things are done differently than in most other cities in the NBA. It is a place where [stars] Karl Malone and John Stockton and [Coach] Jerry Sloan rule, and everybody that enters their world conforms. . . . 'Their work ethic,' [recent acquisition Donyell] Marshall marvels. 'Guys don't come in here and complain about going to practice the next day.'" Sports writers are not just talking about the team. They note how well the team fits the area. Region/religious group images and team images have nearly converged. Multiple correspondences between images of team and region exist: both succeed with little concern for individual glory, both embrace the ethic of hard work, people conform to both or move on, both are boring to many people, both value dogged persistence more than creativity or flair, Mormons' obedient unity parallels the Jazz's precision teamwork, and so forth.

Of course, no analogy fits perfectly; minority status does not differentiate the Jazz in the same way it marks Mormons. The following came from an analysis of George W. Bush's incoming administration: "The China portfolio on the National Security Council will be handled by Garrett Gong. . . . Gong, a Chinese Mormon, is close to business and viewed as 'soft' on China by many conservatives" (Stokes 2001). The term *Mormon* seems out of place. No context situates it, unless it explains the "close to business" phrase (but such an interpretation is by no means certain). One wonders why the author included it at all. Its use parallels the common media practice of identifying race only when referring to racial minorities. I believe that it (and this is hardly an isolated incident) evidences Mormons' continuing minority status in America. Presumably the author thought the term provided its own meaning (DePillis 1996, 5–9). I will not presume to pinpoint that meaning, though images of Mormons in the media typically cluster around certain, not always consistent characteristics: conservative, too nice (lacking savvy), ultra-conforming, super patriotic, congenial, boring, patriarchal, capitalist, hard-working, obedient, intelligent, uncreative, secretive, and lacking critical thinking.

These images are misleading stereotypes. Stereotypes are sometimes untrue for groups and almost always untrue when applied to individuals. These particular stereotypes, however, are not entirely inaccurate. I have pointed in this book to many regional dispositions paralleling these attributes. Stereotypes mislead as much by obscuring history and social relations as by perpetuating inaccurate characterizations. Media images of Mormons and, by extension, the Mormon culture region provide few clues about how and why particular characteristics arose. Such portrayals especially lack an understanding of Mormon (and regional) culture's transformation during Americanization. To the extent that the stereotypes contain some accuracy, it is not because Mormons simply manifest a fundamental Mormon essence. Instead, when stereotypes point to conformity, conservatism, lack of critical thinking, patriotism, patriarchy, and capitalism, Mormons follow a script whose fundamental outlines both Mormons and non-Mormons produced; the script emerged as the product of regional struggle.

I do not literally mean that people always simplistically obey cultural and ideological scripts. Life is always more complex, and people are more intelligent and creative. Yet ideologies can have long lives. Ideologies and dispositions can always be questioned, but there is never any guarantee that particular ones will be examined at certain historical moments (in fact, some are very difficult to investigate because complex cultural and social systems sustain them). Nor is there any guarantee that people will remember why they originated. Some of the Mormon culture region's ideologies and dispositions have assumed a life of their own by the twenty-first century, far removed from the largely forgotten collective memories and struggles that called them into existence. In particular, the region no longer needs the narrow attitudes toward social and cultural difference it once seemed to require. Few people now think, as they did a century ago, that controlling difference within the Mormon culture region would avert a national crisis. Yet the ideologies and dispositions called upon by that long-dead fear persist.

Today a regionalized Mormon–non-Mormon dynamic still exists (special section on "The Unspoken Divide," *Salt Lake Tribune,* 9 December 2001), but its center differs from the active struggle or the collective memory of struggle from past years. To be sure, antagonism between Mormons and non-Mormons still occasionally arises. Mormon numerical dominance of the region has increased since 1920 (Phillips 1999). Complaints over a supposed anti-Mormon bias at the University of Utah surface periodically. Newspapers contain letters to the editor claiming either that the Mormon influence drags the state down or that non-Mormons do not properly respect Utah's cultural heritage. Suspicion of close connections between LDS leadership and state officials never dies. Persistent battles over liquor laws and gambling often appear to be Mormon versus non-Mormon fights. Some Mormons and non-Mormons regulate their children's friendships along religious lines. Some people believe the *Salt Lake Tribune* is still an anti-Mormon newspaper. The debates that led to the impeachment of Arizona's Governor Evan Meacham, a Mormon, in the late 1980s remind us that the dynamic defines a region not strictly equivalent to Utah. Few people living in this region can avoid the dynamic and its periodic episodes of mistrust; residents still often use such phrases as "this is how we do things here." But more than ever, I suspect, many shrug off these episodes as peripheral incidents provoked by a few who wish to continue old battles.

To me, other, subtler operations of the contemporary Mormon–non-Mormon dynamic are more important. One feature of the contemporary Mormon–non-Mormon dynamic—demonstrated in discussions related to the 2002 Winter Olympics—is an inferiority complex vis-à-vis the rest of the United States. Feelings of embarrassment sometimes arise over the need to explain "the way we do things here" (for example, liquor laws, Sunday closings, broadcasts of LDS general conferences that preempt weekend sports, and green jello). A feeling persists that LDS culture prevents this region from being a normal part of America.

Today's Mormon–non-Mormon dynamic has another important effect. It shunts people toward particularly strong and explicit positions on LDS morality. Unlike the dynamic in the 1880s, when people's religious allegiance determined their stances on social issues, today's dynamic more directly centers on morality per se. Disputes often acquire shape in relation to (sometimes narrow) conceptions of LDS morality. Children and teenagers face this most strongly. Debates over morality feature people taking sides in relation to the presumed church stance. Debates over teenage drinking, for example, always find the LDS moral prohibition against alcohol lurking just beneath the surface. People read the row over whether to allow a gay social club in a Salt Lake City high school through the lens of LDS statements about homosexuality. Labor debates encounter the "right-to-work" moralities many church leaders hold. Even the Olympic bribery scandal produced acute regional embarrassment because of an expectation, at least among Mormons, that a specifically Mormon (higher) morality exists. I am not suggesting that LDS morality should not figure in regional debates; I am simply saying that the region may be better off not assuming LDS morality is the opposite of non-LDS morality or the central reference point on most issues. Life in Taiwan taught me that effecting progressive social change is difficult when routing all social debates through a single issue (in Taiwan, independence versus non-independence). One needs to recognize "non-Mormon" as the heterogeneous category it is. Actions assuming its unity recur remarkably often. In breaking apart "non-Mormon," one may also find specifying "Mormon" to be more difficult than stereotypes lead us to believe.

While the Mormon–non-Mormon dynamic is still socially significant, current social conditions chip away at its regional centrality. LDS Church leaders joined with other LDS and non-LDS community representatives in 2001 to work toward reducing LDS–non-LDS tensions. Globalization offers the region a new chance to shape its image without the hindrance of long-seated American assumptions. Karl Malone's regional representations may turn out to be quite helpful. New rounds of immigration force relationships among an ever-changing mix of regional inhabitants. Multiculturalism highlights the concerns of different groups. Issues arise that do not easily break along Mormon–non-Mormon lines. Terry Tempest Williams (whose writings are fundamentally important for political progressives trying to create a brighter regional future) recently wrote, for example, about preserving the natural environment in a way that neither avoided Mormon morality and regional identity nor implied that Mormon–non-Mormon antagonism must result when calling upon those sentiments (1992; on this book, see G. T. Smith 1993, 291–353).

Because of this changing context, regional inhabitants have opportunities to build upon the regional peace created a century ago and to rethink problematic aspects of regional culture. Many thought the 2002 Winter Olympics offered opportunities to shape the region's image to the outside world. It remains to be seen, however, whether internal debates move regional ideologies and dispositions in more progressive directions. Regions pull together many people(s), as well as multiple and shifting processes. By doing so, they create an inherent potential for productive conversations, but there is never any guarantee that such conversations will result (Limerick 1996; Cartier 2001). A century ago, the Mormon–non-Mormon regional conversation promoted vital regional peace between Mormons and non-Mormons, but it rejected more egalitarian visions of American citizenship in favor of the liberalist/nationalist pluralism that emerged. One can only hope that the future region will accommodate a wider conversation.

NOTES

Preface

1. Use of the term *radical* in this book is not meant to indicate either a place on a political continuum or an inclination toward certain political methods; rather, it means a position that challenges a dominant practice or ideology in fundamental ways. By this definition, Mormonism remains theologically radical in relation to mainstream Christianity. My argument in this book is that its social radicalism in relation to mainstream American society diminished. I use the term *conservative* to refer to positions that do not fundamentally challenge the status quo. Unless otherwise stated, the status quo I refer to when using *conservative* is the American status quo. This social conservatism may overlap with what is referred to today as political conservatism, but the terms are not equivalent. The current distinction between political liberalism and political conservatism refers to two positions that are both often deeply conservative socially. Both have a strong interest in maintaining many fundamental elements of the status quo—for example, capitalism. When I refer to political conservatism rather than social conservatism, I use *political conservatism,* while I often use *conservatism* to refer to social conservatism.

Introduction

1. Some readers may find terminology used in this book unfamiliar. *Mormon* refers to a member of the Church of Jesus Christ of Latter-day Saints. I use *Mormons, LDS* (for Latter-day Saints), and *Saints* synonymously. *Non-Mormon* and *non-LDS* refer here to people, almost always white, who do not belong to the LDS Church (I categorize Native Americans and other nonwhite groups separately to match historical categorizations). Non-Mormon is clearly a heterogeneous category and masks much difference within it. I justify its use not because I consider it a unitary category but because it highlights the main social dynamic that runs throughout this book. People holding various other identities were regionally constructed as non-Mormon.

Though I rarely use it, the term *Gentiles* also refers to all those who are not members of the LDS Church, usually even Jews. Nineteenth-century Mormons used the term because they considered themselves God's covenant people of the age. The Mormon culture region can be regarded as that area of the world where the terms *Mormon* and *non-Mormon* and the social distinctions they represent resonate in public discourse. In practical terms, this region consists of the area where Mormons constitute the largest religious grouping—most of Utah, northern Arizona, southern Idaho, and western Wyoming. By *Mormonism* I mean the system of thought linked to LDS doctrine and institutions. Because such thought is not always strictly doctrinal, there is some overlap between the terms *Mormonism* and *Mormon culture* (*Mormon culture* refers more specifically to norms, ideals, and ways of creating meaning that Mormons hold whether or not these are linked to LDS doctrine).

2. To be sure, other geographers have written about this area in the intervening years; perhaps most well-known nationally are Jeanne Kay Guelke (for example, Kay 1997; Kay and Brown 1985; and Morin and Guelke 1998) on environment and gender, Richard Jackson (1978 and 1992) on settlement and environmental perception, Richard Francaviglia (1978) on landscape morphology, and Lowell C. Bennion (1980; Louder and Bennion 1978) on Mormonism's historical geography. But in the discipline of geography, no other single work has had the impact of Meinig's piece.

3. This campaign to Americanize Mormons developed alongside the slowly growing campaign to Americanize white, non-Anglo immigrants; the height of the former (1880s–1915) slightly preceded the apex of the latter (1890s–1920s). On the latter, see Jacobson (1998); and Dinnerstein and Reimers (1999).

4. Even Meinig (1996) glosses too easily over the extent to which Mormon Americanization was also a regionalization.

5. Others speak of LDS "assimilation" (see Mauss 1994, for the best example). I think the term *assimilation,* like *Americanization,* is somewhat problematic, partly because it takes the majority (American) culture too much for granted; it does not subject American norms to enough critical scrutiny. I also think that multiculturalist critiques have revealed that the term encompasses too much desire for national uniformity (see the debates in Takaki [1994]).

6. Donald Meinig suggests that "the single most compelling reason for the recognition of a Mormon region is the simple fact that its residents are aware that [Mormon-Gentile contact and creative tension] still exists" (1965, 215).

7. I thank John Agnew for the expression "advance guard."

Chapter 1: The Region as the Unit of Analysis

1. Donald Meinig has long been interested in this issue (see, for example, 1965, 1971, and 1986). I consider the present work to be an extension of Meinig's concerns—although looking to different sources for answers—not a replacement for them.

2. These examples are chosen deliberately. Just as races and ethnicities do not

exist in some natural, eternal, or essentialistic sense, neither do regions. But just as races or ethnicities exist in the sense that the (contingent) social organizations of people into such groupings produce profoundly important social effects, so, too, can regions.

3. Regional geography and regional history are complex fields. Those wishing to explore their claims and practices in more detail might begin with such sources (beyond those referred to elsewhere in this book) as Gregory (1982); Thrift (1983); Massey (1984); Pudup (1988); Sayer (1989); A. Murphy (1991); Häkli (1998); MacLeod (1998); Limerick, Milner, and Rankin (1991); Cronon, Miles, and Gitlin (1992); Wrobel and Steiner (1997); Matsumoto and Allmendinger (1999); and R. White and Findlay (1999).

4. The object of this study thus differs from that of regional science or that of much of British regional geography; in different ways, both of those pursuits center on preconstituted political administrative units.

5. This changed emphasis parallels concerns of some regional social history. The "New Western History," for example, exhibits a wariness of unitary characterizations of the American West, particularly those that fail to draw attention to relations of dominance (the best example is perhaps Limerick [1987]).

6. It should be clear by now that I am not using *culture* to refer to a whole way of life or as something that somehow exists apart from social contest. In cultural studies, conceptions of culture, while still connoting something of a shared unconscious, have shifted away from something static to something resembling a "structure of improvisation," which allows societies and individuals to assume multiple and shifting positions (within limits) through negotiation and struggle (Greenblatt 1990; see also Jenks 1993). For me, the "cultural" specifies widely utilized patterns of meaning creation (see P. Jackson 1989), while the "social" refers to the (often patterned forms of) relationships between people.

7. Such marginalizations usually result anyway, even if they are not necessary. Theorists imagine identities without oppression (I. Young 1990; Said 1993; West 1994; Massey and Jess 1995; Lippard 1997; Sack 1999).

8. Although see Givens (1997); Flake (2000); and Gordon (2002) on the centrality of religion over a long time period and of polygamy during its heyday, especially to Mormonism's eastern opponents.

9. Particularly helpful are Entrikin (1991, 1996, and 1997); Sack (1997); Proctor and Smith (1999); D. Smith (2000). A few significant geographic treatments of morality focusing less explicitly on place preceded them, including Jackson (1984 and 1989); and Driver (1988). Robert Park, with his notion of "moral regions" (1952), and the traditional regional geographers discussed in Livingstone (1992) are important predecessors of all of these.

10. For other important examples of a similar argument, see J. Allen, Massey, and Cochrane (1998); Amin and Thrift (1994); Harris (1991); and Dear and Wolch (1989).

11. The temporal porosity of regions should also be discussed because the past always exercises a presence.

12. Because I focus on the Mormon–non-Mormon dynamic (and because of personal predilections and sources that are more complete on Mormons than non-Mormons), this book devotes more space to things LDS than to things non-LDS; *Mormon* is always the necessary referent. I make no apologies for the substantive focus but hope others will produce accounts with different emphases.

13. Likewise, because the term *culture* encompasses many processes not necessarily related (Mitchell 1995), someone else's ideas of culture would likely produce a different Mormon culture region than the one I am here suggesting based on socially fundamental moral habits.

14. These are located in a multivolume set generically entitled *Conference Reports of the Church of Jesus Christ of Latter-day Saints, 1880, 1897–1973*, published by various names of publishers (usually connected with *Deseret News*) in Salt Lake City. I refer to them as *Conference Reports* in the Works Cited.

15. To a lesser degree and surely in a distorted manner, these records also hint at what the Ute themselves thought about the opening.

16. I also recognize that every representation of other people reproduces my own ideological distortions (Duncan 1993; Duncan and Ley 1993). It is impossible to fully "let people speak for themselves." Yet when such representations challenge dominant ideologies (as I believe those in this book do), they can be helpful as long as the source of this representational knowledge is properly situated (Haraway 1988; Alcoff 1991–92).

Chapter 2: Moderating Feminist Imaginations

1. Celestial marriage is the LDS doctrine encompassing continued marriage relations in the eternities. For most of the nineteenth century, the church taught that polygamy was the necessary form of celestial marriage.

2. I note here that turn-of-the-century "Mormon feminism" is a problematic concept by today's standards (see also Iversen 1997, 7–10; and Carver 2000, 13–14). But because it promoted an expansive view of women in many ways, I will not multiply scare quotes. I also hope to signal that scholars, for many reasons, ought to reclaim Mormon female activism as a type of feminism.

3. LDS women were objecting to their impending disfranchisement and treatment in polygamy prosecutions.

4. Jessie Embry argues that polygamy did not produce this independent woman at greater rates than monogamy did (1987, 89–104). While there is probably validity to her argument that the rhetoric of independence was greater than the reality, methodological limitations of her study (including oral interviews with children of polygamists long after polygamy ended) make it difficult to measure accurately this gap between discourse and practice.

5. Stanley Ivins observes that plural wives generally had fewer children than did monogamous Mormon women (1992, 176–77).

6. Kirby was once a polygamous wife. When the church excommunicated her

then-husband, William S. Godbe, she apparently lost favor as well. Though she continued to claim membership, the church never advertised her as a member who promoted suffrage and protested antipolygamy legislation, both of which she did (Beeton 1991, 23–24).

7. The "Manifesto," in which church president Wilford Woodruff proclaimed the end of church-endorsed polygamy, did not completely squelch the practice; a few members subsequently contracted secret plural marriages (K. Cannon 1992; Quinn 1985). But the vast majority of church members no longer considered the practice applicable to their own situation.

8. Lawrence was a former Mormon and a Salt Lake City merchant who, by this time, was active in Utah's Socialist Party (McCormick and Sillito 1994).

9. Critiques of nineteenth- and early-twentieth-century Mormonism continually "orientalized" church members (Said 1994). Critics constantly compared Mormons with the so-called oriental races, especially because of the church's polygamy and prophetic leadership structure (*Salt Lake Tribune*, 4 July 1880); by dint of Mormon cultural inheritance, they assumed Latter-day Saints were miserable, ignorant, and incapable of progressive change (Merriam 1894, 108; Vermilye 1912). Franklin Spalding's letter assumes Mormons could not change on their own, despite his rejection of Mormon ignorance and miserableness: "May I ask you to try to understand the difficulty of my position [a Salt Lake City Episcopal reverend who often spoke out against Mormonism]? I think it is generally recognized that it is the duty of all Christian missionaries to believe the best they can about the people among whom they are working. At the Edinburgh Conference last fall the real virtue of heathen races was the point most emphasized. We do not go to China, Japan, India, because the people there are utterly depraved but we go there because their inherent worth, in spite of their superstition and ignorance, constitutes an appeal to give them more light and more truth. You [C. E. Mason, president of the Interdenominational Council of Women for Christian and Patriotic Service], and those who think like you, insist upon making the Mormons an exception to this rule. . . ." Spalding argued that the falsehoods perpetuated about polygamists only made church members more defensive: "Mormons simply cannot understand your point of view. He [*sic*] knows that the awful tales about the misery of plural wives are not true in his experience." See the correspondences between Spalding and Mason, the Right Reverend Charles S. Burch from New York City, and the Reverend William Seeley from Yorkshire in the Spalding collection for an interesting discussion about strategies for ridding Utah of polygamy and Mormonism. The letters exemplify how easy it was for most non-Mormons to close off critical approaches to dominant social norms when they feared a Mormon return to objectionable practices and power.

10. A later example was when Joseph F. Smith, the president of the church, tried to mediate between the somewhat more egalitarian gender position of Anthon H. Lund, his first counselor, and the less egalitarian position of Hyrum M. Smith, his son who was also an apostle, during a 1904 LDS stake conference (Lund n.d., 25:63).

11. But see Newell (1992a and 1992b) on how some early Mormon women claimed partial priesthood power. These claims to priesthood power eroded by about 1930 or 1940, as church leaders gradually but systematically countered them. Women held complex and contradictory positions in nineteenth-century Mormon culture. The culture encompassed much wider views on the issue than is commonly supposed (even within individuals, such as Brigham Young). It is a mistake to take Brigham Young's or anyone else's retrogressive statements and elevate them to "classic [LDS] doctrine" (as in Kern 1981, 190). Contradictory views about women's position existed in the culture, apparently without great tension before 1890, though some viewpoints were more dominant than others (defending a persecuted church provided most faithful Mormons with sufficient cause to overlook intracommunity differences of opinion). Doctrinal codification occurred largely in the twentieth century, as LDS leaders valorized some nineteenth-century cultural elements and discarded others (see also Alexander 1986).

12. Although critiques of monogamy from within the system could still potentially be enacted, Mormon feminism's third radical element—its defense of *polygamic* female authority*—was no longer tenable. It was not so much that the theory behind the defense had been undercut; rather, any defense of polygamy, especially after the so-called Second Manifesto of 1904 (Alexander 1986, 64–66), brought almost universal social ostracism and was *barely* legal (on the only gradually diminishing power of the antipolygamy movement, see Iversen [1997]).

13. I added emphasis because such qualifying sentiments were increasingly added to statements about women's postsuffrage social influence. These "matters pertaining to the uplift and betterment of humanity" tended to operate in only a few sites.

14. This forgetfulness provides additional indication that Americans found it difficult to acknowledge polygamous wives as capable agents. Many felt a polygamous Utah never really belonged to the United States.

15. The *Young Woman's Journal* publicized women's noteworthy accomplishments throughout the world. Such articles continued to appear, even in the *Relief Society Magazine*, but the significance of these articles may have declined because twentieth-century Mormon women of achievement provided strong local role models.

16. The emphasis on health and hygiene as female public-sphere issues mirrored increased attention to health and hygiene in the *Young Woman's Journal* in 1910 and 1920 compared with 1890 and 1900.

17. Evidence that domestic concerns motivated women's public activity can be found in E. Lindsey (n.d., 1–10); "A Word to Women" (1900); R. Penrose (1908); A. W. Cannon (1911, 1912, and 1913); "Women Recognized" (1912); Bradley (1991); Alexander (1995a); Bate (1995, 29–44); Black and McPherson (1995, 12–14); and Carver (2000).

18. Advantages may be said to be deserved either because of individual effort (racial privilege is often justified in this manner) or because nature fitted some people to use those advantages better. The two arguments often converge. Early-twentieth-century LDS culture allowed for both a social and a natural construction of gender

(though most arguments relied on the latter), as in the following statement about courtship: "Society has given the young man the prerogative of selecting the girl he wishes to court, of giving the invitations, making the advances and proposing marriage. It is the prerogative of the woman, however, to decide on and uphold the standards of courtship because, as a rule, she is less liable to be influenced by bad motives or moral weakness; and further she has the prerogative of accepting or refusing courtship or proposal" (Young Men's Mutual Improvement Association n.d.d, 46). Note, however, that the emphasis is on male privilege and female responsibility.

19. Here I follow Aida Hurtado's argument that the presence of un(re)marked categories betrays acceptance of privilege (1996, 137). Hurtado's argument centers on white feminists' general failure to consider whiteness as exceptional and white women's experiences as anything other than the norm upon which feminism should theorize. Self-identification with American whiteness and frustration when others did not extend the privileges of whiteness to the Saints marked turn-of-the-century LDS culture. One might argue that many Mormon women allowed Mormon culture to reinscribe male privilege during this period in exchange for more complete enjoyment of the privileges of whiteness. Susa Young Gates, for example, seemed to combine the increasing LDS urge to learn of one's ancestors (Alexander 1986, 298–300) with this desire to claim white privilege. Her frequent short biographies of leaders of the Young Ladies' Mutual Improvement Association (Gates 1911) teem with references to the noble European stock from which these leaders came.

20. While priesthood was a site of male privilege, the LDS priesthood had a different structure of male privilege than did priesthoods of other Christian religions. The LDS Church had a lay, universal (except for blacks) male priesthood. Priesthood power was exercised in day-to-day activities, even within the family. This installed a sense of male privilege even more strongly in Mormon culture. As Marilyn Warensky points out, women's lack of priesthood authority affects all Mormon women, not just a small group with leadership aspirations (1978, 31). Such a situation creates ambiguous effects. Warensky and Terry Tempest Williams both want a universal Mormon priesthood but emphasize very different implications of the universal male priesthood (Warensky wrote just before priesthood authority was extended to black males; Williams wrote well after that change). Warensky (1978) focuses on women's frustration and undue deference toward men, while Williams (1992) points to family spiritual/emotional power and closeness and to surreptitiously cultivated female spiritual strength.

21. Young men were encouraged to have the same virtue as women in, for example, Brimhall (n.d., 27a, 183a); "Mormon" Women's Protest ([1886], 76–77); Cragan (1895, 254); Lund (n.d.); J. H. Smith (1910b, 12–13); Huntsman (n.d., [Part 4], 85); and McKay (1917, 56).

22. This passage is located in the Book of Mormon, a book of LDS scripture.

23. Her apparent silence toward humanity, however, reinscribed a role of female public deference.

24. See Jesse Hoy's similar conclusions after spending the last quarter of the nine-

teenth century among the Ute and Shoshone of northeastern Utah and northwestern Colorado (n.d., 145, 148, 258). Even to talk of home-centeredness in non-European cultures is often misleading. "Home" is not an interculturally fixed category, Paula Gunn Allen (1986), in particular, reminds us. American Indian women's smaller geographical sphere of activity compared with men's did not necessarily translate into a domestic–non-domestic gender distinction.

25. Cracks began to appear in the American women's movement over the issues surrounding the Smoot controversy. Some suffrage leaders, such as Susan B. Anthony, articulated opinions supporting Smoot and opposing strengthened antidivorce laws in opposition to antipolygamist activists who insisted on women's superior moral authority within the home and played a strong role in the fight to unseat Smoot (Iversen 1997, 213–38).

26. Even Joseph F. Smith, the church president, had to admit that his wives sometimes did not conform to his direction: "I wish they would [go to church meetings], Mr. Chairman, but sometimes they do not go" (U.S. Congress 1906, 1:384).

27. Lystra and Seidman differ over whether these expectations were Victorian or romantic. For my purposes, this debate matters little, since this was a time of transition between Victorian and romantic expectations in American society; norms from both periods existed simultaneously.

28. In Mormon theology, temple marriage is much more highly valued than church or civil marriage. To have a temple marriage, both partners must live according to church teachings.

29. Gates's own life is emblematic of the changes in Mormon gender culture. A daughter of Brigham Young, she played strong roles in LDS women's groups and Utah civic organizations. She founded and edited the *Young Woman's Journal* and the *Relief Society Magazine*. She served on the board of regents at both Brigham Young University and the State Agricultural College (now Utah State University), cofounded the Sons and Daughters of the Utah Pioneers, and was a president of that organization. She also founded the Utah Woman's Press Club and the Utah Daughters of the Revolution. An early relationship resulted in heartache and divorce, but her second marriage brought much more joy. Carolyn Person argues that Gates's early feminism gradually gave way to conservatism and a strong sense of gender hierarchy (1976, 215–20). A spiritual reconversion around her fortieth birthday seems to have been key. After that, she increasingly deferred to men and felt they should lead in domestic, civic, and spiritual matters.

30. See, however, the seriousness that the topic of relationships provoked in the 1912–13 Young Men's Mutual Improvement Association manual (Young Men's Mutual Improvement Association n.d.d, 42–45).

31. Ruth Cowan (1983) notes a similar irony in the technological development of housework's tools. Technologies were supposed to lighten women's housework burdens, but their ideological accompaniment, among other things, was an expectation of increasing levels of household cleanliness. The technologies that were supposed to liberate women kept them just as busy (or busier) with housework.

32. Examples of general conference addresses on motherhood include Ellsworth (1911, 75–77); Herrick (1911, 75–76); C. Hart (1913, 41–43); Callis (1917, 134); and S. L. Richards (1917, 139).

33. I say "almost all" because they clearly hesitated to assert that women ought to have the same responsibility and authority as men in spheres where they believed God had given men the authority (church leadership and leadership of the family, for example). But they believed that God gave men authority in these areas simply because someone had to have authority for order to exist and that men's authority in these areas had little implication for authority in other areas.

34. Daniel Howe makes a similar point about nineteenth-century evangelical Christianity: too many historians treat the movement as either a democratic, liberating power or an austere movement of social control, but not as both (1989, 126–28).

Chapter 3: Privatizing Mormon Communitarianism

1. Part of the pre-Manifesto strategy to diminish Mormon power included limiting immigration of foreign converts. American legislators searched for some time for a legal method to do so. There were some misguided efforts to have Mormon immigrants excluded from immigration as paupers. Although these did not succeed because few Mormon immigrants actually became paupers (Mulder 1957, 299), some Americans outside the region equated Mormon communitarianism with poverty.

2. Jan Shipps (1987) points out more consistently and effectively than other scholars that non-LDS objectors to Mormon actions have historically fallen into two basic categories. On the one hand were those whose chief complaints with the church were religiously based. These have primarily been people strongly identified with mainstream Protestantism. On the other hand were those who cared much less about LDS theology and instead protested the LDS Church's political and economic power. At certain historical junctures (including the late nineteenth century), these groups' criticisms converged.

3. The LDS Church did not by any means abandon all economic influence; it continued as an institution, and its leaders continued as individuals, to participate heavily in many leading regional companies. Nevertheless, such influence remained only because the church and its leaders ever more successfully played by capitalist rules.

4. The YMMIA insisted that lessons on economics presented in the 1910–11 and 1911–12 manuals "have been treated wholly from an economic and practical point of view. No attempt has been made to connect the Church with the interpretation of any fact or theory here presented" (Young Men's Mutual Improvement Association n.d.c, 3). Nevertheless, these manuals' statements about wage labor seem, in the absence of an effective countervailing tendency, to encapsulate what young men learned about their relationship to work.

5. This is not to say that attitudes toward gender hierarchies paralleled those toward economic hierarchies among all individuals.

6. Most Saints distrusted organized labor for two reasons in particular: LDS leaders were increasingly capitalists themselves and expressed their interests more often (and increasingly unsubtly), and western U.S. labor represented itself as anti-Mormon. Non-Mormon labor disliked Mormon communitarian and separatist activities as much as non-Mormon capitalists did. After LDS communitarianism came to an end, this anti-Mormonism persisted much longer within labor than within capital (Alexander 1986, 186–89).

7. Anthon Lund, first counselor to the president of the church, noted in a 1907 journal entry that "David Eccles [an LDS entrepreneur] called on the President [Joseph F. Smith]. He says that we are making too much of the educational work. Our boys are studying and becoming unfit for labor. He says they can not get workmen to keep their factories going" (Lund n.d., 29:6).

8. Whether they would have wanted to or not, LDS leaders did not have the freedom leaders of other churches had to resist the system.

9. William H. Smart, the Wasatch stake president, had an interest in more than just the settlement of individuals. He had been in contact with the church's First Presidency about colonizing the reservation ("reclaiming the waste land of the Uinta Valley"), and he manifestly saw such a project as God's work in expanding Zion. Many officials (including himself as president) of the Wasatch Development Company, the company heavily involved in helping settle the reservation, were church stake leaders, and Smart often conflated the work of the two institutions in his diary. In May, he strategized with Senator Reed Smoot, a Mormon apostle, about reservation matters. While there is no intimation of illegal or radically separatist objectives in Smart's diaries, he gives the impression that the church wanted a dominant presence in this area (W. H. Smart n.d., 60–135, quote on 62; see also Malanson 1985, 14). An early Mormon settler on the reservation, however, recalled that church leaders did not preach such regional dominance from the pulpit (Bartlett 1974, 32). For more details, see W. B. Smart (1982); and Fuller (1990).

10. Craig Fuller regards the LDS stance in the controversy as one of the church leaders' last echoes of nineteenth-century Mormon communitarianism, even as many LDS intended individualistically minded settlement (1990, 219–49).

11. Terryl Givens shows how some recent LDS scholars think it more likely that the Book of Mormon refers to a small group of people who lived between present-day Guatemala City and Veracruz, Mexico, rather than the entire American landmass (2002, 126). If so, the idea (virtually unquestioned in the nineteenth century) that all of the continent's aboriginal inhabitants are of Book of Mormon/Israelite descent becomes much more problematic.

12. While it is possible for a Native American Mormon to favorably compare LDS notions of community and place with her tribal values (Hafen 1998), one should remember that Mormon communitarianism held Native American identity in low regard. (Mormons even assigned non-LDS white communities a lower moral worth than their own communities during LDS communitarianism.)

13. Non-Mormons also perceived a difference but characterized it differently.

Shortly after arriving in Salt Lake City, Franklin Spalding, an Episcopal bishop, remarked, "One breathes a different atmosphere when he crosses the Colorado line. There is a push, a go, an ambition, a confidence in the larger future which is not as general in Utah. When it is remembered that the Mormon Church as an emigration Society has brought to this state many from Europe and the poorer parts of our country, and that the settlers in Colorado are largely the young and progressive men and women from the best parts of the east, the difference is explained. The mormon farmer is easily satisfied, the poorest condition here being better in most cases than he was used to. The young American who has come west for fame and fortune dose [sic] not have the word 'enough' in his vocabulary" (1905a, 7–8).

14. For example, in 1883, Mormons had also distinguished between LDS material contentment and non-LDS zealousness for quick material accumulation. Mary M. Lucke wrote that "'the women of Utah are illustrious examples [of good character],' and are not any behind their sisters of the world in intelligence, culture and morality, with all the intuition of true feminine nature; the same aspirations, the same desires, but with the remarkable difference of living for more than worldly goods . . ." (*Home Writer,* 18 June 1883, 6–7).

15. Although this company clearly blurred the distinction between church and economy, it still garnered private profits. The company encouraged some (perhaps non-Mormon) homesteaders to settle and work the land for a few years, after which the company would buy the land (Barton n.d., 20–22). It must be noted, however, that this company catered much more to Mormons than to non-Mormons (Wasatch Development Company n.d.). Soon after obtaining water rights on the reservation, it turned these over to a subsidiary representing a group of homesteaders (Dry Gulch Irrigation Company), which thereafter aggressively sought communal water development, including "unclaimed" Indian rights to water (Fuller 1990, 269–309); government officers characterized Mormons as particularly seeking a permanent footing in the Uintah Basin (Collett 1905; Code 1907, 1908, and 1911).

16. As Richard Jackson notes, the invented tradition in Mormon culture that the Salt Lake Valley was a barren, desolate place upon the Saints' arrival facilitated reference to the miracle of the desert blossoming as a rose (1978, especially 330–34). The earliest Mormon settlers viewed the Salt Lake Valley as a potentially productive, if somewhat dry, agricultural area, not as a barren desert.

17. Young women needing work were encouraged to find employment from others (or find a husband).

18. Church leaders continued to conflate the people of Utah with the Mormon people, as well.

19. Underwood (1993) is the most recent comprehensive treatment of early Mormon millennialism. He argues against what has been called the Kingdom School of Mormon historiography (Hansen [1967] and Leone [1979] are the most prominent examples). The Kingdom School argues that nineteenth-century Mormonism constituted not only a new belief system but also a fundamental challenge to American society. Underwood makes the valid point that early Mormonism cannot be reduced

to a movement growing out of social dissatisfaction with American society; it also grew out of profoundly spiritual longings. But, besides incorporating an unreasonably tough standard as to what constitutes radicalism, he emphasizes his point too strongly so that he can downplay Mormonism's social content. In focusing on the first decade and a half of Mormonism, he pays too little attention to the continuing interplay between LDS eschatological and social concerns throughout the rest of the nineteenth century. I return to a point made in chapter 2: a key feature of nineteenth-century Mormonism was its *simultaneous* conservatism and radicalism.

20. Zion had other meanings as well. The church itself, with its geographic centers, was called Zion. Zion also meant where the pure in heart dwelled. It referred to the Missouri lands from which the Saints had been evicted in the 1830s and which served as a focus for millennial aspirations. At times it meant the United States or the North and South American continents. Once the Saints arrived in the Great Basin, they usually called areas in which they were dominant "Zion." This regional definition (along with the definition of Zion as the church itself) dominated in the period under study. The present analysis focuses on region-delineating uses of the term *Zion*.

21. In spite of deriving these ideas from ecofeminism, my argument here is not primarily about LDS culture's effect on the environment (on that, see Alexander 1995a; and Kay and Brown 1985); rather, my focus is on the relationship between region, nation, and individual.

22. For a sermon retaining older views of the relationship between region and nation, see J. F. Smith (1918a, 4–5).

23. Smart's sentiment also reflects what Carolyn Merchant calls an organic, pastoral view of a feminized nature (Merchant 1980, 7–9). The land is coded as female, but there are worries about the greater exploitation involved with mining (and perhaps fears of what Merchant terms "disorderly nature"—capable of leading men astray) than with the more legitimate relationship to the land represented by agriculture.

24. Home manufacturers were church-led efforts to develop broad production capacity and employment capability in the region.

25. See also Mulder (1957, 213–14) on the church's changing expectations for Scandinavian immigrants to make a living.

26. On the back-to-the-farm movement, see Merrill (1902, 62); McMurrin (1903); J. F. Smith (1903b, 3; and 1910, 3–4); J. H. Smith (1909, 1910a, and 1910b); Robinson (1915, 106–7); and Irving (1987, 168–90).

27. Anne McClintock argues that "women are typically constructed as the symbolic bearers of the nation but are denied any direct relation to national agency" (1997, 90). The temporal paradox of nationalism—the simultaneously forward and backward glance that Tom Nairn represented with the figure of Janus in his *Faces of Nationalism*—tends to be resolved by assigning women to the inert and men to the progressive characteristics of the nation (McClintock 1997, 91–93). Mormons characterized the region in much the way that women tend to be figured in nation-

alism—as the unchanging rearer of national virtue—vital to, but at a remove from, the shifting fortunes of national development.

28. On the importance of individual work for lasting social progress, see especially Young Men's Mutual Improvement Association (n.d.d; n.d.e, 7–9, 31–49, 62–64; and n.d.l, 3–6); and Utah governor Heber M. Wells's Fourth of July speech (reported in the *Vernal Express*, 11 July 1903).

29. It is assumed that the efficiency of sectors does not vary greatly from state to state and that consumption needs for a state can be defined by the country's sectoral workforce division. The set of total sectors (and definitions of those sectors) varies slightly from census to census. It is therefore more accurate to compare different states' vulnerability indexes with one another in a given year than to chart a state's absolute index from decade to decade.

30. Thomas Alexander (1996 and personal correspondence [18 April 2000]) suggests that this apparent overall level of self-sufficiency masks the beginning of an "old colonial economy" in which unfinished or semimanufactured agricultural and mineral products were shipped out of Utah, while finished manufactures were shipped in.

31. Examples of LDS leaders' ideas about home manufacturing can be found in Clawson (1906, 30–33); G. A. Smith (1906, 52–53); J. F. Smith (1909, 7; 1910, 3–4; and 1918a, 2–5); Grant (1913, 90–91; and 1919a, 75–76); and F. Lyman (1916, 26–27).

32. Discussion of charges of personal profiteering by church leaders are in U.S. Congress (1906, 1:691, 2:196–97, 2:211–12, 2:297, 3:142–60, 3:284–85, 3:324–34, 4:78–83, 4:257–63, 4:374–98); and Alexander (1986, 74–92).

33. On home industry, see Brimhall (n.d., 44); Smoot (1900, 6–7); F. Lyman (1904, 15–17); Ellsworth (1909, 61–62); Kimball (1909, 31–34); C. Penrose (1913, 23); and J. F. Smith (1917, 2–3).

34. LDS First Presidency member Anthon H. Lund's diaries make clear that while charges continued to be made against church involvement in *capitalist* economics through 1920, church leaders were not seriously concerned with these, except for the monopoly probe against the Utah-Idaho Sugar Company (n.d., 32:26). They took charges against church political involvement much more seriously. Most capitalists had little against church capitalist involvement, except where church-dominated corporations were competitors.

35. A few years earlier, church president Joseph F. Smith had seemed more concerned about this changed state of affairs:"Formerly [immigrants] were assigned to the various wards as they came in, with recommendations to the Bishops and leading men to look after them, to provide them labor, and assist them in their inexperience, that they might . . . eventually establish themselves in independency and prosperity by the results of their own labor" (1899, 41).

36. Anthon Lund's diaries indicate that church leaders did not give up their assumption of authority over such matters quite so immediately as Smoot implies, though this assumption did diminish, especially after the hearings (see especially n.d., 28:48, 29:2).

37. Since Mormon leaders knew that American culture did not value members of minority groups representing themselves, Smoot employed non-Mormon lawyers (Smoot 1903; First Presidency 1903).

38. Some non-Mormons saw the making of both Indians and Mormons into non-communal individuals as related projects (Gordon 2002, 204).

39. See, for example, the common attribution of savagery in the creation of an organization remembering the "heroics" of Mormons who fought against these groups (E. Lindsey n.d.).

40. Identifying Indians as Israelites and suggesting that Indians were a degenerate race were not original to Mormons (see Berkhofer 1978, 35–38), but linking such beliefs to their scriptural canon (through the Book of Mormon) and their particularly strong adherence to historic dispensationalism gave these beliefs a stronger currency to Mormons than to almost any other whites.

41. Although see also a Mormon attempt to liken Indian experiences to their own unjust removal from Nauvoo (S. Young 1912, 37). This attempt did not understand that Native Americans assigned greater importance to specific lands than did Mormons.

42. Mormons boasted of this claim (as they still do) in the midst of occupying Native Americans' lands, thus removing their means of subsistence, despite LDS sentiment, mentioned earlier, that providing the means for subsistence is better than feeding people in idleness (Young Men's Mutual Improvement Association n.d.j, 71).

43. Sentiments for teaching agriculture to Native Americans are found in Walsh (1898); Brosius (1899); Waddell (1904, 1905, and 1906); Mercer (1905); Peais (1905); and Spalding (1905b).

44. Hoy, incidentally, also admired nineteenth-century Mormons for taking the Constitution into their own hands when they were not protected by it. Few Mormons turned their own oppression into fundamental concern about other groups' oppression.

45. Mormons were not averse to defining themselves through other groups' "deficiencies" either. "Oriental" cultures failed to give the individual the same rights that "higher civilization" or "Christianity" did (Young Men's Mutual Improvement Association n.d.c, 23–26; Gates 1911, 261). Chinese Americans were said to live in conditions not fit for any one "of our race, and above all none of us" (Young Men's Mutual Improvement Association n.d.j, 78). Ironically, Asian Americans and Mormons have held similar positions of otherness in relation to dominant American culture since the nineteenth century (Bunker and Bitton 1983; Chen 2000).

46. After Snow became church president, Apostle Brigham Young Jr. suggested reestablishing the Law of Consecration as a precursor to reestablishing the United Order. Snow opted for the more individualistically oriented and politically acceptable alternative of tithing to bolster the church and redeem Zion (Alexander 1986, 6).

47. This short section on socialism, communism, and the United Order interrupts the manual's main project of laying out University of Wisconsin professor Richard Ely's left-tending but still mainstream economic principles. A later manual (likely

the 1912–13 edition) may have pushed the socialist comparison further, but it was recalled and replaced by the YMMIA board (including many in the First Presidency and the apostles) because its section on public utilities was deemed too socialistic (Smoot 1997, 116; Lund n.d., 32:48–49). The manuals' left leanings are usually attributed to B. H. Roberts, whose political feuds with some Republican church leaders were well known.

48. I suspect many contemporary Mormons agree with Cowley's reasoning on socialism yet see no irony in allying with a conservative social agenda apart from the LDS Church. Cowley was consistent. He blasted any non-LDS attempts to institute practices similar to LDS practices.

49. This is hardly a new argument. In 1922, a University of Chicago-trained LDS scholar wrote, "Thus the business man's standards and point of view is rapidly developing among [church] leaders. There is a growing tendency to take sides with the capitalist class and with large corporations against the laboring classes. The philosophy of the church leaders was at one time radical and socialistic; it is now conservative and capitalistic. . . . The present economic order is accepted by them as right and proper. In fact their philosophy seems to have completely changed in this respect from that held forty years ago. The United Order is as far from their minds as is socialism from the minds of the owners of large corporations" (Ericksen [1922] 1975, 72).

50. See Stryker (1992) on how Mormons made a similar claim about their key to knowledge.

51. In some senses, such silences are understandable. No Mormon socialism movement analogous to Christian socialism brought the issue to the fore (on the latter, see Cort 1988). Moreover, since Mormons clearly called themselves Christians, discussions of Christian socialism might have been thought to cover Mormonism. Yet Mormons' and mainstream Christians' predominant attitude toward each others' agendas was mutual rejection. Socialists had a national project they felt was more directly addressed through reference to Christianity than to Mormonism. This preference supports my point. Silence about Mormonism implied an unwillingness to take regional society seriously. Socialists appealed primarily to those who thought regional life was unimportant in a capitalist nation-state.

52. Reports of traveling socialists' speeches in the *Morning Examiner* are in the columns of 1 November 1906, 3 March 1907, 10 March 1907, and 7 October 1907. The *Duchesne (Utah) Record,* however, notes that a Dr. Herold spoke in 1916 to the convention of Duchesne County socialists on the topic of "The Economics of Mormonism" (9 September 1916). I have not yet located any record of what was said in the speech.

53. The Brotherhood of the Co-operative Commonwealth attempted—with little success—to unite all U.S. socialists. In 1897, Myron Reed, a Denver-based Christian socialist, tried to establish a colony in Utah under its auspices but with no success (Denton 1997).

54. Although see 28 April 1907 and 30 June 1907 for some theoretical commitments to local action.

55. Examples of local issues arising near elections can be found in the paper on 5 November 1905, 23 September 1906, and 27 October 1907.

56. Examples of columns in which local issues were discussed apart from election topics include 17 September 1905, 24 June 1906, 27 January 1907, 10 February 1907, and 4 August 1907.

57. The column's editorial staff clearly wanted more written about socialism than they could produce themselves. They relied heavily on reprinting nonlocal articles. Still, a universalistic approach characterized even most local socialists' writings.

58. See also the philosophically pitched "Debate on Socialism" in the *Duchesne (Utah) Record* (10 July 1915 through 11 September 1915). The short-lived socialist column in the *Nephi (Utah) Record* made much more effort to explain local farming production systems and other local issues from a socialist viewpoint, however (5 August 1904 through 23 September 1904). The socialist column in the *Vernal Express* also appealed to local conditions (in out-of-the-way eastern Utah) by arguing that under socialism the prices of shipping would be uniform (25 April 1903). One column in which the Ogden socialists came close to evaluating local production was when they denounced Mormon and Gentile capitalists alike and criticized the Salt Lake County Socialist Party's alliance with the anti-Mormon American Party in the 1905 election (*Ogden Morning Examiner,* 19 November 1905). This attack still remained more polemical than analytical, however. Also, a column once tried to explain how local agricultural waste resulted from capitalist inefficiency (3 November 1907).

59. Like Susa Young Gates and John Wells, Isaac Russell, a *New York Times* reporter, had at one time found hope in Mormonism as a social vision. He thought it paralleled socialist ideals, but he found church leaders' increasing involvement in capitalist extractive trusts difficult to swallow. In a letter to Spalding, he confided, "I was born a Mormon and loved to think our Church had struck an ideal working basis between cooperation and individual initiative. Sometimes I could feel that in the shaking loose of old shackles, and the general uprising against exploitive capital, and government and churches under its control, the Mormon philosophy was going to edge its way in with compelling force. But right on top of that there was the spectacle of the close partnership between the Mormon leaders and the exploitive program being carved out there in salt, sugar, coal, and smelting to contemplate" (1910).

60. LDS leaders' growing opposition to organized labor is documented in Lund (n.d., 25:36); Nibley (1906, 63–64); Grant (1919b, 12–15); Alexander (1986, 186–89; and 1991). Ironically, given charges against the church, church leaders argued that organized labor minimized individual economic freedom.

61. Some argue that Mormons directed their egalitarian values inward in the twentieth century. Dean May (1997) contends that the church turned away from economic communalism to protect social communalism—a viable option as long as the church acted like a Protestant church (see also Alexander 1986). While some scholars argue that egalitarian nineteenth-century LDS rhetoric cannot be trusted

since Mormons perpetuated capitalist inequalities in spite of it, May turns this argument around and suggests that present LDS rhetoric (dominated by unrelenting capitalist ideology) is less important than LDS actions (egalitarian within church confines).

Chapter 4: Re-presenting America

1. Scholars have ever since been arguing about Mormon intentions. Some claim that the Saints did intend to create an independent commonwealth (Hansen [1967] is the classic statement of this "Kingdom School"; see also Stryker 1992). Others (Underwood [1993] is a more recent example) find that the Kingdom School inflates the significance of rhetoric meant either to protest abuses of the Saints' rights or, more figuratively, to refer to a millennial spiritual kingdom that the Saints expected Christ to usher in. This rhetoric, they say, stemmed from a participationist, rather than a separatist, relationship with the United States. Others find evidence that the Saints were neither wholly separationist nor entirely nonseparationist. Relations with America at various historical moments led to episodes of greater or lesser separatism (Arrington 1958; Hill 1989; Winn 1989).

2. At least the church ended its practice of frequently prescribing political action. Some instances of direct political dictates continued to occur, though less openly and less often. It also took church leaders decades before they generally refrained from publicly promoting their political preferences. Early-twentieth-century debates revolved around whether such public pronouncements constituted church mandates or the exercise of individual citizenship.

3. Deseret was the name for the state Mormons leaders originally envisioned. The federal government turned down more than a half-dozen applications for statehood between 1850 and 1896. Rather than permit a Mormon-dominated state, the government created a territory, with the Indian-derived name of Utah.

4. A few additional examples of LDS protests against persecution are J. Taylor 1880, 102; *Home Writer*, 14 July 1882, 3–4; *"Mormon" Women's Protest* [1886]; *Deseret Evening News*, 3 July 1890; and Young Men's Mutual Improvement Association 1891, 58.

5. Before the 1890s, the Mormon People's Party and the non-Mormon Liberal Party were the two major parties in Utah. Neither had much connection to national political parties or even national political issues. Instead, they operated, respectively, as the voice of the Mormon church for the establishment of its Zion and the voice of those opposing the Mormon church and trying to Americanize Utah.

6. Walter M. Wolfe, a former Mormon, testified at the Smoot hearings that "there is an undercurrent among the older [LDS] people—and I have not noticed it among the younger people—that the conditions under which Utah was settled were oppressive, that the United States Government interfered with their liberty in many ways, and there is a feeling of resentment among the older people. In fact it . . . is often expressed that the Latter-Day [*sic*] Saints will some day rule the earth" (U.S.

Congress 1906, 4:28). Smoot's opponents in the hearings pursued fear of this resentment and lingering LDS aspirations in many ways, most notably through Chairman Julius Caesar Burrows's persistent questioning into whether LDS temple oaths enjoined members to be disloyal to the nation and an entering of some of the more militant LDS hymns into the record (4:64–67). Smoot's lawyers responded with testimony by many LDS witnesses that they felt nothing but loyalty to the nation and that the church was more apt to sing patriotic hymns in contemporary meetings than militant ones (4:275–81).

7. Some Mormon leaders clearly hoped to reestablish, at least partially, the old ways after a period in which tensions between Mormons and the federal government decreased. A few leaders, contrary to church pledges, continued some practices as secretly as possible. Non-Mormons were alert to such trends, even if they did not have all the details.

8. The *Tribune* staunchly supported disciplining the church in the 1880s. In the 1890s, it became much more conciliatory with the Americanization and statehood campaigns. In the early years of the twentieth century, however, it complained about Mormon power and practices in language that hearkened back to the 1880s.

9. As late as 1915, church leaders feared that the American Party would reconstitute itself. They feared, at the least, that the party would bring harassing legal action against church members and, at the most, that the party would attempt to disfranchise Mormons, as the Liberal Party did during the 1880s (Lund n.d., 36:2, 46). This fear partially explains why the church insisted on maintaining political party influence (even as it denied that it was doing so), just as continuing church influence partially explains why some non-Mormons continued threatening to revive the party.

10. I do not want to imply that nineteenth-century concern for oppression stemmed more from altruistic motives than from self-interest. Both Mormons and non-Mormons spoke of rights mostly when they were victims of oppression. Each group had difficulty seeing how it was simultaneously the oppressor and the oppressed. Nevertheless, a regionally active discourse concerned with oppression was more available in the late nineteenth century than in later decades.

11. Of course Teasdale could not have anticipated the LDS culture's recent fight against homosexuals in Utah schools, the church's mobilization against the Equal Rights Amendment in the 1970s and 1980s, or any of the battles countenanced by Mormon culture against nonmainstream political views in the latter half of the twentieth century. Part of the aim of this book is explaining how LDS culture came to allow for such petitions against "any handfull of people."

12. From one viewpoint, it is difficult to see why Mormons between 1890 and 1910 began claiming their rights had been upheld. After all, Mormons had little choice but to relinquish earlier practices; the federal government did not give in to Mormon demands. But from another viewpoint, the one that Mormons must have increasingly taken, statehood, regional peace, and the church's continued existence constituted a victory for Mormon liberty.

13. Throughout the 1910s, many church leaders regarded the Mexican Revolution as a form of anarchy (Robinson 1912, 80–81; J. F. Smith 1912, 5–7); these sentiments surely derived at least partly from concern for the safety of the LDS Mexican colonists, many of whom had settled there to escape polygamy prosecutions (Smoot 1997, especially 80, 98, 143–45, 164–66, 221–23). It is almost remarkable that one leader viewed that revolution as a battle over rights, analogous to the American Revolution (R. Pratt 1916, 144–47; and 1918, 97–98).

14. In the early part of the Saints' exodus from Nauvoo, the federal government asked for five hundred men to fight against Mexico. The Saints complied, even though many healthy men were therefore unable to help with the trek (their service raised much-needed cash for provisions, however).

15. Many regional inhabitants did not agree with aggressively prosecuting continued plural living by those married before the Manifesto. Although virtually all non-Mormons agreed that America should not tolerate polygamy, they differed on how best to rid Mormonism of it. Most hoped polygamy would disappear, but disagreements occurred on whether aggressive prosecution would best achieve that result.

16. As far as I can tell, these specific references to "race suicide" are directed more toward American identity than white identity. Nevertheless, Mormons could not have entirely escaped the racial overtones of the national anti-race-suicide movement that postulated a major crime existed when those carrying "civilization" did not reproduce such civilization through procreation.

17. Among other sources on the requirements of good citizenship, see Editorial, *Deseret Evening News,* 23 July 1890; G. Cannon (1897, 40–42); a speech by Utah's Governor Heber M. Wells reported in *Vernal Express,* 11 July 1903; J. H. Smith (1910a, 36–37); Austin (1917a); Young Men's Mutual Improvement Association (n.d.b; n.d.c; n.d.d, 63–64; n.d.e; and n.d.m, 83). Most of these statements about economic responsibility were directed to men. As chapter 2 argues, regional culture normatively removed women from "public" economic life.

18. I refer here to the philosophy of classical liberalism, not to the political liberalism that today is figured as the primary rival of conservatism.

19. Additional examples of Mormons claiming American civilization are in "Program of the Utah Pioneer Jubilee" (1897); J. F. Smith (1912); Young Men's Mutual Improvement Association (n.d.j, 77–78); and Reed Smoot's 1917 speech about Indian Wars veterans in E. Lindsey (n.d.). A. Ivins (1917, 51–52) is more ambivalent.

20. Salt Lake City's Americanization Day celebration conveyed similar ideas (*Salt Lake Tribune,* 5 July 1916). However, when wartime prejudice against German Americans and others began, some church leaders pled with the Saints to understand that old loyalties do not die easily and to be tolerant of one another (such a move was similar to that made by the national Protestant Federal Council of Churches during the war [Handy 1989, 287]). Even then, they argued there were no separate nationalities in the church (Lund 1917, 13; J. F. Smith 1917, 11–12; Alexander 1986, 47–48).

21. Evidence of Mormon attitudes toward minorities is in Bernice Anderson (1974, 3–4); Kurumada (1975, 10–13); Mitsunaga (1975, 9); Papanikolas and Kasai (1976, 342–43); Stipanovich (1976, 381–82); Yano (1976, 6, 17); Murakami (1976, 19); Uchida (1976, 8–9); Inouye (1979, 2); and Masaoka (1982, 11–12; and 1987, 30).

22. For just a few examples of the argument that LDS politics and religion were not separated enough, see U.S. Congress (1906, 1:1–23, 1:688, 2:1006–7, 2:363, 2:962–67, 3:470–94, 4:107, 4:468–69); and Kearns (1905a).

23. See Flake (2000, 109–89) on how Smoot's and Joseph F. Smith's similar, if more evasive, claims produced a semicrisis among some members who felt their leaders had abandoned the faith; church leaders in this case were required to a greater-than-usual degree to reassert their authority to speak and act as mouthpieces of God.

24. Smoot's attitude was neither unheard of nor dominant in Mormonism at the time, but it has since become almost canonically inscribed into LDS culture.

25. See C. Brian Hardy (1995) on how the professionalization of teachers in Mormon-controlled "public" schools helped establish this separation before the turn of the century.

26. Edward Leo Lyman (1986) argues that, even before the Manifesto and statehood, opponents of the church often put partisan politics ahead of philosophical disagreements with the church when church actions (or as here—Smoot's retaining his position) benefited their party.

27. Although becoming politically Protestant, the church retained theological distinctiveness from religious Protestantism through, for example, its nontrinitarian deity, belief in scriptures and prophetic revelation beyond the Bible, and emphasis on temples. This incomplete Protestantization of Mormonism also derives from a changed climate. By 1920, U.S. Protestants were somewhat more tolerant of theological pluralism (Handy 1991; Flake 2000).

28. Thatcher said he knew nothing of the rule when he decided to run; it could well have been formulated after he declared his candidacy. The rule was not part of formal church doctrine and was created to deal with the post-1891 relationship between the LDS Church and the state.

29. With many elements of Americanization, some Mormon leaders attempted to retain more influence than they publicly admitted. Some polygamy continued for a time amid denials. Church leaders continued (though less frequently) to claim jurisdiction over some noninstitutional economic contests (Lund n.d.; Smoot 1997). Some leaders implied that partisan political messages represented the church position (Democratic church leaders likely would have done so as much as Republicans if they could have). Church leaders took longer than most ordinary members to give up old practices (Alexander 1986). Significant differences existed among church leaders, however; some accepted new ways, while others wanted quietly to perpetuate the old order until a more propitious time for full reinstatement. Two opinions expressed by apostles in the same 1900 quorum meeting illustrate this. "I am aware of the feeling growing among the people that plural families are unpopular. They are growing less. [But t]hey will never die out. This principle will never be taken from the Earth. . . . There

are some who think the Church is going back upon the principle. I tell them this is not so," Marriner W. Merrill declared (quoted in Lund n.d., 18:33). In contrast, Francis M. Lyman thought the church should let polygamy die. Just as the Saints no longer followed the Law of Consecration, they could also manage without plural marriage. Instead, Lyman thought, the church should say little about plural marriage and instead "talk up" marriage itself (Lund n.d., 18:38). Some individuals even accommodated some of the changes but resisted others. Reed Smoot did not mourn the passing of polygamy, but he expected to have special influence over Utah's voters by virtue of his apostleship. As Merrill's statement intimates, ordinary Mormons increasingly acted on the assumption that plural marriage and church political and economic control were inevitably declining. To some extent, then, church leaders could not control the enormous cultural changes taking place.

30. As with much of the hearings' reasoning (by both Mormons and non-Mormons), this argument teemed with contradictions. The Mormon church had improperly infringed on one of its leaders' political opportunities, Smoot's opponents claimed. But, instead of opening up political opportunities for church leaders, they argued the government should never let church leaders hold political office. To them, this was not a contradiction because they assumed that anyone church leaders "allowed" to run for office must be an official church candidate.

31. Arguments over the Roberts case also contained their share of contradictions. Although originally against the "rule" about consulting with other church leaders before running for office, Roberts reached an understanding with the church by 1898. The church, he said, in giving permission to leaders to run was merely offering a leave of absence, not an endorsement (U.S. Congress 1906, 1:724). He received the church's blessing to run for a seat in the House as a Democrat. Without any uproar about the church's trying to influence Utah politics through his candidacy, he won the election. Nevertheless, the House refused to seat him then because he still lived with the multiple wives he had married before the 1890 Manifesto. Yet in the Smoot hearings, Smoot's opponents' lawyers argued by pointing to Roberts's early resistance to the rule that the church was unduly supporting Republicans and restricting the political opportunities of its Democratic members.

32. In reality, Smoot was at least Joseph F. Smith's candidate. Smith seemingly wanted Smoot in the Senate less to reinstate theocratic control over Utah politics than to ensure that someone in Washington would dependably look out for the institutional survival of the church (Flake 2000). As much as Smoot took this charge from his church leader seriously, it would be a mistake to reduce his three-decade senatorial career to this "calling."

33. Just as political independence was being forced on Mormons to mean separation of the individual from the communal (church) body, so, too, did some Mormon leaders try to force an individualization in the economic sphere. Mormon leaders came to regard independence and "manhood" to mean not "surrendering" to labor unions on issues of when to work and strike (Grant 1919b, 13–14). American conceptions of manliness were not race-neutral either (Bederman 1995).

34. Robert Booth Fowler argues that the most coherent and logically aware forms of liberalism tend to view even political parties with great distaste (1994, 204).

35. One of America's liberal conceits is that religious belief had little to do with political voting in the United States. As Robert Swierenga (1989) argues, throughout most of the nineteenth century, until no more than ten years before the Smoot hearings, religious affiliation was perhaps the strongest determinant of American voting patterns. Though the relation between religious affiliation and party voting became more complex after the mid-1890s (Handy 1989, 292–98), these norms separating religious experience from party voting were norms other Americans, at best, were just beginning to follow themselves.

36. Just as the relegation of women to the private sphere aids the myth of the independent man, the shunting of religion to the private sphere props up the ideology of independent politics (see Gordon [2002, 222] on the antipolygamist connection made between private religion and monogamous relationships).

37. I believe that what Carl Esbeck calls a structural-pluralist stance toward American church-state relations is more desirable (1994, 15–18). That is, the religious sphere ought not be completely separate from the political sphere. While government should not establish religion, neither should it deny religion a voice any more than it does other nongovernmental institutions, such as businesses, unions, or families. Religious people should feel free to incorporate their religious and other identities into politics. Although Mormons needed to learn to participate with non-Mormons politically, they should not have been required to check their religious identities at the door.

38. For public schools' treatment of Utah history, see Utah State Text Book Committee ([1897], 72–76); State Department of Public Instruction (1918a, 84–89; and 1918b, 90–91); Cranley (1942, 5–107); Moffitt (1944, 116–21); and Rampton (1969, 48–60); see also Banker (1993). Frederick Buchanan (1996) argues that well into the twentieth century Mormons and non-Mormons struggled over a localist versus centralist curriculum orientation. Yet the converging treatment of Utah history suggests that even if they sought to emphasize the local more than the national, Mormons had already developed significant faith in American progress.

39. For additional examples and evidence of this discourse that grew increasingly dominant over time, see Carter (1899); U.S. Congress (1906, 4:290); Redding (1910, 166–67); Hansen (1992, 231–38); and Young Men's Mutual Improvement Association (n.d.i, 101–3; and n.d.m, 77–91).

40. Bodnar (1992) contains a somewhat different interpretation of a similar celebratory shift nationally.

41. Incidentally, church leaders who argued for the right to continue living plurally seemed to sense the value of liberal individualist arguments. Smith, for example, agreed that living plurally was not only against the law of the land but also against the (post-Manifesto) law of the church. Nevertheless, he said, his justification for continued plural living was an individual one: he had made an individual pact

with God and with his wives not to abandon them, and this agreement superseded any more communal forms of pressure.

42. See also indications of regional inhabitants' (including non-Mormons') growing exasperation with those who insisted on not admitting Mormons and Mormon history into the national narrative (Smoot 1997, 103).

43. Kathleen Flake offers one explanation (2000, 173–75): Joseph F. Smith forgave the nation during Americanization. Joseph F. Smith Jr.'s later (1916) condemnation of the nation for its iniquity was a new sentiment that developed fully only after 1920. Joseph F. Smith Jr. located civilization's degradation in abandoning the previous generation's moral virtues for the pleasures of modern life rather than (as in earlier Mormon critiques) for failing to allow people to live the moral principles it hypocritically espoused.

44. Seeds of this change previously existed in Mormonism. Joseph Smith had called North and South America the land of Zion, yet Mormons downplayed this usage in favor of a regional definition of Zion until near the turn of the century. The regional definition did not fade into the background altogether, but it became less important.

45. To be sure, LDS attitudes toward difference should not be completely equated with mainstream American attitudes. For example, a key distinction between Mormon missionaries in Polynesia (including Joseph F. Smith many times during the nineteenth century) and those of other Christian denominations was that LDS missionaries did not separate their dwelling spaces from those of local peoples, did not require local peoples to support them financially, were willing to learn local languages, and generally treated local peoples with much respect (Maffly-Kiff 2000).

Chapter 5: A New Type of Home

1. Some people were more intensively socialized into these regional processes than others. Most Native Americans, twentieth-century immigrants, and African Americans, for example, were less directly affected by the struggles between Mormons and non-Mormons than were native-born whites. These people experienced a different region (different regionalized sociocultural processes assumed priority). Nevertheless, even they usually did not avoid the Mormon–non-Mormon dynamic altogether (as when both Mormons and non-Mormons used them in definitional struggles).

2. See T. Hafen (1997) on how the church found public relations valuable during the last third of the nineteenth century by creating spaces in Salt Lake City that conveyed the gentility and order valued by eastern elites.

3. Of course, the region did not become an apolitical space in reality. The separation between political and nonpolitical spaces is always itself a political act. Instead, the representation of the region as a relatively apolitical space narrowed the regional conversation by denying differences that might have led to a broader regional politics.

4. National participation in debates between Mormons and non-Mormons was often figured as *eastern* meddling. Regional inhabitants increasingly identified themselves as westerners.

5. To be sure, some contemporary Mormons still cultivate such a mentality. Hardline right-wingers do so most strongly, yet more mainstream Mormons still argue, in order to motivate religious/community zeal, that the world is attacking Mormon moral values. But, except among the right-wingers, such sentiments do not often preclude cooperation and friendship with non-Mormons.

6. To be sure, some non-Mormons still feel like strangers, though not as they did in the 1870s and 1880s (Barber 1995); the region, like most of the country, still does not offer as welcoming a hand to nonwhites as it should; and most regional inhabitants have hardly begun to examine the implications of their colonialist culture.

7. Carolyn Cartier offers a stimulating analogous analysis of regional desires to manage regional difference in an era of globalization through the concepts of cosmopolitan and cosmopolitical (2001, 239–42). The cosmopolitical critique, without giving in to visions of separatist cultures, understands the cosmopolitan agenda as an ultimately elite desire to manage difference through obliterating uncomfortable difference under cover of "liberal" universal ethics.

WORKS CITED

Agnew, John A. 1999. "Regions on the Mind Does Not Equal Regions of the Mind." *Progress in Human Geography* 23: 91–96.

Agnew, John A., and James S. Duncan, eds. 1989. *The Power of Place: Bringing Together Geographical and Sociological Imaginations.* Boston: Unwin Hyman.

Alcoff, Linda. 1991–92. "The Problem of Speaking for Others." *Cultural Critique* 20 (Winter): 5–32.

Alexander, Thomas G. 1974. "The Burgeoning of Utah's Economy, 1910–18." In *A Dependent Commonwealth: Utah's Economy from Statehood to the Great Depression,* edited by Dean L. May, 35–55. Provo, Utah: Brigham Young University Press.

———. 1986. *Mormonism in Transition: A History of the Latter-day Saints, 1890–1930.* Urbana: University of Illinois Press.

———. 1991. *Things in Heaven and Earth: The Life and Times of Wilford Woodruff, a Mormon Prophet.* Salt Lake City: Signature Books.

———. 1992. "'To Maintain Harmony': Adjusting To External and Internal Stress." In *The New Mormon History: Revisionist Essays on the Past,* edited by D. Michael Quinn, 247–66. Salt Lake City: Signature Books.

———. 1995a. "Cooperation, Conflict, and Compromise: Women, Men, and the Environment in Salt Lake City, 1890–1930." *BYU Studies* 35 (1): 7–39.

———. 1995b. *Utah, the Right Place: The Official Centennial History.* Salt Lake City: Gibbs Smith.

———. 1996. "Some Meanings of Utah History." *Utah Historical Quarterly* 64: 155–67.

Alexander, Thomas G., and James B. Allen. 1984. *Mormons and Gentiles: A History of Salt Lake City.* Boulder, Colo.: Pruett.

Allen, Annie Maria. 1909. Letter from Castle Dale, Utah, to Ada Ostberg, Spring Glen, Utah, 18 January. Spring Glen Ward, Carbon Stake, Relief Society Papers. Archives, Church of Jesus Christ of Latter-day Saints Historical Department, Salt Lake City.

Allen, James, Doreen Massey, and Allan Cochrane. 1998. *Rethinking the Region*. London: Routledge.

Allen, Paula Gunn. 1986. *The Sacred Hoop: Recovering the Feminine in American Indian Traditions*. Boston: Beacon.

Amethyst. 1890. "Home, Husband, Motherhood." *Contributor* 11: 269–70.

Amin, Ash, and Nigel Thrift. 1994. "Living in the Global." In *Globalization, Institutions, and Regional Development in Europe*, edited by Ash Amin and Nigel Thrift, 1–22. Oxford: Oxford University Press.

Anderson, Benedict. 1983. *Imagined Communities: Reflections on the Origin and Spread of Nationalism*. London: Verso.

Anderson, Bernice Gibbs. 1974. Interview by Phil Notarianni and Greg Thompson, 15 August. Golden Spike Oral History Project. Manuscript Division, Special Collections, Marriott Library, University of Utah, Salt Lake City.

Anderson, Kay J., and Fay Gale. 1992. Introduction to *Inventing Places: Studies in Cultural Geography*, edited by Kay Anderson and Fay Gale, 1–12. Melbourne: Longman Cheshire.

Anderson, Nephi. 1890. "Mary: A Story of Sage-Brush Bench." *Contributor* 12: 22–29.

———. 1898. *Added Upon: A Story*. Salt Lake City: Deseret News.

Anglin, Mary K. 1992. "A Question of Loyalty: National and Regional Identity in Narratives of Appalachia." *Anthropological Quarterly* 65: 105–16.

Anthony, Susan B. 1900. Letter from Rochester, N.Y., to Elmina S. Taylor, Salt Lake City, 30 March. Anstis Elmina Shepard Taylor Correspondence. Archives, Church of Jesus Christ of Latter-day Saints Historical Department, Salt Lake City.

Appadurai, Arjun. 1990. "Disjuncture and Difference in the Global Cultural Economy." *Theory, Culture and Society* 7 (2–3): 295–310.

Arrington, Leonard J. 1958. *Great Basin Kingdom*. Cambridge, Mass.: Harvard University Press.

———. 1974. "The Commercialization of Utah's Economy: Trends and Developments." In *A Dependent Commonwealth: Utah's Economy from Statehood to the Great Depression*, edited by Dean L. May, 3–34. Provo, Utah: Brigham Young University Press.

Arrington, Leonard J., Feramorz Y. Fox, and Dean L. May. 1992. *Building the City of God: Cooperation and Community among the Mormons*. 2d ed. Urbana: University of Illinois Press.

Austin, Heber C. 1917a. Address. In *Conference Reports*, April, 80–82. Salt Lake City: Deseret News.

———. 1917b. Address. In *Conference Reports*, October, 99–100. Salt Lake City: Deseret News.

Ayers, Edward L., and Peter S. Onuf. 1996. Introduction to *All over the Map: Rethinking American Regions*, edited by Edward L. Ayers, Patricia Nelson Limerick, Stephen Nissbaum, and Peter S. Onuf, 1–10. Baltimore: Johns Hopkins University Press.

Ballard, Melvin J. 1913a. Address. In *Conference Reports*, April, 16–21. Salt Lake City: Deseret News.

———. 1913b. Address. In *Conference Reports*, October, 123–27. Salt Lake City: Deseret News.

———. 1920. Address. In *Conference Reports*, October, 76–83. Salt Lake City: Deseret News.

Banker, Mark T. 1993. *Presbyterian Missions and Cultural Interaction in the Far Southwest, 1850–1950*. Urbana: University of Illinois Press.

Barber, Phyllis. 1995. "Culture Shock." In *A World We Thought We Knew: Readings in Utah History*, edited by John S. McCormick and John R. Sillito, 393–410. Salt Lake City: University of Utah Press.

Bartlett, Ross. 1974. Interview by Craig Fuller, 26 February. Transcript. Utah State Historical Society Oral History Project. Utah State Historical Society, Salt Lake City.

Barton, William C. n.d. Autobiography. Typescript. Utah State Historical Society, Salt Lake City.

Bate, Kerry William, ed. 1992. "Diary of Mary Elizabeth (May) Stapley, a Schoolteacher in Virgin, Utah." *Utah Historical Quarterly* 60: 158–67.

———. 1995. "Kanarraville Fights World War I." *Utah Historical Quarterly* 63: 24–49.

Bederman, Gail. 1995. *Manliness and Civilization: A Cultural History of Gender and Race in the United States, 1880–1917*. Chicago: University of Chicago Press.

Beecher, Maureen Ursenbach. 1976. "The Eliza Enigma: The Life and Legend of Eliza R. Snow." In *Essays on the American West, 1974–1975*, edited by Thomas G. Alexander, 29–46. Provo, Utah: Brigham Young University Press.

———. 1992. "The 'Leading Sisters': A Female Hierarchy in Nineteenth-Century Mormon Society." In *The New Mormon History: Revisionist Essays on the Past*, edited by D. Michael Quinn, 29–46. Salt Lake City: Signature Books.

———. 1993. "Each in Her Own Time: Four Zinas." *Dialogue: A Journal of Mormon Thought* 26 (2): 119–35.

Beeton, Beverly. 1976. "Woman Suffrage in the American West, 1869–1896." Ph.D. diss., University of Utah.

———. 1991. "A Feminist among the Mormons: Charlotte Ives Cobb Godbe Kirby." *Utah Historical Quarterly* 59: 23–31.

Bennion, Lowell C. 1980. "Mormon Country a Century Ago: A Geographer's View." In *The Mormon People, Their Character and Traditions*, edited by Thomas G. Alexander, 1–26. Provo, Utah: Brigham Young University Press.

Berdoulay, Vincent. 1989. "Place, Meaning, and Discourse in French Language Geography." In *The Power of Place: Bringing Together Geographical and Sociological Imaginations*, edited by John A. Agnew and James S. Duncan, 124–39. Boston: Unwin Hyman.

Berkhofer, Robert F., Jr. 1978. *The White Man's Indian: Images of the American Indian from Columbus to the Present*. New York: Alfred A. Knopf.

Berry, Brian J. L. 1992. *America's Utopian Experiments: Communal Havens from Long-Wave Crises.* Hanover, N.H.: University Press of New England.

Bishop, M. Guy, and Richard Neitzel Holzapfel. 1993. "The 'St. Peter's of the New World': The Salt Lake Temple, Tourism, and a New Image for Utah." *Utah Historical Quarterly* 61: 137–49.

Black, Marcia, and Robert S. McPherson. 1995. "Soldiers, Savers, Slackers, and Spies: Southeastern Utah's Response to World War I." *Utah Historical Quarterly* 63: 4–23.

Bodnar, John. 1992. *Remaking America: Public Memory, Commemoration, and Patriotism in the Twentieth Century.* Princeton, N.J.: Princeton University Press.

Bordo, Susan. 1993. *Unbearable Weight: Feminism, Western Culture, and the Body.* Berkeley: University of California Press.

Bourdieu, Pierre. 1977. *Outline of a Theory of Practice.* Cambridge: Cambridge University Press.

Boyer, S. A. 1893. "The Ballot for Women." *Woman's Exponent* 22: 66.

Bradley, Martha S. 1991. "Protect the Children: Child Labor in Utah, 1880–1920." *Utah Historical Quarterly* 59: 52–71.

Brimhall, George H. n.d. "Diary of George Brimhall, 1881–1932." Dean R. Brimhall Papers. Manuscript Division, Special Collections, Marriott Library, University of Utah, Salt Lake City.

Brosius, S. M. 1899. Letter from Washington, D.C., to Commissioner of Indian Affairs, 2 December. "Selected Documents Relating to the Ute Indians, 1881–1939" (microform), reel 3, frame 1135–37. Record Group 75, Records of the Bureau of Indian Affairs. National Archives, Washington, D.C.

Brown, Jean. 1914. "The New Freedom for Women." *Young Woman's Journal* 25: 688–91.

Brown, Michael P. 1997. *RePlacing Citizenship: AIDS Activism and Radical Democracy.* New York: Guilford.

Buchanan, Frederick S. 1996. *Culture Clash and Accommodation: Public Schooling in Salt Lake City, 1890–1994.* Salt Lake City: Smith Research Associates in Association with Signature Books.

Bunker, Gary L., and Davis Bitton. 1983. *The Mormon Graphic Image, 1834–1914: Cartoons, Caricatures, and Illustrations.* Salt Lake City: University of Utah Press.

Bunker, Gary L., and Carol B. Bunker. 1991. "Woman Suffrage, Popular Art, and Utah." *Utah Historical Quarterly* 59: 22–31.

Burgess-Olsen, Vicky. n.d. "Mary Ann Burnham Freeze, 1845–1912: 'The Letter Killeth but the Spirit Giveth Life.'" Typescript. Utah State Historical Society, Salt Lake City.

Bush, Lester E., Jr., and Armand L. Mauss, eds. 1984. *Neither White Nor Black: Mormon Scholars Confront the Race Issue in a Universal Church.* Midvale, Utah: Signature Books.

Cactus. 1890. "Leaves from the Journal of a Medical Student." *Young Woman's Journal* 1: 265–68, 472–74.

———. 1894. "Cactus Papers No. 1: Unbidden Thoughts." *Woman's Exponent* 23: 209–10.

Callis, Charles A. 1917. Address. In *Conference Reports*, April, 133–36. Salt Lake City: Deseret News.

Campbell, Ella. 1890. "A Dream, and Occurrence Which Took Place on Dec. 23, 1889." *Young Woman's Journal* 1: 169–70.

Campbell, Eugene E. 1987. "Pioneers and Patriotism: Conflicting Loyalties." In *New Views of Mormon History: A Collection of Essays in Honor of Leonard J. Arrington,* edited by Davis Bitton and Maureen Ursenbach Beecher, 307–22. Salt Lake City: University of Utah Press.

Campbell, Eugene E., and Bruce L. Campbell. 1992. "Divorce among Mormon Polygamists: Extent and Explanations." In *The New Mormon History: Revisionist Essays on the Past,* edited by D. Michael Quinn, 181–200. Salt Lake City: Signature Books.

Cannon, Ann M. 1910. "In the Hills." *Young Woman's Journal* 21: 545–49.

Cannon, Annie Wells. 1911. "Utah Women at Chicago." *Woman's Exponent* 40: 29.

———. 1912. "Suffrage No Failure in Utah." *Woman's Exponent* 40: 69.

———. 1913. "The Legislature." *Woman's Exponent* 41: 44.

———. 1923. "From the Curtained Alcove to the United States Senate: A Suffrage Retrospective." *Relief Society Magazine* 10: 57–62.

Cannon, David H. 1913. Address. In *Conference Reports,* April, 103–8. Salt Lake City: Deseret News.

Cannon, George Q. 1884. "Discourse by President Geo. Q. Cannon, Delivered in the New Tabernacle, Salt Lake City, Sunday, June 25, 1882." In *Journal of Discourses by President John Taylor, His Counsellors, and the Twelve Apostles and Others,* vol. 24, reported by George F. Gibbs, John Irvine, and Others, 38–50. Liverpool: John Henry Smith.

———. 1897. Address. In *Conference Reports,* October, 37–43. Salt Lake City: Deseret News.

———. 1898a. Address. In *Conference Reports,* April, 83–86. Salt Lake City: Deseret News.

———. 1898b. Address. In *Conference Reports,* October, 3–6. Salt Lake City: Deseret News.

———. 1899. Address. In *Conference Reports,* October, 46–53. Salt Lake City: Deseret News.

Cannon, Hugh J. 1913. Address. In *Conference Reports,* October, 82–84. Salt Lake City: Deseret News.

Cannon, Kenneth L., II. 1992. "After the Manifesto: Mormon Polygamy, 1890–1906." In *The New Mormon History: Revisionist Essays on the Past,* edited by D. Michael Quinn, 201–20. Salt Lake City: Signature Books.

Cannon, M. Hughes. 1894. [Speech Reported under Title] "A Woman's Assembly." *Woman's Exponent* 22: 113–14.

Carmer, Carl. 1962. "The 'Peculiar People' Prosper." *New York Times Magazine,* 15 April, 36+.

Carroll, Elsie C. 1920–21. "The Strength of the Hills." *Young Woman's Journal* 31: 549–52, 623–26, 680–83; 32: 21–24, 72–76, 148–52, 207–13.

Carter, L. R. 1899. Letter to "My Beloved Daughter," 25 July. Special Collections Archives, Harold B. Lee Library, Brigham Young University, Provo, Utah.

Cartier, Carolyn. 2001. *Globalizing South China.* Oxford: Blackwell.

Carver, Sharon Snow. 2000. "Club Women of the Three Intermountain Cities of Denver, Boise, and Salt Lake City between 1893 and 1929." Ph.D. diss., Brigham Young University.

Chen, Chiung Hwang. 2000. "From Pariah to Paragon: Mormon and Asian American Model Minority Discourse in News and Popular Magazines." Ph.D. diss., University of Iowa.

Chen, Chiung Hwang, and Ethan Yorgason. 1999. "'Those Amazing Mormons': The Media's Construction of Latter-day Saints as a Model Minority." *Dialogue: A Journal of Mormon Thought* 32 (2): 107–28.

Chun, Allen. 1996. "Discourses of Identity in the Changing Spaces of Public Culture in Taiwan, Hong Kong and Singapore." *Theory, Culture and Society* 13 (1): 51–75.

Clark, Lucy A. 1896. [Speech Reported under Title] "Conference N.A.W.S.A.: Conference of the National American Woman Suffrage Association; Held at Salt Lake City, Utah, May 13, and 14, 1895." *Woman's Exponent* 24: 77.

Clawson, Rudger. 1899. Address. In *Conference Reports,* April, 3–5. Salt Lake City: Deseret News.

———. 1906. Address. In *Conference Reports,* April, 29–33. Salt Lake City: Deseret News.

———. 1910. Address. In *Conference Reports,* April, 65–68. Salt Lake City: Deseret News.

Code, W. H. 1907. Letter from Los Angeles to Secretary of the Interior, 30 October. "Selected Documents Relating to the Ute Indians, 1881–1939" (microform), reel 4, frame 0–6. Record Group 75, Records of the Bureau of Indian Affairs. National Archives, Washington, D.C.

———. 1908. Letter from Los Angeles to Secretary of the Interior, 9 November. "Selected Documents Relating to the Ute Indians, 1881–1939" (microform), reel 4, frame 84–94. Record Group 75, Records of the Bureau of Indian Affairs. National Archives, Washington, D.C.

———. 1911. Letter from Los Angeles to Secretary of the Interior, 17 October. "Selected Documents Relating to the Ute Indians, 1881–1939" (microform), reel 4, frame 100–110. Record Group 75, Records of the Bureau of Indian Affairs. National Archives, Washington, D.C.

Cohen, Anthony. 1986. "Of Symbols and Boundaries." In *Symbolising Boundaries: Identity and Diversity in British Cultures,* edited by Anthony Cohen, 1–19. Manchester, England: Manchester University Press.

Collett, R. S. 1905. Letter from Vernal, Utah, to C. G. Hall, 8 December. "Indian

Archives, 1880–1934." Record Group 75, Records of the Bureau of Indian Affairs. National Archives, Washington, D.C. Also in Manuscript Division, Special Collections, Marriott Library, University of Utah, Salt Lake City.

Collins, Patricia Hill. 1990. *Black Feminist Thought: Knowledge, Consciousness, and the Politics of Empowerment*. New York: Routledge.

Committee of Homesteaders. 1905. Letter from Vernal, Utah, to C. G. Hall, 5 October. "Indian Archives, 1880–1934." Record Group 75, Records of the Bureau of Indian Affairs. National Archives, Washington, D.C. Also in Manuscript Division, Special Collections, Marriott Library, University of Utah, Salt Lake City.

Conetah, Fred A. 1982. *A History of the Northern Ute People*. Edited by Kathryn L. MacKay and Floyd A. O'Neil. Salt Lake City: Unitah-Ouray Ute Tribe.

Cort, John C. 1988. *Christian Socialism: An Informal History*. Maryknoll, N.Y.: Orbis.

Cowan, Ruth Schwartz. 1983. *More Work for Mother: The Ironies of Household Technology from the Open Hearth to the Microwave*. New York: Basic Books.

Cowley, Matthias F. 1899a. Address. In *Conference Reports*, April, 59–61. Salt Lake City: Deseret News.

———. 1899b. Address. In *Conference Reports*, October, 8–11. Salt Lake City: Deseret News.

———. 1900. Address. In *Conference Reports*, October, 17–23. Salt Lake City: Deseret News.

———. 1903. Address. In *Conference Reports*, October, 52–57. Salt Lake City: Deseret News.

Cox, A. L. 1893. "Equal Suffrage." *Woman's Exponent* 22: 49–50.

Cragan, Katie Halladay. 1895. "Social Purity." *Woman's Exponent* 23: 254–55.

Cranley, Doris Elizabeth. 1942. "The Development of the Social Studies Courses of Study in the Salt Lake City Public Schools since 1893." Master's thesis, University of Utah.

Cronon, William, George Miles, and Jay Gitlin, eds. 1992. *Under an Open Sky: Rethinking America's Western Past*. New York: W. W. Norton.

Crosby, Jesse W. 1902. Address. In *Conference Reports*, October, 67–68. Salt Lake City: Deseret News.

Cuba, L., and D. M. Hummon. 1993. "A Place to Call Home: Identification with Dwelling, Community, and Region." *Sociological Quarterly* 34: 111–31.

Curry, Michael R. 1999. " 'Hereness' and the Normativity of Place." In *Geography and Ethics: Journeys in a Moral Terrain*, edited by James D. Proctor and David M. Smith, 95–105. London: Routledge.

Davies, Douglas. 1989. "Mormon History, Identity, and Faith Community." In *History and Ethnicity*, edited by Elizabeth Tonkin, Maryon McDonald, and Malcolm Chapman, 168–82. London: Routledge.

Dawson, Janice P. 1993. "An Economic Kaleidoscope: The Stephen Hales Family of Bountiful." *Utah Historical Quarterly* 61: 63–78.

Daynes, Kathryn M. 2001. *More Wives Than One: Transformation of the Mormon Marriage System, 1840–1910*. Urbana: University of Illinois Press.

Dear, Michael, and Jennifer Wolch. 1989. "How Territory Shapes Social Life." In *The Power of Geography: How Territory Shapes Social Life,* edited by Jennifer Wolch and Michael Dear, 3–18. Boston: Unwin Hyman.

Deloria, Vine, Jr. 1999. *For This Land: Writings on Religion in America.* New York: Routledge.

Denton, James A. 1997. *Rocky Mountain Radical: Myron W. Reed, Christian Socialist.* Albuquerque: University of New Mexico Press.

DePillis, Mario S. 1996. "The Emergence of Mormon Power since 1945." *Journal of Mormon History* 22 (1): 1–32.

Dinnerstein, Leonard, and David M. Reimers. 1999. *Ethnic Americans: A History of Immigration.* 4th ed. New York: Columbia University Press.

Donaldson, Laura E. 1992. *Decolonizing Feminisms: Race, Gender, and Empire-Building.* Chapel Hill: University of North Carolina Press.

Done, Willard. 1900. "Women of the Bible: Sarah—a Character Sketch." *Young Woman's Journal* 11: 360–64.

Donnelly, Sally B. 1991. "Mixing Business and Faith." *Time,* 29 July, 22–24.

Driver, Felix. 1988. "Moral Geographies: Social Science and the Urban Environment in Mid-Nineteenth Century England." *Transactions of the Institute of British Geographers* 13: 275–87.

Dudley, Kathryn Marie. 1994. *The End of the Line: Lost Jobs, New Lives in Postindustrial America.* Chicago: University of Chicago Press.

Duncan, James S. 1993. "Sites of Representation: Place, Time and the Discourse of the Other." In *Place/Culture/Representation,* edited by James Duncan and David Ley, 39–56. London: Routledge.

Duncan, James S., and David Ley. 1993. "Introduction: Representing the Place of Culture." In *Place/Culture/Representation,* edited by James Duncan and David Ley, 1–21. London: Routledge.

Dunfey, Julie. 1984. " 'Living the Principle' of Plural Marriage: Mormon Women, Utopia, and Female Sexuality in the Nineteenth Century." *Feminist Studies* 10: 523–36.

Dushku, Judith Rasmussen. 1976. "Feminists." In *Mormon Sisters: Women in Early Utah,* edited by Claudia L. Bushman, 177–97. Cambridge, Mass.: Emmeline.

Dushku, Judith Rasmussen, and Patricia Gadsby. 1977. " 'I Have Risen Triumphant': A Personal View of Emmeline B. Wells." Typescript. Utah State Historical Society, Salt Lake City.

Dyal, Donald H. 1989. "Mormon Pursuit of the Agrarian Ideal." *Agricultural History* 63 (4): 19–35.

Dye, Nellie D., Mary Lyons, and Mary E. Freeman. 1907. "A Tribute." *Woman's Exponent* 36: 31.

E. S. 1894. "Woman." *Woman's Exponent* 22: 107.

Eagleton, Terry. 1991. *Ideology: An Introduction.* London: Verso.

Earle, Carville. 1992. *Geographical Inquiry and American Historical Problems.* Stanford: Stanford University Press.

Eberhardt, Nancy. 1988. Introduction to *Gender, Power, and the Construction of the Moral Order: Studies from the Thai Periphery*, edited by Nancy Eberhardt, 3–10. Madison: Center for Southeast Asian Studies, University of Wisconsin at Madison.

"Editorial." 1877. *Young Ladies Diadem* 1 (6): n.p. Manuscript. Young Women of St. George, 1877–78, Collection. Utah State Historical Society, Salt Lake City.

Editorial. 1894a. *Equal Rights Banner: The Ballot, the Key to All Reform*, 16 May. Manuscript. Beaver, Utah, Woman Suffrage Association Papers, 1892–95. Special Collections Archives, Harold B. Lee Library, Brigham Young University, Provo, Utah.

Editorial. 1894b. *Equal Rights Banner: The Ballot, the Key to All Reform*, 16 August. Manuscript. Beaver, Utah, Woman Suffrage Association Papers, 1892–95. Special Collections Archives, Harold B. Lee Library, Brigham Young University, Provo, Utah.

Elazer, Daniel J. 1994. *American Mosaic: The Impact of Space, Time, and Culture on American Politics*. Boulder, Colo.: Westview.

Elias, Norbert. 1996. *The Germans: Power Struggles and the Development of Habitus in the Nineteenth and Twentieth Centuries*. New York: Columbia University Press.

Ella. 1890. "Kate's Sacrifice." *Young Woman's Journal* 1: 171–73.

Ellsworth, German E. 1909. Address. In *Conference Reports*, October, 58–63. Salt Lake City: Deseret News.

———. 1911. Address. In *Conference Reports*, October, 74–77. Salt Lake City: Deseret News.

Embry, Jessie L. 1987. *Mormon Polygamous Families: Life in the Principle*. Salt Lake City: University of Utah Press.

Entrikin, J. Nicholas. 1991. *The Betweenness of Place: Towards a Geography of Modernity*. Baltimore: Johns Hopkins University Press.

———. 1996. "Place and Region 2." *Progress in Human Geography* 20: 215–21.

———. 1997. "Place and Region 3." *Progress in Human Geography* 21: 263–68.

Ericksen, Ephraim Edward. [1922] 1975. *The Psychological and Ethical Aspects of Mormon Group Life*. Reprint, Chicago: University of Chicago Press.

Esbeck, Carl H. 1994. "A Typology of Church-State Relations in Current American Thought." In *Religion, Public Life, and the American Polity*, edited by Luis E. Lugo, 3–34. Knoxville: University of Tennessee Press.

"Ethics for Young Girls: Lesson II—the Social Unit." 1900. *Young Woman's Journal* 11: 94–95.

Evans, Vella Neil. 1992. "Empowerment and Mormon Women's Publications." In *Women and Authority: Re-Emerging Mormon Feminism*, edited by Maxine Hanks, 49–68. Salt Lake City: Signature Books.

Faragher, John Mack, Mari Jo Buhle, Daniel Czitrom, and Susan H. Armitage. 2000. *Out of Many: A History of the American People*. 3d (combined) ed. Upper Saddle River, N.J.: Prentice Hall.

Faust, Elsie Ada. 1897. "The New Woman." *Woman's Exponent* 25: 111–12.

First Presidency of the Church of Jesus Christ of Latter-day Saints, 1903. Letter from Salt Lake City to Reed Smoot, Washington D.C., 17 November. Reed Smoot Papers. Special Collections Archives, Harold B. Lee Library, Brigham Young University, Provo, Utah.

FitzSimmons, Margaret. 1990. "The Social and Environmental Relations of U.S. Regions." In *Technological Change and the Rural Environment*, edited by Philip Lowe, Terry Marsden, and Sarah Whatmore, 8–32. London: David Fulton.

Flake, Kathleen. 2000. "Mr. Smoot Goes to Washington: The Politics of American Religious Identity, 1900–1920." Ph.D. diss., University of Chicago.

Fogarty, Robert S. 1990. *All Things New: American Communes and Utopian Movements, 1860–1914*. Chicago: University of Chicago Press.

Foote, Kenneth E. 1997. *Shadowed Ground: America's Landscapes of Violence and Tragedy*. Austin: University of Texas Press.

Forest, Benjamin. 1995. "West Hollywood as Symbol: The Significance of Place in the Construction of Gay Identity." *Environment and Planning D: Society and Space* 13: 133–57.

Foster, Lawrence. 1991. *Women, Family, and Utopia: Communal Experiments of the Shakers, the Oneida Community, and the Mormons*. Syracuse: Syracuse University Press.

Foucault, Michel. 1990. *The History of Sexuality*. Vol. 1, *An Introduction*. Translated by Robert Hurley. New York: Vintage Books.

"Four More States for Suffrage." 1912. *Woman's Exponent* 41: 21.

Fowler, Robert Booth. 1994. "Religion and Liberal Culture: Unconventional Partnership or Unhealthy Co-Dependency." In *Religion, Public Life, and the American Polity*, edited by Luis E. Lugo, 201–21. Knoxville: University of Tennessee Press.

Fox, Ruth May [R. M. F.]. 1895. "Lecture on Suffrage." *Woman's Exponent* 24: 41–42.

——— [told to Feramorz Y. Fox]. n.d. "My Story." Typescript. Utah State Historical Society, Salt Lake City.

Francaviglia, Richard V. 1978. *The Mormon Landscape: Existence, Creation, and Perception of a Unique Image in the American West*. New York: AMS.

Freeze, Grace. 1900. "Some Women of the Bible." *Young Woman's Journal* 11: 369–70.

Frost, Grace Ingles. 1920. "Mothers of Men." *Improvement Era* 23: 315.

Fuller, Craig Woods. 1990. "Land Rush in Zion: Opening of the Uncompahgre and Uintah Indian Reservations." Ph.D. diss., Brigham Young University.

Furniss, Norman F. 1960. *The Mormon Conflict, 1850–1859*. New Haven, Conn.: Yale University Press.

Gallaher, Carolyn. 1997. "Identity Politics and the Religious Right: Hiding Hate in the Landscape." *Antipode* 29: 256–77.

Gardener, Helen B., and Quenton T. Bowler. 1993. "The People's Progressive Telephone Company, 1912–17: The Dream and the Reality." *Utah Historical Quarterly* 61: 79–94.

Gates, Susa Young. 1901. "Domestic Science." *Woman's Exponent* 29: 82.

———. 1909. *John Stevens' Courtship: A Story of the Echo Canyon War.* Salt Lake City: Deseret News.

———. 1911. *History of the Young Ladies' Mutual Improvement Association of the Church of Jesus Christ of Latter-day Saints, from November 1869–June 1910.* Salt Lake City: Deseret News.

———. 1918. "Brigham Young and the United Order." *Improvement Era* 21: 668–70.

———. [1920a]. "History of Women." Manuscript. Susa Amelia Young Gates Collection. Archives, Church of Jesus Christ of Latter-day Saints Historical Department, Salt Lake City.

———. 1920b. "Suffrage Won by Mothers." *Relief Society Magazine* 7: 251–75.

Gellner, Ernest. 1983. *Nations and Nationalism.* Ithaca, N.Y.: Cornell University Press.

Gilbert, Anne. 1988. "The New Regional Geography in English and French Speaking Countries." *Progress in Human Geography* 12: 208–28.

Givens, Terryl L. 1997. *The Viper on the Hearth: Mormons, Myths, and the Construction of Heresy.* New York: Oxford University Press.

———. 2002. *By the Hand of Mormon: The American Scripture That Launched a New World Religion.* New York: Oxford University Press.

Goddard, Benjamin. 1915. Address. In *Conference Reports,* October, 63–65. Salt Lake City: Deseret News.

Gordon, Sarah Barringer. 2002. *The Mormon Question: Polygamy and Constitutional Conflict in Nineteenth Century America.* Chapel Hill: University of North Carolina Press.

Gosner, Kevin. 1992. *Soldiers of the Virgin: The Moral Economy of a Colonial Maya Rebellion.* Tucson: University of Arizona Press.

Grant, Heber J. 1913. Address. In *Conference Reports,* October, 86–92. Salt Lake City: Deseret News.

———. 1919a. Address. In *Conference Reports,* June, 74–76. Salt Lake City: Deseret News.

———. 1919b. Address. In *Conference Reports,* October, 3–35. Salt Lake City: Deseret News.

Green, Arnold H. 1999. "Gathering and Election: Israelite Descent and Universalism in Mormon Discourse." *Journal of Mormon History* 25 (1): 195–228.

Green, James R. 1978. *Grass-Roots Socialism: Radical Movements in the Southwest, 1895–1943.* Baton Rouge: Louisiana State University Press.

Greenblatt, Stephen. 1990. "Culture." In *Critical Terms for Literary Studies,* edited by F. Lentricchia and S. Greenblatt, 225–32. Chicago: University of Chicago Press.

Greenwood, Annie Pike. 1920. " 'Skip-to-My-Lou-My Darling.' " *Young Woman's Journal* 31: 258–66.

Gregory, Derek. 1982. *Regional Transformation and Industrial Revolution: A Geography of the Yorkshire Woolen Industry.* London: Macmillan.

———. 1994. *Geographical Imaginations.* Cambridge, Mass.: Blackwell.

Gregory, Derek, and John Urry, eds. 1985. *Social Relations and Spatial Structures.* New York: Macmillan.

Griffin, Susan. 1978. *Woman and Nature: The Roaring inside Her.* New York: Harper and Row.

———. 1995. *The Eros of Everyday Life: Essays on Ecology, Gender and Society.* New York: Doubleday.

Grover, Hannah. 1900. "The Law of Intellectual Development, with One Practical Application." *Young Woman's Journal* 11: 359–60.

H. F. 1987. "Salt Lake City Diarist: This Is the Place." *New Republic,* 2 March, 42.

Hafen, P. Jane. 1998. "The Being and Place of a Native American Mormon." In *New Genesis: A Mormon Reader on Land and Community,* edited by Terry Tempest Williams, William B. Smart, and Gibbs M. Smith, 35–41. Salt Lake City: Gibbs Smith.

Hafen, Thomas K. 1997. "City of Saints, City of Sinners: The Development of Salt Lake City as Tourist Attraction, 1869–1900." *Western Historical Quarterly* 28: 343–77.

Häkli, Jouni. 1998. "Discourse in the Production of Political Space: Decolonizing the Symbolism of Provinces in Finland." *Political Geography* 17: 331–63.

Handy, Robert T. 1989. "Protestant Theological Tensions and Political Styles in the Progressive Period." In *Religion and American Politics: From the Colonial Period to the 1980s,* edited by Mark A. Noll, 281–301. New York: Oxford University Press.

———. 1991. *Undermined Establishment: Church-State Relations in America, 1880–1920.* Princeton, N.J.: Princeton University Press.

Hansen, Klaus. 1967. *Quest for Empire.* East Lansing: Michigan State University Press.

———. 1981. *Mormonism and the American Experience.* Chicago: University of Chicago Press.

———. 1992. "The Metamorphosis of the Kingdom of God: Toward a Reinterpretation of Mormon History." In *The New Mormon History: Revisionist Essays on the Past,* edited by D. Michael Quinn, 221–46. Salt Lake City: Signature Books.

Haraway, Donna. 1988. "Situated Knowledges: The Science Question in Feminism and the Privilege of Partial Perspective." *Feminist Studies* 14: 575–99.

Hardy, C. Brian. 1995. "Education and Mormon Enculturation: The Ogden Public Schools, 1849–1896." Ph.D. diss., University of Utah.

Hardy, Carmon. 1991. *Solemn Covenant: The Mormon Polygamous Passage.* Urbana: University of Illinois Press.

Harmston, Ed. F. 1905. Letter from Vernal, Utah, to C. G. Hall, 7 October. "Indian Archives, 1880–1934." Record Group 75, Records of the Bureau of Indian Affairs. National Archives, Washington, D.C. Also in Manuscript Division, Special Collections, Marriott Library, University of Utah, Salt Lake City.

Harris, Cole. 1991. "The Historical Mind and the Practice of Geography." In *Historical Geography: A Methodological Portrayal*, edited by D. Brooks Green, 285–98. Savage, Md.: Rowman and Littlefield.

Hart, Charles H. 1909. Address. In *Conference Reports*, October, 114–20. Salt Lake City: Deseret News.

———. 1913. Address. In *Conference Reports*, October, 40–43. Salt Lake City: Deseret News.

Hart, John Fraser. 1982. "The Highest Form of the Geographer's Art." *Annals of the American Association of Geographers* 72: 1–29.

Harvey, David. 1985. *The Urbanization of Capital*. Baltimore: Johns Hopkins University Press.

Hatch, Nathan O. 1989. "The Democratization of Christianity and the Character of American Politics." In *Religion and American Politics: From the Colonial Period to the 1980s*, edited by Mark A. Noll, 92–120. New York: Oxford University Press.

Herrick, John L. 1911. Address. In *Conference Reports*, April, 74–79. Salt Lake City: Deseret News.

Hill, Marvin S. 1989. *Quest for Refuge: The Mormon Flight from American Pluralism*. Salt Lake City: Signature Books.

Hinckley, Bryant S. 1916. Address. In *Conference Reports*, October, 81–83. Salt Lake City: Deseret News.

Hobsbawm, Eric J. 1990. *Nations and Nationalism since 1780: Programme, Myth, Reality*. Cambridge: Cambridge University Press.

Holmén, Hans. 1995. "What's New and What's Regional in the 'New Regional Geography'"? *Geografiska Annaler* 77B: 47–63.

"Home Builders." 1900. *Young Woman's Journal* 11: 376–79.

Homespun [Susa Young Gates]. 1890. "A Vivid Dream." *Young Woman's Journal* 1: 258–61.

———. 1901. "What Hath the Century Wrought." *Woman's Exponent* 29: 70–71.

Home Writer: Representing the YM and YLMIA Association. Manuscript. Young Men's and Young Ladies' Mutual Improvement Associations of Manti, Utah, 1881–83. George T. Brooks Papers. Manuscript Division, Special Collections, Marriott Library, University of Utah, Salt Lake City.

Honig, Bonnie. 1994. "Difference, Dilemmas, and the Politics of Home." *Social Research* 63: 563–97.

hooks, bell. 1984. *Feminist Theory: From Margin to Center*. Boston: South End.

———. 1990. *Yearning: Race, Gender, and Cultural Politics*. Boston: South End.

Horne, M. Isabella. 1895. [Speech Reported under Title] "Conference N.A.W.S.A.: Conference of the National American Woman Suffrage Association; Held at Salt Lake City, May 13, and 14, 1895." *Woman's Exponent* 24: 77.

Howe, Daniel Walker. 1989. "Religion and Politics in the Antebellum North." In *Religion and American Politics: From the Colonial Period to the 1980s*, edited by Mark A. Noll, 121–45. New York: Oxford University Press.

Howell, Philip. 1995. "'Diffusing the Light of Liberty': The Geography of Political Lecturing in the Chartist Movement." *Journal of Historical Geography* 21: 23–38.

Hoy, Jesse S. n.d. "The J. S. Hoy Manuscript." Typescript. Manuscript Division, Special Collections, Marriott Library, University of Utah, Salt Lake City.

Hughes, Frank. 2001. "After Seven Years, Donyell Hits It Big." *ESPN.Com,* 1 March.

Hughey, Michael W. 1983. *Civil Religion and Moral Order: Theoretical and Historical Dimensions.* Westport, Conn.: Greenwood.

Hunt, Andrew. 1993. "Beyond the Spotlight: The Red Scare in Utah." *Utah Historical Quarterly* 61: 357–80.

Hunter, Milton R. 1973. *Brigham Young the Colonizer.* Santa Barbara, Calif.: Peregrine Smith.

Huntsman, Orson W. n.d. "Orson W. Huntsman Diary." Typescript. Manuscript Division, Special Collections, Marriott Library, University of Utah, Salt Lake City.

Hurtado, Aida. 1996. *The Color of Privilege: Three Blasphemies on Race and Feminism.* Ann Arbor: University of Michigan Press.

Inouye, Yukus. 1979. Interview by Geoffrey Crisp, 17 October. Brigham Young University Oral Histories, Oral History Project of the Charles Redd Center for Western Studies. Manuscript Division, Special Collections, Marriott Library, University of Utah, Salt Lake City.

International Council for Patriotic Service. [1912]. Letter from New York City to Potential Donors. Papers of the Right Reverend Franklin Spencer Spalding, Episcopal Register of the Protestant Episcopal Church. Manuscript Division, Special Collections, Marriott Library, University of Utah, Salt Lake City.

"In the Home." 1900. *Young Woman's Journal* 11: 84–85.

Irving, Gordon. 1987. "Coming of Age in a Western Farm Community: Union, Utah, 1900–1910." In *New Views of Mormon History: A Collection of Essays in Honor of Leonard J. Arrington,* edited by Davis Bitton and Maureen Ursenbach Beecher, 162–96. Salt Lake City: University of Utah Press.

Iversen, Joan. 1984. "Feminist Implications of Mormon Polygyny." *Feminist Studies* 10: 504–22.

———. 1997. *The Antipolygamy Controversy in U.S. Women's Movements, 1880–1925: A Debate on the American Home.* New York: Garland.

Iverson, Heber C. 1908. Address. In *Conference Reports,* April, 68–72. Salt Lake City: Deseret News.

Ivins, Anthony W. 1910. Address. In *Conference Reports,* April, 13–17. Salt Lake City: Deseret News.

———. 1911. Address. In *Conference Reports,* April, 115–22. Salt Lake City: Deseret News.

———. 1917. Address. In *Conference Reports,* April, 50–55. Salt Lake City: Deseret News.

———. 1919. Address. In *Conference Reports,* June, 80–85. Salt Lake City: Deseret News.

Ivins, Stanley S. 1992. "Notes on Mormon Polygamy." In *The New Mormon History: Revisionist Essays on the Past,* edited by D. Michael Quinn, 169–80. Salt Lake City: Signature Books.

Jackson, Peter. 1984. "Social Disorganization and Moral Order in the City." *Transactions of the Institute of British Geographers* 9: 168–80.

———. 1989. *Maps of Meaning: An Introduction to Cultural Geography.* London: Unwin Hyman.

Jackson, Richard H. 1978. "Mormon Perception and Settlement." *Annals of the Association of American Geographers* 68: 317–34.

———. 1992. "The Mormon Experience: The Plains as Sinai, the Great Salt Lake as the Dead Sea, and the Great Basin as Desert-cum-Promised Land." *Journal of Historical Geography* 18: 41–58.

Jacobson, Matthew F. 1998. "Malevolent Assimilation: Immigrants and the Question of American Empire." In *Beyond Pluralism: The Conception of Groups and Group Identities in America,* edited by Wendy F. Katkin, Ned Landsman, and Andrea Tyree, 154–81. Urbana: University of Illinois Press.

Jakeman, Ellen. 1890. "We Tread the Dust." *Young Woman's Journal* 1: 103–13.

———. 1890–91. "The Western Boom." *Young Woman's Journal* 1: 241–46, 302–9, 341–45, 385–90, 433–38; 2: 15–22, 54–59, 103–10, 197–202, 251–57, 303–9, 353–57, 400–405, 450–54, 494–500.

Jenks, Chris. 1993. *Culture.* London: Routledge.

Jensen, Richard L. 1987. "Mother Tongue: Use of Non-English Languages in the Church of Jesus Christ of Latter-day Saints, 1850–1983." In *New Views of Mormon History: A Collection of Essays in Honor of Leonard J. Arrington,* edited by Davis Bitton and Maureen Ursenbach Beecher, 273–303. Salt Lake City: University of Utah Press.

Jenson, Andrew. 1908a. Address. In *Conference Reports,* April, 45–50. Salt Lake City: Deseret News.

———. 1908b. Address. In *Conference Reports,* October, 21–23. Salt Lake City: Deseret News.

———. 1914. Address. In *Conference Reports,* April, 73–79. Salt Lake City: Deseret News.

———. 1915. Address. In *Conference Reports,* April, 25–29. Salt Lake City: Deseret News.

Johnston, R. J. 1991. *A Question of Place.* Oxford: Blackwell.

Jonas, Andrew. 1988. "A New Regional Geography of Localities." *Area* 20: 101–10.

Jorgensen, Danny L. 2001. "The Mormon Gender-Inclusive Image of God." *Journal of Mormon History* 27 (1): 95–126.

July Twenty-Fourth, Celebration of Pioneer Day; also Pioneer Sunday School, the Large Tabernacle, Commencing at 10 A.M., July 24th, 1888. [1888]. Juvenile Instructor Print. Utah State Historical Society, Salt Lake City.

Kandiyoti, Deniz. 1994. "Identity and Its Discontents: Women and the Nation." In

Colonial Discourse and Post-Colonial Theory: A Reader, edited by Patrick Williams and Laura Chrisman, 376–91. New York: Columbia University Press.

Kay, Jeanne. 1997. "Sweet Surrender, but What's the Gender? Nature and the Body in the Writing of Nineteenth-Century Mormon Women." In *Thresholds in Feminist Geography: Difference, Methodology, Representation,* edited by John Paul Jones III, Heidi J. Nast, and Susan M. Roberts, 361–82. New York: Rowman and Littlefield.

Kay, Jeanne, and Craig J. Brown. 1985. "Mormon Beliefs about Land and Natural Resources, 1847–1877." *Journal of Historical Geography* 11: 253–67.

Kearns, Thomas. 1905a. *Conditions in Utah: Speech of Hon. Thomas Kearns of Utah in the Senate of the United States Feb. 28, 1905.* Washington D.C.: n.p.

———. 1905b. Letter from Salt Lake City to C. G. Hall, 25 May. "Indian Archives, 1880–1934." Record Group 75, Records of the Bureau of Indian Affairs. National Archives, Washington, D.C. Also in Manuscript Division, Special Collections, Marriott Library, University of Utah, Salt Lake City.

———. 1905c. Letter from Salt Lake City to C. G. Hall, 13 June. "Indian Archives, 1880–1934." Record Group 75, Records of the Bureau of Indian Affairs. National Archives, Washington, D.C. Also in Manuscript Division, Special Collections, Marriott Library, University of Utah, Salt Lake City.

Kelley, Heidi. 1994. "The Myth of Matriarchy: Symbols of Womanhood in Galician Regional Identity." *Anthropological Quarterly* 67: 71–80.

Kelly, George Armstrong. 1984. *Politics and Religious Consciousness in America.* New Brunswick, N.J.: Transaction Books.

Kern, Louis J. 1981. *An Ordered Love: Sex Roles and Sexuality in Victorian Utopias—The Shakers, the Mormons, and the Oneida Community.* Chapel Hill: University of North Carolina Press.

Kesler, Donnette Smith. 1920. "Three Important Conventions." *Young Woman's Journal* 31: 271–76.

Kimball, Andrew. 1909. Address. In *Conference Reports,* October, 30–35. Salt Lake City: Deseret News.

———. 1911. Address. In *Conference Reports,* October, 81–83. Salt Lake City: Deseret News.

Kimball, Sarah M. 1891. Letter from Salt Lake City to A. L. Cox, 24 November. Beaver, Utah, Woman Suffrage Association Papers, 1892–95. Special Collections Archives, Harold B. Lee Library, Brigham Young University, Provo, Utah.

Kong, Lily. 1996. "Popular Music in Singapore: Exploring Local Cultures, Global Resources, and Regional Identities." *Environment and Planning D: Society and Space* 14: 273–92.

Kurumada, Tsuru. 1975. Interview by Paul Kato, 11 November. Japanese-American Oral History Program. Utah State Historical Society, Salt Lake City.

Lambert, J. N. 1921. Address. In *Conference Reports,* April, 50–54. Salt Lake City: Deseret News.

Lambourne, Alfred. 1890. "Fiametta: Sketch for a Love Tale of the Sierras." *Contributor* 11: 252–57.

Lamont, Ruby. 1895. "Woman Suffrage." *Woman's Exponent* 24: 6–8.

Lancaster, Florence L. 1910. "The Carlyles and Their House at Chelsea." *Improvement Era* 13: 413–17.

Landsman, Ned. 1998. "Pluralism, Protestantism, and Prosperity: Crèvecoeur's American Farmer and the Foundations of American Pluralism." In *Beyond Pluralism: The Conception of Groups and Group Identities in America,* edited by Wendy F. Katkin, Ned Landsman, and Andrea Tyree, 105–24. Urbana: University of Illinois Press.

Lang, Gottfied Otto. 1954. "The Ute Development Program: A Study in Culture Change in an Underdeveloped Area within the United States." Ph.D. diss., Cornell University.

Larson, Gustive. 1971. *The "Americanization" of Utah for Statehood.* San Marino, Calif.: Huntington Library.

Leech, Dwight. 1967. Interview by Sandra Caruthers, 25 March. Interview 297, Transcript. American Indian Oral History: The Duke Collection. Manuscript Division, Special Collections, Marriott Library, University of Utah, Salt Lake City.

Leone, Mark P. 1979. *Roots of Modern Mormonism.* Cambridge, Mass.: Harvard University Press.

"Lesson III—The Push of Poverty." 1920. *Young Woman's Journal* 31: 532–34.

"Lesson V—The Obligations of Wealth." 1920. *Young Woman's Journal* 31: 584–87.

"Lesson VI—The Responsibility of Wealth." 1920. *Young Woman's Journal* 31: 587–89.

"Lesson XV—Eternal Domesticity: Part I—Husbandhood and Wifehood." 1920. *Improvement Era* 23: 336–39.

"Life Story of B. H. Roberts." n.d. Manuscript. Utah State Historical Society, Salt Lake City.

Limerick, Patricia Nelson. 1987. *The Legacy of Conquest: The Unbroken History of the American West.* New York: W. W. Norton.

———. 1996. "Region and Reason." In *All over the Map: Rethinking American Regions,* edited by Edward L. Ayers, Patricia Nelson Limerick, Stephen Nissbaum, and Peter S. Onuf, 83–104. Baltimore: Johns Hopkins University Press.

Limerick, Patricia Nelson, Clyde A. Milner II, and Charles E. Rankin, eds. 1991. *Trails: Toward a New Western History.* Lawrence: University Press of Kansas.

Lindsey, Emma. n.d. "Scrapbook I." Emma Lindsey Correspondence, Scrapbooks, Miscellaneous Items. Manuscript Division, Special Collections, Marriott Library, University of Utah, Salt Lake City.

Lindsey, Robert. 1986. "The Mormons: Growth, Prosperity, and Controversy." *New York Times Magazine,* 12 January, 19+.

Lippard, Lucy R. 1997. *Lure of the Local: Senses of Place in a Multicentered Society.* New York: New Press.

Livingstone, David N. 1992. *The Geographical Tradition: Episodes in the History of a Contested Enterprise.* Oxford: Blackwell.

London, Jack. 1919. *The Star Rover.* New York: Macmillan.

Loraine, Sybil. 1900. "'Near and Yet Far.'" *Young Woman's Journal* 11: 348–55.

Louder, Dean, and Lowell C. Bennion. 1978. "Mapping Mormons across the Modern West." In *The Mormon Role in the Settlement of the West,* edited by Richard H. Jackson, 135–67. Provo, Utah: Brigham Young University Press.

Lula. 1890. "To A. A." *Young Woman's Journal* 1: 251.

Lund, Anthon H. 1897. Address. In *Conference Reports,* October, 2–3. Salt Lake City: Deseret News.

———. 1899. Address. In *Conference Reports,* April, 11–13. Salt Lake City: Deseret News.

———. 1907. Address. In *Conference Reports,* October, 8–13. Salt Lake City: Deseret News.

———. 1910. Address. In *Conference Reports,* April, 8–13. Salt Lake City: Deseret News.

———. 1911. Address. In *Conference Reports,* October, 11–16. Salt Lake City: Deseret News.

———. 1917. Address. In *Conference Reports,* April, 12–15. Salt Lake City: Deseret News.

———. n.d. "Anthon Hendrik Lund, 1844–1921, Diaries 1860–1921." Typescript, 41 vols. Archives, Church of Jesus Christ of Latter-day Saints Historical Department, Salt Lake City.

Lyman, Edward Leo. 1986. *Political Deliverance: The Mormon Quest for Utah Statehood.* Urbana: University of Illinois Press.

Lyman, Francis M. 1899. Address. In *Conference Reports,* April, 37–40. Salt Lake City: Deseret News.

———. 1904. Address. In *Conference Reports,* October, 15–17. Salt Lake City: Deseret News.

———. 1907. Address. In *Conference Reports,* October, 13–18. Salt Lake City: Deseret News.

———. 1909a. Address. In *Conference Reports,* April, 118–21. Salt Lake City: Deseret News.

———. 1909b. Address. In *Conference Reports,* October, 13–20. Salt Lake City: Deseret News.

———. 1916. Address. In *Conference Reports,* April, 24–30. Salt Lake City: Deseret News.

Lystra, Karen. 1989. *Searching the Heart: Women, Men, and Romantic Love in Nineteenth-Century America.* New York: Oxford University Press.

MacKay, Kathryn L. 1995. "The Strawberry Valley Reclamation Project and the Opening of the Uintah Indian Reservation." In *A World We Thought We Knew: Readings in Utah History,* edited by John S. McCormick and John R. Sillito, 249–66. Salt Lake City: University of Utah Press.

MacLeod, Gordon. 1998. "In What Sense a Region? Place Hybridity, Symbolic Shape, and Institutional Formation in (Post-)Modern Scotland." *Political Geography* 17: 833–63.

Madsen, Carol Cornwall. 1987. "Schism in the Sisterhood: Mormon Women and Partisan Politics, 1890–1900." In *New Views of Mormon History: A Collection of Essays in Honor of Leonard J. Arrington,* edited by Davis Bitton and Maureen Ursenbach Beecher, 212–41. Salt Lake City: University of Utah Press.

———. 1995. "Decade of Detente: The Mormon-Gentile Female Relationship in Nineteenth-Century Utah." *Utah Historical Quarterly* 63: 298–319.

Maffly-Kiff, Laurie F. 2000. "Looking West: Mormonism and the Pacific World." *Journal of Mormon History* 26 (1): 40–63.

Malanson, George P. 1985. "The Rise and Fall of the Uintah Valley Indian Reservation: Perception and Policy." *Utah Geological Association Publication* 12: 11–15.

Mangum, Garth, and Bruce Blumell. 1993. *The Mormons' War on Poverty: A History of LDS Welfare, 1830–1990.* Salt Lake City: University of Utah Press.

Marie. 1895. "Affectionately Inscribed to My Husband." *Woman's Exponent* 24: 11.

Marshall, W. G. 1881. *Through America; or, Nine Months in the United States.* London: Sampson Low, Marston, Searle, and Riverton.

Masaoka, Mike. 1982. Interview by S. E. [probably Eric Saul], 20 August. Mike M. Masaoka Papers. Manuscript Division, Special Collections, Marriott Library, University of Utah, Salt Lake City.

Masaoka, Mike, with Bill Hosokawa. 1987. *They Call Me Moses Masaoka: An American Saga.* New York: William Morrow.

Mason, C. E. 1909. Letter from New York City to the Reverend Franklin S. Spalding, Salt Lake City, 8 December. Papers of the Right Reverend Franklin Spencer Spalding, Episcopal Register of the Protestant Episcopal Church. Manuscript Division, Special Collections, Marriott Library, University of Utah, Salt Lake City.

———. 1911. Letter from New York City to the Reverend Franklin S. Spalding, Salt Lake City, 9 March. Papers of the Right Reverend Franklin Spencer Spalding, Episcopal Register of the Protestant Episcopal Church. Manuscript Division, Special Collections, Marriott Library, University of Utah, Salt Lake City.

Massey, Doreen. 1984. *Spatial Divisions of Labour: Social Structures and the Geography of Production.* London: Macmillan.

———. 1994. *Space, Place, and Gender.* Minneapolis: University of Minnesota Press.

Massey, Doreen, and Pat Jess, eds. 1995. *A Place in the World? Places, Culture and Globalization.* Oxford: Oxford University Press.

Matless, David. 1995. "Culture Run Riot? Work in Social and Cultural Geography, 1994." *Progress in Human Geography* 19: 395–403.

Matsumoto, Valerie J., and Blake Allmendinger, eds. 1999. *Over the Edge: Remapping the American West.* Berkeley: University of California Press.

Mauss, Armand L. 1994. *The Angel and the Beehive: The Mormon Struggle with Assimilation.* Urbana: University of Illinois Press.

———. 1999. "In Search of Ephraim: Traditional Mormon Conceptions of Lineage and Race." *Journal of Mormon History* 25 (1): 131–73.

May, Dean, ed. 1974. *A Dependent Commonwealth: Utah's Economy from Statehood to the Great Depression.* Provo, Utah: Brigham Young University Press.

———. 1987. *Utah: A People's History.* Salt Lake City: University of Utah Press.

———. 1992. "A Demographic Portrait of the Mormons, 1830–1980." In *The New Mormon History: Revisionist Essays on the Past,* edited by D. Michael Quinn, 121–35. Salt Lake City: Signature Books.

———. 1997. "One Heart and Mind: Communal Life and Values among the Mormons." In *America's Communal Utopias,* edited by Donald E. Pitzer, 135–58. Chapel Hill: University of North Carolina Press.

McClintock, Anne. 1997. " 'No Longer in a Future Heaven': Gender, Race and Nationalism." In *Dangerous Liaisons: Gender, Nation, and Postcolonial Perspectives,* edited by Anne McClintock, Aamir Mufti, and Ella Shohat, 89–112. Minneapolis: University of Minnesota Press.

McCormick, John S. 1982. "Hornets in the Hive: Socialists in Early Twentieth-Century Utah." *Utah Historical Quarterly* 50: 225–40.

McCormick, John S., and John R. Sillito. 1994. "Henry W. Lawrence: A Life in Dissent." In *Differing Visions: Dissenters in Mormon History,* edited by Roger D. Launius and Linda Thatcher, 220–40. Urbana: University of Illinois Press.

McKay, David O. 1909. Address. In *Conference Reports,* April, 62–68. Salt Lake City: Deseret News.

———. 1912. Address. In *Conference Reports,* April, 52–58. Salt Lake City: Deseret News.

———. 1917. Address. In *Conference Reports,* October, 55–60. Salt Lake City: Deseret News.

———. 1920. Address. In *Conference Reports,* April, 114–19. Salt Lake City: Deseret News.

McMurrin, Joseph W. 1903. Address. In *Conference Reports,* October, 24–27. Salt Lake City: Deseret News.

———. 1905. Address. In *Conference Reports,* October, 84–87. Salt Lake City: Deseret News.

"Medical Colleges Open Doors to Women." 1917. *Relief Society Magazine* 4: 605.

Meinig, Donald W. 1965. "The Mormon Culture Region: Strategies and Patterns in the Geography of the American West, 1847–1964." *Annals of the Association of American Geographers* 55: 191–220.

———. 1971. *Southwest: Three Peoples in Geographical Change, 1600–1970.* New York: Oxford University Press.

———. 1986. *The Shaping of America: A Geographical Perspective on 500 Years of History.* 3 vols. New Haven, Conn.: Yale University Press.

———. 1996. "The Mormon Nation and American Empire." *Journal of Mormon History* 22 (1): 33–51.

Memmi, Albert. 1965. *The Colonizer and the Colonized.* New York: Orion.

Mercer, W. A. 1905. Letter from Carlisle, Pa., to C. G. Hall, 7 August. "Indian Archives, 1880–1934." Record Group 75, Records of the Bureau of Indian Affairs. National Archives, Washington, D.C. Also in Manuscript Division, Special Collections, Marriott Library, University of Utah, Salt Lake City.

Merchant, Carolyn. 1980. *The Death of Nature: Women, Ecology, and the Scientific Revolution.* San Francisco: Harper and Row.

———. 1989. *Ecological Revolutions: Nature, Gender, and Science in New England.* Chapel Hill: University of North Carolina Press.

Merriam, Florence A. 1894. *My Summer in a Mormon Village.* Boston: Houghton, Mifflin.

Merrill, Marriner W. 1899. Address. In *Conference Reports*, April, 13–17. Salt Lake City: Deseret News.

———. 1902. Address. In *Conference Reports*, October, 62–65. Salt Lake City: Deseret News.

Meyer, F. F., Jr. [?]. 1905. Letter from New York City to C. G. Hall, 20 June. "Indian Archives, 1880–1934." Record Group 75, Records of the Bureau of Indian Affairs. National Archives, Washington, D.C. Also in Manuscript Division, Special Collections, Marriott Library, University of Utah, Salt Lake City.

Milner II, Clyde A. 1992. "The View from Wisdom: Four Layers of History and Regional Identity." In *Under an Open Sky: Rethinking America's Western Past*, edited by William Cronon, George Miles, and Jay Gitlin, 202–22. New York: W. W. Norton.

Minshull, Roger. 1967. *Regional Geography: Theory and Practice.* London: Hutchinson University Library.

"Minutes of Beaver, Utah Woman Suffrage Association Meeting." n.d. Manuscript. Beaver, Utah, Woman Suffrage Association Papers, 1892–95. Special Collections Archives, Harold B. Lee Library, Brigham Young University, Provo, Utah.

Mitchell, Don. 1995. "There's No Such Thing as Culture: Towards a Reconceptualization of the Idea of Culture in Geography." *Transactions of the Institute of British Geographers* 20: 102–16.

Mitsunaga, Shizuko. 1975. Interview by Paul Kato, 8 December. Japanese-American Oral History Program. Utah State Historical Society, Salt Lake City.

Moffitt, J. C. 1944. *A Century of Public Education in Provo, Utah.* Provo, Utah: n.p.

Moi, Toril. 1991. "Appropriating Bourdieu: Feminist Theory and Pierre Bourdieu's Sociology of Culture." *New Literary History* 22: 1017–49.

Mollie. 1890. "A Pen Picture." *Young Woman's Journal* 1: 253–54.

Monson, Walter P. 1918. Address. In *Conference Reports*, April, 56–61. Salt Lake City: Deseret News.

Morin, Karen M., and Jeanne Kay Guelke. 1998. "Strategies of Representation, Relationship, and Resistance: British Women Travelers and Mormon Plural Wives, ca. 1870–1890." *Annals of the Association of American Geographers* 88: 436–62.

"'Mormon' Women Physicians." 1915. *Relief Society Magazine* 2: 351–56.

"Mormon" Women's Protest: An Appeal for Freedom, Justice and Equal Rights.

The Ladies of the Church of Jesus Christ of Latter-day Saints Protest against the Tyranny and Indecency of Federal Officials in Utah, and against Their Own Disfranchisement without Cause. Full Account of Proceedings at the Great Mass Meeting, Held in the Theatre, Salt Lake City Utah, Saturday, March 6, 1886. [1886]. Salt Lake City: Deseret News.

"Mother and Home." 1890. *Contributor* 11: 273.

A Mugwump. 1898. "Politics." *Woman's Exponent* 26: 73–74.

Mulder, William. 1957. *Homeward to Zion: The Mormon Migration from Scandinavia.* Minneapolis: University of Minnesota Press.

Murakami, Yorimoto. 1976. Interview by Paul Kato, 17 January. Japanese-American Oral History Program. Utah State Historical Society, Salt Lake City.

Murphy, Alexander B. 1991. "Regions as Social Constructs: The Gap between Theory and Practice." *Progress in Human Geography* 15: 22–35.

Murphy, Thomas W. 1999. "From Racist Stereotype to Ethnic Identity: Instrumental Uses of Mormon Racial Doctrine." *Ethnohistory* 46: 451–80.

Newell, Linda King. 1992a. "A Gift Given, a Gift Taken: Washing, Anointing, and Blessing the Sick among Mormon Women." In *The New Mormon History: Revisionist Essays on the Past,* edited by D. Michael Quinn, 101–20. Salt Lake City: Signature Books.

———. 1992b. "The Historical Relationship of Mormon Women and Priesthood." In *Women and Authority: Re-Emerging Mormon Feminism,* edited by Maxine Hanks, 23–48. Salt Lake City: Signature Books.

Nibley, Charles W. 1906. Address. In *Conference Reports,* October, 62–65. Salt Lake City: Deseret News.

———. 1914. Address. In *Conference Reports,* April, 120–22. Salt Lake City: Deseret News.

———. 1916. Address. In *Conference Reports,* April, 131–34. Salt Lake City: Deseret News.

———. 1917. Address. In *Conference Reports,* October, 73–76. Salt Lake City: Deseret News.

Oakes, T. S. 1993. "The Cultural Space of Modernity: Ethnic Tourism and Place Identity in China." *Environment and Planning D: Society and Space* 11: 47–68.

O'Dea, Thomas. 1954. "Mormonism and the Avoidance of Sectarian Stagnation: A Study of Church, Sect, and Incipient Nationality." *American Journal of Sociology* 60: 285–93.

———. 1957. *The Mormons.* Chicago: University of Chicago Press.

O'Leary, Celia Elizabeth. 1999. *To Die For: The Paradox of American Patriotism.* Princeton, N.J.: Princeton University Press.

Onuf, Peter S. 1996. "Federalism, Republicanism, and the Origins of American Sectionalism." In *All Over the Map: Rethinking American Regions,* edited by Edward L. Ayers, Patricia Nelson Limerick, Stephen Nissbaum, and Peter S. Onuf, 11–37. Baltimore: Johns Hopkins University Press.

Paasi, Anssi. 1991. "Deconstructing Regions: Notes on the Scales of Spatial Life." *Environment and Planning A* 23: 239–56.

Palmer, Michael Dalton. 1982. "A Welded Link: Family Imagery in Mormonism and American Culture." Ph.D. diss., University of California at Santa Barbara.

Papanikolas, Helen Z., and Alice Kasai. 1976. "Japanese Life in Utah." In *The Peoples of Utah,* edited by Helen Z. Papanikolas, 333–62. Salt Lake City: Utah State Historical Society.

Park, Robert. 1952. *Human Communities: The City and Human Ecology.* Glencoe, Ill.: Free Press.

Parry, Keith. 1985. "Joseph Smith and the Clash of Sacred Cultures." *Dialogue: A Journal of Mormon Thought* 18 (4): 65–80.

Pascoe, Peggy. 1990. *Relations of Rescue: The Search for Female Moral Authority in the American West, 1874–1939.* New York: Oxford University Press.

Pateman, Carole. 1989. *The Disorder of Women: Democracy, Feminism, and Political Theory.* Stanford, Calif.: Stanford University Press.

Pateman, Carole, and Mary Lyndon Shanley. 1991. Introduction to *Feminist Interpretations and Political Theory,* edited by Mary Lyndon Shanley and Carole Pateman, 1–10. University Park: Pennsylvania State University Press.

Peais, H. B. [?]. 1905. Letter from Lawrence, Kans., to C. G. Hall, 21 June. "Indian Archives, 1880–1934." Record Group 75, Records of the Bureau of Indian Affairs. National Archives, Washington, D.C. Also in Manuscript Division, Special Collections, Marriott Library, University of Utah, Salt Lake City.

Peay, Ida Stewart. 1910. "The Star Boarder." *Young Woman's Journal* 21: 223–27.

Peet, Richard. 2000. "Culture, Imaginary, and Rationality in Regional Economic Development." *Environment and Planning A* 32: 1215–34.

Penrose, Charles W. 1912. Address. In *Conference Reports,* October, 59–68. Salt Lake City: Deseret News.

———. 1913. Address. In *Conference Reports,* October, 14–24. Salt Lake City: Deseret News.

Penrose, Romania B. 1908. "Delegate from Utah at the Woman's Congress." *Woman's Exponent* 37: 14–15.

"The Perfect Woman: A Symposium." 1890. *Young Woman's Journal* 1: 451–55.

Person, Carolyn W. D. 1976. "Susa Young Gates." In *Mormon Sisters: Women in Early Utah,* edited by Claudia L. Bushman, 199–223. Cambridge, Mass.: Emmeline.

Peterson, Charles S. 1974. "San Juan in Controversy: American Livestock Frontier vs. Mormon Cattle Pool." In *Essays on the American West, 1972–1973,* edited by Thomas G. Alexander, 45–68. Provo, Utah: Brigham Young University Press.

Philippe, Louis. 1906. Letter from New York City to the Reverend Franklin S. Spalding, Salt Lake City, 20 April. Papers of the Right Reverend Franklin Spencer Spalding, Episcopal Register of the Protestant Episcopal Church. Manuscript Division, Special Collections, Marriott Library, University of Utah, Salt Lake City.

Phillips, Rick. 1999. "The 'Secularization' of Utah and Religious Competition."
    Journal for the Scientific Study of Religion 38: 72–82.
"A Picture." 1894. *Equal Rights Banner: The Ballot, the Key to All Reform,* 16 Au-
    gust. Manuscript. Beaver, Utah, Woman Suffrage Association Papers, 1892–95.
    Special Collections Archives, Harold B. Lee Library, Brigham Young University,
    Provo, Utah.
Pisani, Donald J. 1992. *To Reclaim a Divided West: Water, Law, and Public Pol-
    icy, 1848–1902.* Albuquerque: University of New Mexico Press.
Pitzer, Donald E., ed. 1997. *America's Communal Utopias.* Chapel Hill: University
    of North Carolina Press.
"Place Your Trials in God's Keeping." 1900. *Young Woman's Journal* 11: 379–80.
Poll, Richard D. 1987. "Utah and the Mormons: A Symbiotic Relationship." In
    *New Views of Mormon History: A Collection of Essays in Honor of Leonard J.
    Arrington,* edited by Davis Bitton and Maureen Ursenbach Beecher, 323–41. Salt
    Lake City: University of Utah Press.
Pratt, Caroline Beebe. 1889. "Suffrage Speech." In Caroline Beebe Pratt Notebook,
    1883–1900. Manuscript. Archives, Church of Jesus Christ of Latter-day Saints
    Historical Department, Salt Lake City.
Pratt, Rey L. 1913. Address. In *Conference Reports,* October, 47–50. Salt Lake City:
    Deseret News.
———. 1916. Address. In *Conference Reports,* October, 144–48. Salt Lake City:
    Deseret News.
———. 1918. Address. In *Conference Reports,* April, 94–100. Salt Lake City: De-
    seret News.
Pred, Allan. 1986. *Place, Practice and Structure: Social and Spatial Transformation
    in Southern Sweden, 1750–1850.* Cambridge: Polity.
———. 1990. *Making Histories and Constructing Human Geographies: The Local
    Transformation of Practice, Power Relations, and Consciousness.* Boulder, Colo.:
    Westview Press.
Price, Hannah. 1890. "To the Young Sisters." *Young Woman's Journal* 1: 271.
Proctor, James D., and David M. Smith, eds. 1999. *Geography and Ethics: Jour-
    neys in a Moral Terrain.* London: Routledge.
"Program of the Utah Pioneer Jubilee, July 20th to 24th 1897." 1897. Special Col-
    lections Americana, Harold B. Lee Library, Brigham Young University, Provo, Utah.
"Progress of Women in the Last Seventy Years." 1912. *Woman's Exponent* 40:
    44–45.
Pudup, Mary Beth. 1988. "Arguments within Regional Geography." *Progress in
    Human Geography* 12: 369–90.
Quinn, D. Michael. 1984. "The Mormon Church and the Spanish-American War:
    An End to Selective Pacifism." *Dialogue: A Journal of Mormon Thought* 17 (4):
    11–30.
———. 1985. "LDS Church Authority and New Plural Marriages, 1890–1904."
    Dialogue: A Journal of Mormon Thought 18 (1): 9–105.

———. 1987. "Socio-Religious Radicalism of the Mormon Church: A Parallel to the Anabaptists." In *New Views of Mormon History: A Collection of Essays in Honor of Leonard J. Arrington,* edited by Davis Bitton and Maureen Ursenbach Beecher, 363–86. Salt Lake City: University of Utah Press.

Raivo, P. J. 1997. "The Limits of Tolerance: The Orthodox Milieu as an Element in the Finnish Cultural Landscape, 1917–1939." *Journal of Historical Geography* 23: 327–39.

Rampton, George O. 1969. "The Development of Secondary Social Studies Content in the Public Schools of Utah from 1847–1967." Ed.D. diss., Utah State University.

Reagon, Bernice Johnson. 1998. "Coalition Politics: Turning the Century." In *Race, Class, and Gender: An Anthology,* 3d ed., edited by Margaret L. Andersen and Patricia H. Collins, 517–23. Belmont, Calif.: Wadsworth.

Redding, Bettie Elliott. 1910. "Laverne." *Young Woman's Journal* 21: 166–69.

"The Relief Society Woman and Her Home." 1915. *Relief Society Magazine* 2: 477–81.

Reynolds, David R. 1994. "Political Geography: The Power of Place and the Spatiality of Politics." *Progress in Human Geography* 18: 234–47.

Rich, Ben E. 1908a. Address. In *Conference Reports,* October, 39–42. Salt Lake City: Deseret News.

———. 1908b. Address. In *Conference Reports,* October, 101–4. Salt Lake City: Deseret News.

Richards, Emily S., and (Mrs.) J. Fewson Smith. 1902. "Gains of Suffrage in Utah." *Woman's Exponent* 31: 22–23.

Richards, Franklin S. 1895. *The Suffrage Question: Address of Hon. Franklin S. Richards Delivered in the Constitutional Convention of Utah, March 28, 1895.* N.p.: Utah Woman Suffrage Association.

Richards, George F. 1908. Address. In *Conference Reports,* October, 42–45. Salt Lake City: Deseret News.

Richards, S. W. 1894. "Woman's Sphere." *Woman's Exponent* 22: 129–30.

Richards, Samuel W. 1905. Address. In *Conference Reports,* October, 87–89. Salt Lake City: Deseret News.

Richards, Stephen L. 1917. Address. In *Conference Reports,* April, 136–42. Salt Lake City: Deseret News.

———. 1919. Address. In *Conference Reports,* October, 100–105. Salt Lake City: Deseret News.

———. 1920a. Address. In *Conference Reports,* April, 96–100. Salt Lake City: Deseret News.

———. 1920b. Address. In *Conference Reports,* April, 124–32. Salt Lake City: Deseret News.

Roberts, B. H. 1903. Address. In *Conference Reports,* April, 11–14. Salt Lake City: Deseret News.

———. 1908. Address. In *Conference Reports,* April, 103–12. Salt Lake City: Deseret News.

———. 1912. Address. In *Conference Reports,* October, 30–35. Salt Lake City: Deseret News.

———. 1913. Letter to YMMIA Committee on Vocations and Industries, [Salt Lake City], 3 October. Brigham Henry Roberts Papers. Manuscript Division, Special Collections, Marriott Library, University of Utah, Salt Lake City.

———. 1914. Address. In *Conference Reports,* April, 100–109. Salt Lake City: Deseret News.

Robinson, Joseph E. 1907. Address. In *Conference Reports,* April, 90–96. Salt Lake City: Deseret News.

———. 1908. Address. In *Conference Reports,* April, 74–77. Salt Lake City: Deseret News.

———. 1912. Address. In *Conference Reports,* October, 76–82. Salt Lake City: Deseret News.

———. 1915. Address. In *Conference Reports,* October, 106–8. Salt Lake City: Deseret News.

Rose, Gillian. 1993. *Feminism and Geography: The Limits of Geographical Knowledge.* Minneapolis: University of Minnesota Press.

Russell, Isaac. 1910. Letter from New York City to the Reverend Franklin S. Spalding, Salt Lake City, 28 June. Papers of the Right Reverend Franklin Spencer Spalding, Episcopal Register of the Protestant Episcopal Church. Manuscript Division, Special Collections, Marriott Library, University of Utah, Salt Lake City.

Sack, Robert D. 1997. *Homo Geographicus: A Framework for Action, Awareness, and Moral Concern.* Baltimore: John Hopkins University Press.

———. 1999. "A Sketch of a Geographic Theory of Morality." *Annals of the Association of American Geographers* 89: 26–44.

Said, Edward W. 1993. *Culture and Imperialism.* New York: Alfred A. Knopf.

———. 1994. *Orientalism.* New York: Vintage Books.

Sandel, Michael J., ed. 1984. *Liberalism and Its Critics.* Oxford: Basil Blackwell.

Saxenian, Annalee. 1994. *Regional Advantage: Culture and Competition in Silicon Valley and Route 128.* Cambridge, Mass.: Harvard University Press.

Sayer, Andrew. 1989. "The 'New' Regional Geography and Problems of Narrative." *Environment and Planning D: Society and Space* 7: 253–76.

———. 1992. *Method in Social Science.* 2d ed. London: Routledge.

Scott, James C. 1976. *The Moral Economy of the Peasant: Rebellion and Subsistence in Southeast Asia.* New Haven, Conn.: Yale University Press.

Seidman, Steven. 1991. *Romantic Longings: Love in America, 1830–1980.* New York: Routledge.

Sewall, May Wright. 1901. Letter from Indianapolis, to Elmina S. Taylor, Salt Lake City, 2 December. Anstis Elmina Shepard Taylor Correspondence. Archives, Church of Jesus Christ of Latter-day Saints Historical Department, Salt Lake City.

Sharp, Joanne P. 1996. "Gendering Nationhood: A Feminist Engagement with National Identity." In *Bodyspace: Destabilizing Geographies of Gender and Sexuality,* edited by Nancy Duncan, 97–108. New York: Routledge.

Shepherd, Gordon, and Gary Shepherd. 1984. *A Kingdom Transformed: Themes in the Development of Mormonism.* Salt Lake City: University of Utah Press.

Shipps, Jan. 1985. *Mormonism: The Story of a New Religious Tradition.* Urbana: University of Illinois Press.

———. 1987. "Beyond the Stereotypes: Mormon and Non-Mormon Communities in Twentieth-Century Mormondom." In *New Views of Mormon History: A Collection of Essays in Honor of Leonard J. Arrington,* edited by Davis Bitton and Maureen Ursenbach Beecher, 342–60. Salt Lake City: University of Utah Press.

———. 2000. *Sojourner in the Promised Land: Forty Years among the Mormons.* Urbana: University of Illinois Press.

Sillito, John R. 1981. "Women and the Socialist Party in Utah, 1900–1920." *Utah Historical Quarterly* 49: 220–38.

———. 1992. "The Making of an Insurgent: Parley P. Christiansen and Utah Republicanism, 1900–1912." *Utah Historical Quarterly* 60: 319–34.

Sillito, John R., and Martha Bradley. 1985. "An Episcopal Observer of Mormonism." *Historical Magazine of the Protestant Episcopal Church* 54: 339–49.

Sillito, John R., and John S. McCormick. 1985. "Socialist Saints: Mormons and the Socialist Party in Utah, 1900–1920." *Dialogue: A Journal of Mormon Thought* 18 (1): 121–31.

Skurlock. 1890. "Woman's Power." *Young Woman's Journal* 1: 442–45.

Smart, William B. 1982. "William H. Smart, Builder in the Basin." *Utah Historical Quarterly* 50: 59–67.

Smart, William H. 1902. Address. In *Conference Reports,* October, 31–32. Salt Lake City: Deseret News.

———. n.d. "Diary 15." Manuscript. William H. Smart Diaries. Manuscript Division, Special Collections, Marriott Library, University of Utah, Salt Lake City.

Smith, Bathsheba W., and Emmeline B. Wells. 1909. Letter from Salt Lake City to Dr. Romania B. Penrose, 31 March. Esther Romania Bunnell Penrose Letters. Archives, Church of Jesus Christ of Latter-day Saints Historical Department, Salt Lake City.

Smith, David M. 2000. *Moral Geographies: Ethics in a World of Difference.* Edinburgh: Edinburgh University Press.

Smith, George Albert. 1906. Address. In *Conference Reports,* April, 52–58. Salt Lake City: Deseret News.

———. 1911. Address. In *Conference Reports,* October, 43–46. Salt Lake City: Deseret News.

Smith, Gibbs M. 1969. *Joe Hill.* Salt Lake City: University of Utah Press.

Smith, Grant T. 1993. "I've a Mother There: Identity, Language, and Experience in Mormon Women's Literature." Ph.D. diss., University of Iowa.

Smith, John Henry. 1899. Address. In *Conference Reports,* April, 33–36. Salt Lake City: Deseret News.

———. 1905. Address. In *Conference Reports,* October, 12–15. Salt Lake City: Deseret News.

———. 1906. Address. In *Conference Reports,* October, 20–26. Salt Lake City: Deseret News.

———. 1909. Address. In *Conference Reports,* October, 21–26. Salt Lake City: Deseret News.

———. 1910a. Address. In *Conference Reports,* April, 34–37. Salt Lake City: Deseret News.

———. 1910b. Address. In *Conference Reports,* October, 8–14. Salt Lake City: Deseret News.

Smith, Joseph F. 1898. Address. In *Conference Reports,* October, 21–27. Salt Lake City: Deseret News.

———. 1899. Address. In *Conference Reports,* April, 40–42. Salt Lake City: Deseret News.

———. 1900. Address. In *Conference Reports,* October, 46–49. Salt Lake City: Deseret News.

———. 1901. Address. In *Conference Reports,* October, 1–3. Salt Lake City: Deseret News.

———. 1903a. Address. In *Conference Reports,* April, 72–75. Salt Lake City: Deseret News.

———. 1903b. Address. In *Conference Reports,* October, 1–6. Salt Lake City: Deseret News.

———. 1905. Address. In *Conference Reports,* April, 1–7. Salt Lake City: Deseret News.

———. 1907. Letter from Salt Lake City to Reed Smoot, Washington D.C., 23 February. Reed Smoot Papers. Special Collections Archives, Harold B. Lee Library, Brigham Young University, Provo, Utah.

———. 1909. Address. In *Conference Reports,* October, 2–9. Salt Lake City: Deseret News.

———. 1910. Address. In *Conference Reports,* April, 1–8. Salt Lake City: Deseret News.

———. 1912. Address. In *Conference Reports,* April, 1–11. Salt Lake City: Deseret News.

———. 1917. Address. In *Conference Reports,* April, 2–12. Salt Lake City: Deseret News.

———. 1918a. Address. In *Conference Reports,* April, 2–7. Salt Lake City: Deseret News.

———. 1918b. Address. In *Conference Reports,* April, 168–71. Salt Lake City: Deseret News.

Smith, Joseph F., Jr. 1916. Address. In *Conference Reports,* October, 68–73. Salt Lake City: Deseret News.

Smith, Lizzie. 1890. "The Equality of the Sexes." *Young Woman's Journal* 1: 175–76.

Smith, Paul. 1988. *Discerning the Subject.* Minneapolis: University of Minnesota Press.

Smoot, Reed. 1900. Address. In *Conference Reports,* October, 5–8. Salt Lake City: Deseret News.

———. 1903. Letter from Washington D.C. to Joseph F. Smith, Salt Lake City, 20 November. Reed Smoot Papers. Special Collections Archives, Harold B. Lee Library, Brigham Young University, Provo, Utah.

———. 1909. Address. In *Conference Reports,* October, 68–72. Salt Lake City: Deseret News.

———. 1910. Address. In *Conference Reports,* October, 68–71. Salt Lake City: Deseret News.

———. 1915. Address. In *Conference Reports,* October, 131–33. Salt Lake City: Deseret News.

———. 1997. *In the World: The Diaries of Reed Smoot.* Edited by Harvard S. Heath. Salt Lake City: Signature Books.

Snow, Lorenzo. 1898. Address. In *Conference Reports,* April, 12–14. Salt Lake City: Deseret News.

Socialist State Ticket: Summary of Utah State Socialist Party Platform, 1914. 1914. Rare Books. Special Collections, Marriott Library, University of Utah, Salt Lake City.

Spalding, Franklin S. 1905a. "First Annual Address of the Bishop of Salt Lake, 2 May." Typescript. Papers of the Right Reverend Franklin Spencer Spalding, Episcopal Register of the Protestant Episcopal Church. Manuscript Division, Special Collections, Marriott Library, University of Utah, Salt Lake City.

———. 1905b. "Travel Journals of Bishop Franklin Spencer Spalding, 1905 and 1910." Manuscript. Papers of the Right Reverend Franklin Spencer Spalding, Episcopal Register of the Protestant Episcopal Church. Manuscript Division, Special Collections, Marriott Library, University of Utah, Salt Lake City.

———. 1911. Letter from Salt Lake City to C. E. Mason, New York City, 22 March. Papers of the Right Reverend Franklin Spencer Spalding, Episcopal Register of the Protestant Episcopal Church. Manuscript Division, Special Collections, Marriott Library, University of Utah, Salt Lake City.

———. 1912. *Joseph Smith, Jr. as a Translator: An Inquiry Conducted by the Rt. Rev. F. S. Spalding, D.D., Bishop of Utah, with the Kind Assistance of Capable Scholars.* Salt Lake City: Arrow.

———. n.d. "Onward Christian Workers." Typescript. Papers of the Right Reverend Franklin Spencer Spalding, Episcopal Register of the Protestant Episcopal Church. Manuscript Division, Special Collections, Marriott Library, University of Utah, Salt Lake City.

Spivak, Gayatri Chakravorty. 1988. *In Other Worlds: Essays in Cultural Politics.* New York: Routledge.

Stannard, David E. 1992. *American Holocaust: Columbus and the Conquest of the New World.* New York: Oxford University Press.

State Committee of the Socialist Party. 1908. *Utah State Platform and Constitution of the Socialist Party.* Ogden: Denkers and Son.

State Department of Public Instruction. 1918a. *Utah Course of Study for Elementary Schools and Junior High Schools.* Salt Lake City: Skelton.

———. 1918b. *Utah Course of Study for the Secondary Schools.* Salt Lake City: Skelton.

Stimson, Sarah J., Lovisa Thornton, and Sarah R. Taylor. 1908. "A Tribute." *Woman's Exponent* 36: 64.

Stipanovich, Joseph. 1976. "Falcons in Flight: The Yugoslavs." In *The Peoples of Utah,* edited by Helen Papanikolas, 363–83. Salt Lake City: Utah State Historical Society.

Stokes, Bruce. 2001. "Washington Warming up to Land of Rising Sun." *Taipei Times,* 12 March.

Stone, Ivy Williams. 1920. "Purple Pansies." *Young Woman's Journal* 1: 606–11.

Strongwil, John. 1912. *Your Sister's Keeper (Who Is It?): That Question and Other Questions: Dedicated to Young Men.* Salt Lake City: Equity.

Stryker, Susan O'Neal. 1992. "Making Mormonism: A Critical and Historical Analysis of Cultural Formation." Ph.D. diss., University of California at Berkeley.

Swierenga, Robert P. 1989. "Ethnoreligious Political Behavior in the Mid-Nineteenth Century: Voting, Values, Culture." In *Religion and American Politics: From the Colonial Period to the 1980s,* edited by Mark A. Noll, 146–71. New York: Oxford University Press.

"The Swing of the Pendulum." 1930. *Relief Society Magazine* 17: 620–23.

"Symposium: The Nineteenth and Twentieth Centuries." 1901. *Woman's Exponent* 29: 68–70.

Takaki, Ronald, ed. 1994. *From Different Shores: Perspectives on Race and Ethnicity in America.* New York: Oxford University Press.

Talmage, James E. 1912. Address. In *Conference Reports,* October, 125–29. Salt Lake City: Deseret News.

———. 1919. Address. In *Conference Reports,* October, 93–100. Salt Lake City: Deseret News.

Taylor, John. 1880. Address. In *Conference Reports,* April, 99–103. Salt Lake City: Deseret News.

Taylor, Peter J. 1999. "Places, Spaces and Macy's: Place-Space Tensions in the Political Geography of Modernities." *Progress in Human Geography* 23: 7–26.

Teasdale, George. 1900. Address. In *Conference Reports,* April, 18–20. Salt Lake City: Deseret News.

Thatcher, Linda, and John R. Sillito. 1985. " 'Sisterhood and Sociability': The Utah Women's Press Club, 1891–1928." *Utah Historical Quarterly* 53: 144–56.

Thompson, E. P. 1971. "The Moral Economy of the English Crown in the Eighteenth Century." *Past and Present* 50: 76–136.

Thrift, Nigel. 1983. "On the Determination of Social Action in Space and Time." *Environment and Planning D: Society and Space* 1: 23–57.

————. 1994. "Taking Aim at the Heart of the Region." In *Human Geography: Society, Space, and Social Science,* edited by Derek Gregory, Ron Martin, and Graham Smith, 200–231. Minneapolis: University of Minnesota Press.

Tuan, Yi-Fu. 1977. *Space and Place.* London: Arnold.

Uchida, Take. 1976. Interview by Paul Kato, 24 January. Japanese-American Oral History Program. Utah State Historical Society, Salt Lake City.

Underwood, Grant. 1993. *The Millenarian World of Early Mormonism.* Urbana: University of Illinois Press.

U.S. Congress. Senate. Committee on Privileges and Elections. 1906. *Proceedings before the Committee on Privileges and Elections of the United States Senate, in the Matter of the Protests against the Right of Hon. Reed Smoot, a Senator from the State of Utah, to Hold His Seat.* 4 vols. 59th Cong., 1st sess. S. Doc. 486. Washington D.C.: Government Printing Office.

Utah State Text Book Committee. [1897]. *Course of Study for the Public Schools of the State of Utah Excepting Cities of the First and Second Class.* Salt Lake City: Cannon House.

Van Wagenen, Lola. 1994. "Sister-Wives and Suffragists: Polygamy and the Politics of Woman Suffrage, 1870–1896." Ph.D. diss., New York University.

Van Wagoner, Richard S. 1986. *Mormon Polygamy: A History.* Salt Lake City: Signature Books.

————. 1991. "The Lehi Sugar Factory—100 Years in Retrospect." *Utah Historical Quarterly* 59: 189–204.

Vermilye, Elizabeth B. 1912. "Non-Christian Faiths in America." Typescript. Papers of the Right Reverend Franklin Spencer Spalding, Episcopal Register of the Protestant Episcopal Church. Manuscript Division, Special Collections, Marriott Library, University of Utah, Salt Lake City.

Waddell, Oscar M. 1904. Letter from Randlett, Utah, to W. A. Mercer, 17 February. "Indian Archives, 1880–1934." Record Group 75, Records of the Bureau of Indian Affairs. National Archives, Washington, D.C. Also in Manuscript Division, Special Collections, Marriott Library, University of Utah, Salt Lake City.

————. 1905. Letter from Ouray, Utah, to C. G. Hall, 21 February. "Indian Archives, 1880–1934." Record Group 75, Records of the Bureau of Indian Affairs. National Archives, Washington, D.C. Also in Manuscript Division, Special Collections, Marriott Library, University of Utah, Salt Lake City.

————. 1906. Letter from Whiterocks, Utah, to C. G. Hall, 12 November. "Indian Archives, 1880–1934." Record Group 75, Records of the Bureau of Indian Affairs. National Archives, Washington, D.C. Also in Manuscript Division, Special Collections, Marriott Library, University of Utah, Salt Lake City.

Walker, Ronald W. 1992. "Sheaves, Bucklers, and the State: Mormon Leaders Respond to the Dilemmas of War." In *The New Mormon History: Revisionist Essays on the Past,* edited by D. Michael Quinn, 267–301. Salt Lake City: Signature Books.

————. 1998. *Wayward Saints: The Godbeites and Brigham Young.* Urbana: University of Illinois Press.

Walsh, Herbert. 1898. Letter from Philadelphia to Commissioner of Indian Affairs, 3 January. "Selected Documents Relating to the Ute Indians, 1881–1939" (microform), reel 3, frame 861. Record Group 75, Records of the Bureau of Indian Affairs. National Archives, Washington, D.C.

Wang, Horng-luen. 1997. "Rethinking the Global and the National: Reflections on National Imaginations in Taiwan." *Theory, Culture and Society* 17 (4): 93–117.

Warensky, Marilyn. 1978. *Patriarchs and Politics: The Plight of the Mormon Woman.* New York: McGraw-Hill.

Wasatch Development Company. n.d. *Uintah Indian Reservation: Information upon the Opening, August 18, 1905.* Heber City, Utah: Wasatch Development Company.

Weinstein, James. 1984. *The Decline of Socialism in America, 1912–1925.* New Brunswick, N.J.: Rutgers University Press.

Wells, Emmeline B. 1895a. Letter from Salt Lake City to Mary A. White, 14 January. Beaver, Utah, Woman Suffrage Association Papers, 1892–95. Special Collections Archives, Harold B. Lee Library, Brigham Young University, Provo, Utah.

———. 1895b. "Woman Suffrage Column: Utah W.S.A." *Woman's Exponent* 23: 233–34.

———. 1908. Letter to Dr. R. B. Penrose, 15 March. Esther Romania Bunnell Penrose Letters. Archives, Church of Jesus Christ of Latter-day Saints Historical Department, Salt Lake City.

———. 1910. Letter from Salt Lake City to Dr. Romania B. Penrose, Liverpool, England, 7 April. Esther Romania Bunnell Penrose Letters. Archives, Church of Jesus Christ of Latter-day Saints Historical Department, Salt Lake City.

Wells, John. 1914. "Thoughts on the United Order." Typescript. Archives, Church of Jesus Christ of Latter-day Saints Historical Department, Salt Lake City.

West, Cornel. 1994. *Race Matters.* New York: Vintage Books.

Whalen, Sarah. 1900. "Nature Studies for Young Mothers." *Young Woman's Journal* 11: 364–67.

"What Happened in Dreamland." 1900. *Young Woman's Journal* 11: 69–77.

"What Women Will Do with the Suffrage." 1920. *Relief Society Magazine* 7: 291–94.

White, Jean Bickmore. 1975. "Woman's Place Is in the Constitution: The Struggle for Equal Rights in Utah in 1895." In *Essays on the American West, 1973–1974,* edited by Thomas G. Alexander, 81–104. Provo, Utah: Brigham Young University Press.

White, Richard, and John M. Findlay, eds. 1999. *Power and Place in the North American West.* Seattle: University of Washington Press.

Whitney, Orson F. 1895. "Bishop O. F. Whitney." *Woman's Exponent* 24: 9–10.

———. 1907. Address. In *Conference Reports,* October, 45–54. Salt Lake City: Deseret News.

———. 1909. Address. In *Conference Reports,* April, 72–77. Salt Lake City: Deseret News.

———. 1910. Address. In *Conference Reports,* April, 85–88. Salt Lake City: Deseret News.

————. 1916a. Address. In *Conference Reports*, April, 64–69. Salt Lake City: Deseret News.

————. 1916b. Address. In *Conference Reports*, October, 51–57. Salt Lake City: Deseret News.

————. 1917. Address. In *Conference Reports*, October, 49–55. Salt Lake City: Deseret News.

Williams, Raymond. 1961. *The Long Revolution*. London: Chatto and Windus.

Williams, Terry Tempest. 1992. *Refuge: An Unnatural History of Family and Place*. New York: Vintage Books.

Winn, Kenneth H. 1989. *Exiles in a Land of Liberty: Mormons in America, 1830–1846*. Chapel Hill: University of North Carolina Press.

"'Woman's Day.'" 1920. *Young Woman's Journal* 31: 285–86.

"Woman's Opportunity." 1894. *Woman's Exponent* 22: 148.

"Woman's Sphere." 1894. *Equal Rights Banner: The Ballot, the Key to All Reform*, 16 September. Manuscript. Beaver, Utah, Woman Suffrage Association Papers, 1892–95. Special Collections Archives, Harold B. Lee Library, Brigham Young University, Provo, Utah.

"Women in Politics." 1896. *Woman's Exponent* 25: 52–53.

"Women Past and Present." 1913. *Woman's Exponent* 41: 37.

"Women Recognized." 1912. *Woman's Exponent* 41: 12.

Woodruff, Abraham O. 1898. Address. In *Conference Reports*, April, 19–22. Salt Lake City: Deseret News.

————. 1899. Address. In *Conference Reports*, October, 6–8. Salt Lake City: Deseret News.

————. 1902. Address. In *Conference Reports*, October, 32–34. Salt Lake City: Deseret News.

Woodruff, Asahel H. 1902. Address. In *Conference Reports*, October, 15–18. Salt Lake City: Deseret News.

Woodruff, Wilford. 1880. Address. In *Conference Reports*, April, 5–14. Salt Lake City: Deseret News.

Woods, Clyde. 1998. *Development Arrested: Blues and Plantation Power in the Mississippi Delta*. London: Verso.

"A Word to Women." 1900. *Woman's Exponent* 29: 29.

Worster, Donald. 1985. *Rivers of Empire: Water, Aridity, and the Growth of the American West*. New York: Pantheon.

————. 1992. *Under Western Skies: Nature and History in the American West*. Oxford: Oxford University Press.

Wright, John B. 1993. *Rocky Mountain Divide: Selling and Saving in the West*. Austin: University of Texas Press.

Wrobel, David M., and Michael C. Steiner, eds. 1997. *Many Wests: Place, Culture, and Regional Identity*. Lawrence: University Press of Kansas.

Wuthnow, Robert. 1987. *Meaning and Moral Order: Explorations in Cultural Analysis*. Berkeley: University of California Press.

Yano, Suga. 1976. Interview by Paul Kato, 3 January. Japanese-American Oral History Program. Utah State Historical Society, Salt Lake City.

Young, Brigham. 1871. "Discourse by President Brigham Young, Delivered in the New Tabernacle, Salt Lake City, July 11, 1869." In *Journal of Discourses by President Brigham Young, His Two Counsellors, and the Twelve Apostles*, vol. 13, reported by D. W. Evans and John Grimshaw, 139–50. Liverpool: Horace S. Eldredge.

Young, Emily Dow Partridge. n.d. "Diary of Emily Dow Partridge Young." Typescript. Emily Dow Partridge Smith Young Papers. Manuscript Division, Special Collections, Marriott Library, University of Utah, Salt Lake City.

Young, Iris Marion. 1990. *Justice and the Politics of Difference*. Princeton, N.J.: Princeton University Press.

Young, Levi Edgar. 1915. "Utah." *Young Woman's Journal* 26: 395–403.

Young, Rhoda M. [?] 1878. *Young Ladies Diadem* 1, (8): n.p. Manuscript. Young Women of St. George, 1877–78, Collection. Utah State Historical Society, Salt Lake City.

Young, Richard W. 1906. Address. In *Conference Reports*, October, 100–103. Salt Lake City: Deseret News.

———. 1919. Address. In *Conference Reports*, October, 147–54. Salt Lake City: Deseret News.

Young, Seymour B. 1899. Address. In *Conference Reports*, October, 55–60. Salt Lake City: Deseret News.

———. 1906a. Address. In *Conference Reports*, April, 11–13. Salt Lake City: Deseret News.

———. 1906b. Address. In *Conference Reports*, October, 89–94. Salt Lake City: Deseret News.

———. 1912. Address. In *Conference Reports*, October, 35–38. Salt Lake City: Deseret News.

Young, Zina D. H. 1894. [Speech Reported under Title] "A Woman's Assembly." *Woman's Exponent* 22: 102.

Young Ladies' Mutual Improvement Association. n.d. [1900]. *Young Ladies' Mutual Improvement Association, Guide to the Second Year's Course of Study in the Young Ladies' Mutual Improvement Association*. Salt Lake City: George Q. Cannon and Sons.

Young Men's Mutual Improvement Association. 1891. *Latter-day Saints Young Men's Mutual Improvement Associations Manual, Part 1, 1891–'92*. Salt Lake City: Published by Authority.

———. 1895. *Latter-day Saints Young Men's Mutual Improvement Associations, the First Twelve Lessons of Manual, Part 2, 1894–5*. Salt Lake City: Contributor.

———. 1899. *Young Men's Mutual Improvement Associations Manual, 1899–1900, Subject: Dispensation of the Fullness of Times, Part 1 (1805–1839)*. Salt Lake City: Deseret News.

———. 1900. *Young Men's Mutual Improvement Associations Manual, 1900–1901,*

Subject: Dispensation of the Fullness of Times, Part II (1838–1846). Salt Lake City: Deseret News.

———. n.d.a. *Young Men's Mutual Improvement Associations Manual, 1902–1903, Subject: Principles of the Gospel, Part II*. Salt Lake City: General Board of the Y.M.M.I.A.

———. n.d.b. *Young Men's Mutual Improvement Associations, Manual, 1910–11, Subject: The Making of a Citizen I—Lessons in Economics*. Salt Lake City: General Board of the Y.M.M.I.A.

———. n.d.c. *Young Men's Mutual Improvement Associations, Manual, 1911–12, Subject: The Making of a Citizen—Problems in Economics—Agriculture and Public Finance*. Salt Lake City: General Board of the Y.M.M.I.A.

———. n.d.d. *Young Men's Mutual Improvement Associations, Manual, 1912–13, Subject: The Individual and Society*. Salt Lake City: General Board of the Y.M.M.I.A.

———. n.d.e. *Young Men's Mutual Improvement Associations, Manual for Senior Classes, 1913–14, Subject: Man in Relation to His Work*. Salt Lake City: General Board of the Y.M.M.I.A.

———. n.d.f. *Young Men's Mutual Improvement Associations, Manual for Senior Classes, 1914–15, Subject: The Vocations of Man*. Salt Lake City: General Board of the Y.M.M.I.A.

———. n.d.g. *Young Men's Mutual Improvement Associations, Manual for Senior Classes, 1915–16, Subject: Conditions of Success*. Salt Lake City: General Board of the Y.M.M.I.A.

———. n.d.h. *Young Men's Mutual Improvement Associations, Manual for Junior Classes, 1916–17, Subject: The Development of Character I—Lessons on Courage*. Salt Lake City: General Board of the Y.M.M.I.A.

———. n.d.i. *Young Men's Mutual Improvement Associations, Manual for Senior Classes, 1916–17, Subject: The Church as an Organization for Social Service*. Salt Lake City: General Board of the Y.M.M.I.A.

———. n.d.j. *Young Men's Mutual Improvement Associations, Manual for Junior Classes, 1917–18, Subject: The Development of Character II—Lessons on Conduct*. Salt Lake City: General Board of the Y.M.M.I.A.

———. n.d.k. *Young Men's Mutual Improvement Associations, Manual for Senior Classes, 1917–18, Subject: Life and Work under Spiritual Guidance*. Salt Lake City: General Board of the Y.M.M.I.A.

———. n.d.l. *Young Men's Mutual Improvement Associations, Manual for Junior Classes, 1918–19, Subject: The Development of Character III—Lessons on Success*. Salt Lake City: General Board of the Y.M.M.I.A.

———. n.d.m. *Young Men's Mutual Improvement Associations, Manual for Senior Classes, 1918–19, Subject: Some Epoch-Making Events in Church History*. Salt Lake City: General Board of the Y.M.M.I.A.

Zukin, Sharon. 1991. *Landscapes of Power: From Detroit to Disney World*. Berkeley: University of California Press.

INDEX

African Americans, 215n1
Agnew, John A., 194n7
Alexander, Thomas G., 29, 108, 120, 141–
42, 155; on Mormon culture, 109, 154,
169; on regional economy, 106, 205n30
Allen, Paula Gunn, 200n24
Americanization, 6, 17, 42, 150, 185,
194n5; economic, 83, 128–29, 215n2;
economic norms and, 90, 78–79, 126,
208n60; gender and, 61–62, 72, 76,
184–85; geographical scale and, 168; in-
adequacy of term, 129, 172–73; Mormonism and, 3, 150, 154, 159–62; non-
Mormons and, 137, 159, 168–69; region
and, viii, 4, 24–25, 42, 132, 171–72,
194n3; social difference and, 150–51,
185. *See also* Liberalism; Mormon culture; Mormon culture region; Mormonism; Mormon–non-Mormon dynamic;
Non-Mormons; Pluralism; Protestantization; Smoot hearings; United States federal government
Americanization Day, 211n20
American Party, 29–30, 93, 137, 138, 168,
210n9
American West, vii–viii, 24, 132, 159–61,
162, 183
American Woman Suffrage Association, 55
Arrington, Leonard J., 78–79, 106, 128
Ayers, Edward L., 132

Back-to-the-farm movement, 89–90, 204n26
Bailey, Joseph W., 156

Ballard, Melvin J., 99
Bate, Kerry William, 146
Beaver County Woman Suffrage Associa-
tion, 43
Beecher, Maureen Ursenbach, 48, 72
Beeton, Beverly, 35, 36
Berkhofer, Robert F., Jr., 115
Bodnar, John, 214n40
Bolshevik Revolution, 99, 126, 147
Bourdieu, Pierre, 19
Boyer, S. A., 47
Breeden, M. A., 146–47
Brigham City, Utah, 81, 110
Brimhall, George H., 113
Brotherhood of the Co-operative Common-
wealth, 123, 207n53
Brown, H. C., 159
Brown, William Thurston, 124
Buchanan, Frederick S., 214n38
Buchanan, James, 133
Burch, Charles S., 197n9
Burrows, Julius Caesar, 210n6
Bush, George W., 189

Callis, Charles A., 146, 180
Cannon, Angus M., 61–62
Cannon, David H., 121
Cannon, George Q., 91, 97, 101, 139, 166
Cannon, Martha Hughes, 33, 58, 62
Capitalism: morality and, 20, 127–28, 178–
79; Mormonism and, 6, 109; region and,
6, 7, 8, 23, 29, 82–83. *See also* Economy
Cartier, Carolyn, 216n7

Fox, Ruth May, 60
Francaviglia, Richard V., 194n2
Fuller, Craig Woods, 202n10

Gates, Susa Young, 118, 181, 199n19; gender and, 52, 57, 61, 68, 70–72, 200n29
Gathering, LDS doctrine of, 116–17. *See also* Communitarianism
Gender, 19, 22, 204n27; in Mormonism, 37, 62–63, 103, 136–37; spheres, 49–50, 54, 55–58, 198n17; Victorian and romantic ideals of, 37, 38, 63–69, 200n27. *See also* Feminism; Gender authority; Gender codes; Gender roles; Male privilege; Mormon feminism, Mormon women; Mutual Improvement Associations; *Woman's Exponent*, Woman's movement; Woman suffrage; Women politicians; Women's clubs; *Young Woman's Journal*
Gender authority, 33, 61; in Mormon culture region, 9, 76–77; Mormonism and, 6–7, 32–33, 35, 38, 48, 74. *See also* Gender
Gender codes, 102–5, 204 nn. 21, 23, 204–5n27
Gender roles, 85–86, 88–89; the home and, 48, 69–72, 175–80, 200n31
General conference, LDS, 27–28, 72, 118, 196n14, 201n32
Generation, 5–6, 15, 19, 43, 146, 162
Gentile boycott, 81, 110
Gentiles. *See* Non-Mormons
Gilbert, Anne, 16
Givens, Terryl L., 202n11
Globalization, 24–25, 187, 191, 216n7. *See also* Region, geographical scale and
Godbe, William S., 197n6
Goddard, Benjamin, 117
Gong, Garrett, 189
Goodwin, C. C., 160
Government. *See* United States federal government
Gregory, Derek, 40–41
Griffin, Susan, 102
Guelke, Jeanne Kay, 194n2

Habitus, 19, 40, 129
Hafen, P. Jane, 95
Hafen, Thomas K., 215n2
Half-mast incident, 130

Hamblin, Jacob, 113
Hansen, Klaus, 203n19, 209n1
Haraway, Donna, 149
Hardy, C. Brian, 212n25
Hart, Charles H., 146
Hatch, Nathan O., 164
Haywood, William (Big Bill), 124
Heber City Wasatch Wave, 92, 94, 95–96
Hill, Joe, 126
Hilliard, Kate, 122, 124
Historiography, vii–viii, 203n19, 209n1. *See also* History
History, 30; regional, ix, 195nn3, 5. *See also* Historiography; Memory
Hoar, George Frisbie, 62
Home: as basic unit of society, 175, 176, 177, 179–80; citizenship and, 176, 178–79; diversity of types, 56, 177; feminist views of, 18, 72, 200n24; Mormonism and the ideal American, 72, 174–81; politics of, 8, 172, 173–74, 183–84; region and, 18, 173, 175–76; *See also* Americanization; Gender; Region
Home manufacturing, 204n24, 205nn31, 33
Homespun [pseud.]. *See* Gates, Susa Young
Home Writer, The, 60, 84, 144, 159
Honig, Bonnie, 172, 183–84
Horne, M. Isabella, 52, 179
Howe, Daniel Walker, 201n34
Hoy, Jesse S., 199–200n24
Hughes, Frank, 188
Hughey, Michael W., 135–36
Hurtado, Aida, 199n19
Hyphenated Americans, 151

Identity, viii–ix, 73–74, 195n7; Mormon, viii–ix, 19, 66–68, 96, 169, 206n37; Mormon and American, 211n19; regional, 15–19, 132, 162–63, 182, 215n42, 216n6; western, 216n4. *See also* Culture; Mormon culture; Mormon culture region
Ideology, 22, 189–90
Immigrants, 82, 151, 201n1. *See also* Minorities
Improvement Era, 26, 71. *See also* Mormon youth literature
Independence Day. *See* Patriotic celebrations
International Council for Patriotic Service (Interdenominational Council of Women

Stalker, William Hyde, 44, 157
Stockton, John, 188
Structures of expectation, 19–20, 127. *See also* Moral order; Region
Stryker, Susan O'Neal, 109, 143, 154, 169, 207n50
Suffrage. *See* Woman suffrage
Swierenga, Robert P., 158, 214n35

Taiwan, 187, 191
Talmage, James E., 111, 142, 163
Taylor, John, 81, 84, 140, 134–35, 143–44, 165
Teasdale, George, 139, 210n11
Thatcher, Arizona, 120
Thatcher, Moses, 154–55, 212n28
Thomas, Arthur L., 144
Thrift, Nigel, 26
Tithing. *See* United Order
Tuan, Yi-Fu, 18

Uintah Indian Reservation, 28, 91–96, 115, 202n9, 203n15. *See also* Native Americans
Underwood, Grant, 203–4n19, 209n1
United Order, 80, 81, 110, 117–21, 206n46; *See also* Communitarianism
United States federal government, 6, 27. *See also* Americanization; Smoot Hearings
Utah, 3, 82–83, 133–34, 187–88, 209n3, 214nn38, 39
Utah Idaho Sugar Company, 110, 204n34
Utah Jazz, 187, 188–89
Utah War, 68, 133
Utah Woman Suffrage Associations, 47, 52–53; *See also* Woman suffrage; Mormon feminism; Woman's movement
Ute Indians. *See* Native Americans

Van Wagenen, Lola, 25, 26, 59
Vernal Express, 94, 95, 208n58
Victorian gender ideals. *See* Gender, Victorian and romantic ideals of
Vulnerability index, 106–8, 205nn29, 30

Wage labor, 48, 84–90, 201n4, 203n17
Walker, Ronald W., 145–46
Warensky, Marilyn, 199n20

Wasatch Development Company, 96, 202n9, 203n14
Wasatch stake, 92
Wasatch Wave. See *Heber City Wasatch Wave*
Wealth, 90–91, 93–99. *See also* Economy
Welfare, 98. *See also* Economy
Wells, Emmeline B., 35–36, 38, 43, 46, 51, 180–81
Wells, John, 118–19
West, Cornel, ix
"The Western Boom" (Jakeman), 32
"What Happened in Dreamland," 66–67
Whitecotton, W. J. N., 156–57
Whiteness. *See* Race
Whitney, Orson F., 116, 166
Williams, Raymond, 19
Williams, Terry Tempest, 191, 199n20
Wolfe, Walter M., 209n6
Woman's Exponent, 27, 35, 43, 51–52, 62–63, 70
Woman's movement, 76–77, 200n25. *See also* Woman suffrage.
Woman suffrage, 36, 136–37; arguments over, 37, 47, 49–51; Mormon–non-Mormon alliances, 27, 47–48; polygamy and, 27, 43, 198n14; in Utah, 27, 33, 35, 36, 55. *See also* American Woman Suffrage Association; Beaver County Woman Suffrage Association; Gender; Gender authority; Mormon feminism; Mormon women; National Suffrage Association; Utah Woman Suffrage Association; Woman's movement
Women politicians, 57–58
Women's clubs, 33, 48
Woodruff, Abraham O., 97
Woodruff, Asahel H., 117
Woodruff, Wilford, 46, 84–85, 96–97, 114–15; on LDS institutions, 100, 117, 144
World War I, 146, 167–68
Wuthnow, Robert, 22

Young, Brigham, 2, 5, 14, 26, 113, 122–23; on economic issues, 28, 80, 84, 91, 99–100, 105–6
Young, Brigham, Jr., 206n46

ETHAN R. YORGASON is an adjunct assistant professor in the College of Arts and Sciences at Brigham Young University at Hawai'i. He received his Ph.D. in geography from the University of Iowa. He has published articles in *Cultural Geographies; Antipode: A Radical Journal of Geography; Social Science Journal,* and *Dialogue: A Journal of Mormon Thought.*

The University of Illinois Press
is a founding member of the
Association of American University Presses.

———————————————————

Composed in 10/13 Sabon
with Sabon display
by Type One, LLC
for the University of Illinois Press
Designed by Dennis Roberts
Manufactured by Sheridan Press

University of Illinois Press
1325 South Oak Street
Champaign, IL 61820-6903
www.press.uillinois.edu